Tip of the Spear

Tip of the Spear

U.S. Marine Light Armor in the Gulf War

G. J. Michaels

NAVAL INSTITUTE PRESS
ANNAPOLIS, MARYLAND

Naval Institute Press
291 Wood Road
Annapolis, MD 21402

First Naval Institute Press paperback edition published in 2008.

ISBN-13 978-1-59114-498-4

Library of Congress Cataloging-in-Publication Data
Michaels, G. J., 1966–
    Tip of the spear : U.S. Marine light armor in the Gulf War / G.J. Michaels.
        p. cm.
      ISBN 1-55750-599-3 (alk. paper)
        1. United States. Marine Corps—History—Persian Gulf War, 1991.
I. Title.
DS79.72.M483   1998
97-51651
956.7044'245—dc21

Printed in the United States of America on acid-free paper ∞

14 13 12 11   9 8 7 6 5 4 3
Cover image courtesy of Greg E. Mathieson, MAI Photo News Agency

For Alec, Christopher, and Nicholas:
I hope that within these pages
you find something from which
to draw strength.

Preface

THIS BOOK is the story of the shared experience of leaders within a United States Marine Corps light armored vehicle battalion in Operation Desert Shield and Desert Storm in Saudi Arabia and Kuwait. It is a chronicle of unselfish sacrifice and commitment. All of the people in it are real; the events are told the way they occurred. If I played a direct role in a particular situation, my description of it in this book is based upon what I remember, what I recorded on tape, and what I extracted from letters I wrote to my wife. My accounts of incidents that took place outside my direct observation are based on the recollections of the marines involved, taped conversations, and official Marine Corps history.

Depending upon one's position in the overall scheme of the operation, Desert Storm was everything from a horrific ordeal to a sterile interlude. Many have belittled the experience. *It wasn't a war; it was a huge live-fire exercise. The Iraqis didn't even fight back.* These words are founded in reality, and for some people they are completely true. And yet while I myself may find some truth in them too, I believe there is greater truth beyond them.

How can anyone who buries comrades accept a judgment of our presence in the Persian Gulf as trivial or meaningless? To do so is a grave injustice to everyone who fought and died in that war. Neither is such a judgment fair to those who still lie awake at night thinking of those moments during the war that they wish they could change. But past events cannot be changed—marines cannot be brought back to life, and mistakes cannot be undone. What remains, and what will always be, is the story. There is a story to be told here, and I will try to tell it.

My purpose is not to glamorize the part I played in this story but to record the service of a group of individuals whose actions should be remembered. There are lessons to be learned from such a chronicle. You will laugh at times. You might cry. And even if you have never lived through events similar to these, you may still find yourself to be a part of the narrative. I hope so.

There are two vital points that I need to establish here at the outset. The first centers on the overriding reason that my company returned to the United States without having experienced any casualties in Saudi Arabia: my commanding officer, Capt. Michael Shupp. When I first met him, I thought he was crazy. He worked us to death doing all sorts of things that, although they needed to be done, could have been accomplished in a less intense manner. Only when we finally went to the Persian Gulf did I realize just how important it was to have a leader of his caliber. Captain Shupp is the type of leader you definitely want to have when there is an imminent threat of war. And though this book is not the story of Captain Shupp, the very fact that I relate many of these events from my own perspective demands that he play a major role in it. I may never work with Captain Shupp again, but no memory of my experience in Alpha Company passes through my head without his image being attached to it.

My second point concerns the marine light armor noncommissioned officers. The reason that the light armored infantry (LAI) battalion had so much success in Desert Storm was the professional and heroic conduct of these marines. This story is partially told through their eyes: Sgt. Randy Buntin, 1st LAI Battalion, Company B; Sgt. Richard Smith, 2d LAI Battalion, Company C; Sgt. Aniceto Hernandez, 1st LAI Battalion, Company C; and Sgt. Roland Ramirez, 1st LAI Battalion, Headquarters and Service Company. I was in 1st LAI Battalion, Company A.

It was a distinct honor for me to serve with these marines during the Gulf War—as it is for me to continue to work with all four of them today. They are currently assigned to train officers and staff noncommissioned officers who are joining the light armor community, and I cannot overstate the degree to which their professionalism and expertise operate to shape the quality product they are putting out. I want you to feel the huge burden of responsibility they carried in the Persian Gulf War and to understand the significance of their abilities and their actions on the battlefield. Most importantly I want you to know why their story has to be told and to understand just how important these individuals were to the shared success of our unit.

I have assigned fictitious names to almost all of the characters in this book. The aforementioned marines and public figures are called by their real names. In addition, some ranks and details of hierarchy have been made ambiguous to allow for anonymity.

On the walls of my home now hang three flags. Each flag is stained by the very oil that many people believe to have been the primary reason for the Gulf War. The first one, the flag of the United States of America, reminds me that although freedom is given to many, it comes at a price that is paid by a select few and that under the blue field of stars and stripes of white and red, the price is life itself. The second, the scarlet and gold flag of the United States Marine Corps, is a reminder that those who sacrifice their lives for freedom make the choice to go into harm's way for reasons only they can fully explain, yet they fight and die unselfishly nonetheless. The third, the flag of the nation of Kuwait, is a constant reminder that freedom can indeed be lost. Today this flag flies over a capital city eight thousand miles away from America as a testament that for a price—in this case, one paid in important measure by men and women of these other two flags—lost freedom can indeed be regained.

Acknowledgments

I WAS ASKED during a command-sponsored PME (professional military education) to describe what the words *honor, courage,* and *commitment* meant to me. That thought-provoking question, which I could not answer in just a few sentences, became the reason for my writing the work that is now in your hands: I told Staff Sergeant Ramirez, a fellow member of Task Force Shepherd, that I was going to explain those three words by writing a book.

I feel good about the story you are about to read, but it took the dedication and efforts of the people in this book during the Gulf War to make the story as wonderful as it is. Each of the marines I interviewed while writing this book put up with my poor use of a tape recorder and less-than-spectacular questioning technique. I thank each of them for their patience, but most of all, I thank them for living the theme of this book. So thank you, Randy Buntin, Rolando Ramirez, Aniceto Hernandez, and Richard Smith.

I also owe a special thanks to my wonderful wife, Angie, whose patience with my crazy writing hours was nothing short of remarkable. In addition to the hours of transcription work she did for me, I appreciate her for tolerating the cold dinners that were hot when she called for me, for cleaning the dirty dishes that appeared out of nowhere late in the night, and finally, for killing the fleas in my writing room (another story itself).

Jenny was my first editor. Her ideas led to the first rewrite and to what I believe to be the key to the readability of this story. Then as my first "publisher" she presented a wonderful Christmas gift to us all with the first printed version of this book. Thank you, Jenny.

To Bill, thanks for letting me put wear and tear on your printer. And to those who read the book as I worked on it, thanks for the timely and positive (most of the time) feedback.

Finally, I would be negligent if I did not recognize Capt. Michael Shupp, my commanding officer during Desert Shield and Desert Storm. Captain Shupp is one of the reasons that I used *Honor, Courage, Commitment* as the working title for this book—he lived the words and set a shining example. Semper Fi!

Tip of the Spear

1

ALPHA COMPANY of the 1st Light Armored Infantry Battalion was just north of the burning al-Burqan oil fields of Kuwait. We were making our way here, through Iraqi troops and the natural obstacles of the desert, en route to Kuwait City. It was the morning of 25 February 1990, and I could clearly see the Iraqi troops to my front. It was readily obvious that these soldiers, unlike many others we had encountered, were not intent on surrendering. They huddled behind protective earthworks and watched us from about eight hundred meters across a huge depression. They didn't fire at us but moved with a tactical posture between fixed positions throughout the morning. All the previous evening I had watched their green forms through the nightscope as they raced quickly, heads down, rifles slung at the ready, from one position to another.

We did have surrendering Iraqi soldiers marching across the west side of the depression carrying white flags. To my left front I watched somewhere between fifty and a hundred Iraqi soldiers walking with their hands high in the air. They were allowed to come all the way to the positions of the unit on our left and were then quickly gathered by swift moving, professional marines.

Lieutenant Tice, my platoon commander, realized that the troops to our front were of a different nature than the surrendering ones. For hours we had watched the surrendering action, but these troops to the front never

1

changed their tactical posture. Tice had given them every opportunity to give up, but the time had now come when the threat they presented had to be dealt with.

I was talking on the radio to him about the troops, and he told me to go ahead and eliminate the threat. I acknowledged, grabbed the joystick that moved the turret, and laid my gunner on the center of the Iraqi line. I issued a fire command directing Uke, my vehicle gunner, to treat the target as an area target. I wanted him to fire 25-mm high-explosive rounds at the center of the Iraqi troops and then to traverse and fire as rapidly as possible across the frontage of the troops for the surprise effect.

Uke had just energized the turret hydraulics, laid the reticle on the center of the target, and announced "Identified!" when the radio call came in. Just seconds before I was to give the command to fire, one of the anti-tank vehicles attached to us transmitted on the platoon net, "Hey! Wait! I see a white flag going up."

I looked, and sure enough the Iraqis on the left edge of the target area had started to surrender. I grabbed my joystick, overriding the gunner, and gave the command to cease fire. Those Iraqi troops lived to surrender.

I have watched the footage, taken from an aircraft gun camera, of the Iraqi who crossed the bridge just moments before the American bomb destroyed it. The media called this individual the luckiest man in Iraq. As far as I was concerned, these soldiers in front of us were the luckiest Iraqis in Kuwait. Had they waited one more second to raise the white flag, they would have been killed by a vicious rain of explosive steel.

Behind us the battalion had arranged for LVSs carrying fuel bladders to replenish our thirsty vehicles. Captain Shupp, Alpha Company's commanding officer, ordered that we refuel "by element"—a command requiring each section in the company to move back and refuel one section (two vehicles) at a time. While refueling was in progress, the company retained 95 percent of its combat power forward in the screen line.

On the company's flank I was the last section to refuel. My wingman and I left the line and traveled the kilometer distance to the LVSs. Just as we approached their position, two friendly F-18s appeared from the clouds and swooped down over us. They were only a hundred meters above us when they passed over, and I watched them bank into tight turns as if to head back toward us. I looked around and saw that my section and the LVSs were the only vehicles in the area. I could not see another vehicle anywhere.

I knew that the F-18s were coming back. They had disappeared into the clouds, but their movement led me to believe they were turning tightly to engage us, thinking we were Iraqi armor. With one hand I grabbed and held tightly the green star-cluster that was supposed to be fired to identify us as friendly. I wasn't sure if the aircraft would be able to see it in the cloud cover. With the other hand I transmitted on the company radio net to the forward air controller in the LAV-C2 (light armored vehicle—command and control). "Wildman, Wildman, this is Blue 5 at the FARP [forward area rearm-refuel point]. I've got two F-18s in the pop on me. Can you get them off me?"

Wildman acknowledged me, and we spent the next few minutes looking skyward, ready to launch the green star-cluster into the air. After what seemed like forever, the F-18s materialized from the clouds and passed over us, heading north. When they appeared, I realized there was no way I could fire the green star in time to stop anything. They moved so fast that by the time I could move my hand to fire the flare, they would be gone. I don't know if Wildman got through to anyone, and I didn't ask. I told him that whatever he did worked, and then I went to refuel.

These two events epitomize much of what the light armored vehicle companies dealt with during the ground war of Desert Storm: enemies that might or might not surrender, and the ever-present threat of friendly fire.

Marines are thoroughly trained to do many things: they are able to conduct a myriad of missions, operate multimillion-dollar pieces of equipment, and fight the enemy in the face of uncertainty. Unfortunately no amount of training prepares a marine to face friendly fire from an aircraft or to confront the moral dilemma of engaging prisoners of war. These skills are learned on the job, and that job is almost always in a hostile environment where mistakes mean death.

To explain how we came to be in the middle of Kuwait, I will start from the beginning with Company A, 1st Light Armored Infantry (LAI) Battalion. I joined the company as a newly promoted corporal in 1988. The company was in search of an identity at the time. Alpha Company had never been outside the United States and had never been tested in any challenging situation. Officers and staff noncommissioned officers (SNCOs) were exploring the venues of their leadership and trying to learn how to lead in a light armored unit.

One of the continuing problems in the LAV community has always been identity. *What is our mission? For whom do we work?* These questions

frequently surfaced and governed our daily lives. Our doctrine for employment was not very helpful, and every link in the chain of command had
what seemed to be a different point of view. To some the LAV was strictly a
reconnaissance asset to be used by the division commander. To others the
LAV was a support asset for the infantry battalions in their mission of seeking out, closing with, and destroying the enemy. Whatever the point of
view, there is doctrine written by the army to support the opinion. The
events in this book are recounted from the small-unit level, so I will also
try to explain in general detail how a platoon and a company of LAVs are
organized.

Marine Corps doctrine requires the LAV to serve in the reconnaissance
and security role, but for the past thirteen years that role has never been
clearly defined. The LAV has certainly fulfilled the division commander's
requirement for accurate intelligence on a rapidly changing battlefield, but
as the story I record here illustrates, reconnaissance and security missions
take on various forms. At times those forms may look like the BFVs (Bradley fighting vehicles) conducting an attack with dismounted infantry or
like a cavalry troop holding its ground against superior forces. Because of
the many possible variations, the identity of the Marine Corps light
armored units has been poorly defined.

This poorly defined identity can be tracked by following the actual
name changes of the light armored vehicle unit over the years. The first
designation, "light armored vehicle" battalion, focused on the importance
of the actual vehicle platform to the mission. Then in the late 1980s these
units became "light armored infantry" battalions. The shift from *vehicle* to
infantry was more than just a name change. As late as 1986 the LAV battalions "borrowed" personnel from the infantry battalions to use as a dismounted element. These infantrymen—the scouts—rode in the back of
the vehicles, and without them the battalion could not accomplish its mission. Appropriately the new name had placed the focus on something
other than vehicles. But because the light armored infantry battalion was
truly a reconnaissance element, it was soon renamed "light armored
reconnaissance" (LAR) to reflect that role. Each of the four light armor battalions made the final name change at different times over a two-year
period, however.[1] And throughout that process, marines within every battalion had to struggle to understand who they were as a unit. At the time
the events I recount in this book took place, the battalions were light
armored *infantry* battalions. The leap to *reconnaissance* had not yet been
made by any one of them.

The base vehicle in the light armored infantry battalion (LAIB) is the LAV-25. This is the workhorse of the unit, the element around which everything else in the battalion revolves. The LAV-25 is named for its weapon: the 25-mm automatic chain gun. The chain gun is mounted in a continuous traverse, two-man hydraulic turret. The Bushmaster chain gun fires either high-explosive (HE) or armor-piercing (AP) rounds at a rate of two hundred per minute at targets in excess of three kilometers. The sighting system is magnified to seven and eight power for the acquisition of targets in day and night, respectively. The gunners can fire at stationary or moving targets from a stationary or moving LAV because the whole system is stabilized by electronically powered gyros.

The turret of the LAV-25 is mounted into the baseline hull of the LAV family of vehicles. The hull is a twenty-foot-long, six-foot-tall, twenty-thousand-pound shell of ballistic, cold rolled steel. It houses a six-cylinder, 275-horsepower diesel engine, capable of moving the fourteen-ton LAV-25 at speeds in excess of sixty miles per hour on hard surfaces and almost that fast off-road. Unlike most platforms, the LAV has wheels instead of tracks. The eight driving wheels enhance the overall mobility of the vehicle by allowing it to traverse a variety of obstacles while still maintaining a reasonable cruising range and on- and off-road mobility.

The LAV-25 is manned by a crew of seven. The driver sits in the front next to the engine; the gunner and the vehicle commander sit side by side in the turret. In the back of the LAV-25 rides the scout team, a four-man group of infantrymen who have been specially trained to operate with the LAV. Each team has a leader and carries the same firepower as the Marine Corps fire team in the infantry squad. Besides their basic infantry skills, these marines have been trained extensively in mounted and dismounted reconnaissance, reporting, and limited engineering.

Filling out the LAV unit are the LAV mission role variants, or MRVs, which fulfill a range of functions. For command and control the variant LAV-C2 allows the commander to set up command cells at radio banks and map boards inside the vehicle. The antitank variant (LAV-AT) mounts an electric, dual TOW (tube-launched optically tracked wire-guided) missile-launching turret in the baseline LAV hull. The AT crews can acquire and engage targets out to 3,750 meters with the newest TOW missiles fired from an armored platform.

The baseline hull has also been modified to produce a variant that allows the 81-mm mortar to be fired. The LAV-M (mortar) is equipped with a traversing platform inside the vehicle that allows the mortar to fire and quickly displace to fire again. For the myriad of logistical tasks inherent in a unit of this kind, there is the LAV-L (logistics), which was designed specifically to hold and move all the logistics assets the unit requires. Finally there is the LAV-R (recovery). The baseline hull is fitted with a hydraulic crane that allows maintenance crews the luxury of performing field-expedient repairs, including replacement of the power plant.

All LAVs are equipped with the same ballistic protection, mobility, and basic capabilities: protection from small arms up to 7.62 mm at point-blank range and from 155-mm artillery rounds at fifty feet. This family of vehicles provides the LAI commander the variety of tools he needs to accomplish his primary mission of providing information about the battle-field—reconnaissance.

The LAI battalion is made up of four LAV companies. Each company is made up of LAV platoons. In the 1990s the companies are made up of two six-vehicle (LAV-25) platoons. Each platoon in the company is further broken down into three two-vehicle sections. Usually the platoon commander and his wingman make up one section, the platoon sergeant and his wingman another, and the senior sergeant and his wingman the third.

The company's commanding officer (CO) rides in the 13th LAV-25, and the executive officer (XO) rides in the LAV-C2. Maintenance and logistics functions are managed by the company trains—that is, the company gunnery sergeant and the maintenance element, an LAV-L and an LAV-R. The companies in Desert Storm were attached between two and four LAV-Ms and two to six LAV-ATs. Altogether, the LAV company is a very formidable force.

The organization of the LAV company varies depending on the parent battalion, mission, and commander. The table on page 7 depicts the organization of 1st LAI Battalion during Desert Shield and Storm.

In Desert Shield and Storm, 1st, 2d, 3d, and 4th LAI Battalions deployed to the Persian Gulf to participate in training and combat operations. What was peculiar about the deployment was its size. Never before had all four LAI battalions deployed to the same place in response to a crisis. Further, this was the largest deployment for the Marine Corps since the Vietnam war. Because of the magnitude of the deployment and the continuing commitments the Marine Corps had abroad, composite units were formed on the hot desert sands using personnel from 1st, 2d, 3d, and 4th Marine Divisions.

For 1st LAI Battalion, this meant that Col. C. O. Myers and the command element from Camp Pendleton (the home of 1st LAI Battalion)

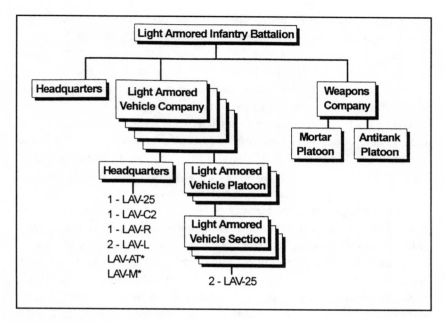

Figure 1. Task organization.

would take command of a battalion made up of two companies from Camp Pendleton (Company A and Company C) and two companies from 3d LAI Battalion from Twentynine Palms, California (Company B and Company D). Initially the unit composed of companies from 1st and 3d LAI Battalions formed in the desert as 1st LAI Battalion. This was fine for those marines from Camp Pendleton, but for the marines from Twentynine Palms it was a loss of identity—a very fragile identity. In fact most of the units in-country were having the same problems: maintaining unit integrity and identity with their composite structure.

Colonel Myers, an insightful and inspiring leader, came up with a recommendation that was implemented: instead of standard battalion and regimental designators, task force names would be used. Hence the composite LAI battalion became known as "Task Force Shepherd."

By the time I joined Alpha, the marines of that company had decided they would call themselves "Cavalry." *Cavalry* is generally not considered a good word in the Marine Corps; *cavalry* is an army word. Furthermore, army cavalry is organized far differently than the LAV battalion (changed to "LAI" battalion shortly thereafter), with the army's version including attack helicopters, tanks, scout BFVs, and infantry BFVs. Yet while other marine companies were "Warhogs" or "Black Knights," we were "Cavalry" —in the old romantic sense of the term, not in the modern army sense. And we operated on the level that we thought reflected that title: we moved fast, exploited the situation whenever possible, conducted mounted and dismounted reconnaissance, and formed pickets.

The company deployed on a WestPac (Western Pacific) cruise in 1989,[2] and we were afforded an opportunity to explore our identity outside the United States. We trained in Thailand, Korea, and the Philippines, and at each location we attempted to validate the mission and role of the LAV company outside the confines of our familiar training areas.

Further complicating the identity problem was the way a unit forms its personality: by adopting that of its commanding officer. When I joined the unit, Captain Shore was the CO. Captain Shore was personality intense— a very friendly and easy-to-talk-to leader. He was focused on the mission but balanced his approach by keeping a constant finger on the unit's pulse. He knew when we were up, he knew when we were down, and he worked with those intuitions during training. Consequently the unit had a very clear-cut, identifiable persona. Problems were openly discussed. Training exercises were debriefed in a manner that didn't hurt anyone's feelings. And it was common for Captain Shore to show up at the ramp (motor pool) and agree with you that what battalion had forced us to do was weird. It was hard to dislike the man.

I don't think we grew professionally as a unit under Captain Shore's tenure, but we were always happy. His personality fitted perfectly with the unit's identity crisis: when we didn't know where we stood, he stood there with us. Looking back, though, I know we were not ready as a unit to wage war. As I say, we were happy, but happy doesn't win battles.

When Alpha returned from the WestPac deployment, the company disintegrated. Officers moved off to different postings, SNCOs moved on to other companies and billets, and NCOs (noncommissioned officers) just moved on. I stayed with what was left of Alpha until we were once again a company. The identity we had found in being "Cavalry" didn't mean as much anymore—the name didn't mean anything special to those who hadn't been there when it was adopted. I accepted that fact as normal since this type of thing usually happened when units reformed.

Introduce Captain Shupp. Captain Shupp could not have been further away on the personality spectrum from Captain Shore if it had been planned that way. Captain Shore was personality intense, and Captain

Shupp was simply intense. I will never forget the first time Captain Shupp spoke to the company (by this time, a skeleton of a company with very few officers and even fewer SNCOs). I stood in formation and listened as the captain explained his focus. The first thing I noticed, and what I will remember forever, was his eyes. As he spoke of being ready for battle and of professional conduct, his eyes moved to make contact with each and every face. They were piercing, focused, and outright scary eyes. I could feel them shoot through me like a laser beam, digging into my very soul in order to read my every thought. From that point on, the one thing that you could expect from Captain Shupp was eye contact. I remember thinking, *What have I got myself into?* . . . *This guy is crazy.* As I look back, I realize he was asking for nothing more than combat readiness. He wanted to lead, and he wanted us to know that we would be led. His personality contrasted with Captain Shore's, though, and in that way it was a shock to the system.

When Sergeant Ramirez checked into 1st LAI Battalion, almost a year before Desert Storm, he had met Captain Shupp, who was then the operations officer (the S-3) for the battalion.[3] Ramirez executed his duties as battalion master gunner under the cognizance of the S-3. After a few encounters with Captain Shupp's intensity, Sergeant Ramirez learned to respect him, and Captain Shupp realized the brightness in Ramirez and left him alone to run his gunnery program.

Sergeant Ramirez always felt that he and Captain Shupp got along well after they understood each other. On a professional level, Ramirez respected Captain Shupp, and when the captain left the S-3 billet to assume command of Alpha Company, Ramirez tried to go with him. In fact Ramirez continued to the end of the Persian Gulf deployment in his effort to get down to Alpha to work with Captain Shupp. That was how much respect he had for the man after the short period they had worked together.

For Alpha the five months after Captain Shupp came aboard were arduous. One of the things the captain did was call in the leaders at 1600 on a Friday afternoon and tell them, "Liberty will be sounded when the company is frequency hopping. Time starts now." What this meant was that the entire company would move to the ramp and transition the SINCGARS (single-channel ground/air radio system) radios from the "off" position to the secure frequency-hopping mode.[4] If you read the technical manuals, the process is fairly simple. You simply turn on the radios, introduce fills (secure code stuff), set the time on the radios, and talk to each other. What happens in real life is usually not so simple, though.

First, if all of the radios are not on the same time clock, you cannot frequency hop. Second, if someone has the wrong position set on a radio's mode switch, it can cause any other radio with the right setting to lose its frequency hopping (FH) sync time (time clock), and you cannot talk. Invariably, out of seventeen vehicles, someone would transmit with the wrong setting.

Additionally, improper loading or filling procedures prevent you from entering the company net, period. All the things that could go wrong usually did, and as a result, at 1900 on a Friday evening, we would be playing SINCGARS games—trying to get the company frequency hopping. It was a fixed game as far as we were concerned: we were destined to fail in the task. Over the months, however, we eventually got it down. Proper switch settings were used, proper filling procedures followed. This didn't change the taste in our mouths for the method Captain Shupp used to accomplish this goal, however. We simply weren't used to his type of leadership. But it was as if he had a premonition of coming events: he wanted combat readiness as soon as possible.

We all lived through the times as best we could. Morale wasn't the highest it had ever been, but we were coping. And we were definitely getting trained. I managed to hold my tongue for the most part. Much of what we did made sense to me. I just had to remember that we were professionals; we were marines: we had to know our craft, and we had to be proficient in our duties.

Some of the training was fun. We exercised like there was no tomorrow. Captain Shupp took us to the pool once or twice a week, where we swam for hours. I actually got into the best shape of my life during those five months.

I learned something that I hadn't known about Captain Shupp through my interview with Sergeant Ramirez: the captain wanted to be a company commander more than anything else in the world. It wasn't so he could say that he was a company commander; instead, it was because he sincerely, deep inside his heart, wanted to train marines. He wanted to train them properly, and he wanted to lead the most proficient marines he possibly could. This was very important to him. With that in mind, it is not hard to figure out why he was pushing Alpha so hard.

The months preceding Desert Shield progressed, and we continued to train. As I look back now, I realize that the NCOs in the company developed rapidly. We had to. In order to fit into this new system of leadership, we had to know our stuff. If we didn't, the SINCGARS drills would last well into the night. We had to become innovative in the way we trained our marines. Not to be innovative would be tantamount to being unprepared for Captain Shupp's newest training exercise. The company was still a skeleton of its former self, but those of us who remained were reaching new plateaus.

When Iraq invaded Kuwait, I was in Bridgeport, California, at Summer Mountain Leader's Course learning how to climb rocks. I was called back from the school as the battalion prepared to deploy. The company, vastly different from when I left, was no longer a skeleton: the battalion commander had moved an entire platoon from another company to augment our company, bringing us up to full strength. Alpha Company was now structured around two full LAV-25 platoons. Each platoon had six LAV-25s, crews for the vehicles, and scouts.

Captain Shupp attempted to integrate the incoming marines into the company without creating a separate entity within the unit. As such, the "new joins" were spread between the platoons. However, the new NCOs were for the most part assigned to 2d Platoon. I was in 1st Platoon, and with few exceptions we remained unchanged. A lieutenant joined the unit and went to 2d Platoon.

We in 1st Platoon had a senior NCO who was in sync with the desires of the company commander: to be combat-ready now. When I met this sergeant, I liked him immediately. A big and burly marine, he always smiled and always had a humorous anecdote about every situation. What I didn't see when I met him was his lack of tactical proficiency. He was a great guy, but he didn't have the tactical knowledge required to lead an LAV platoon in combat. His experience in LAVs was limited, and that fact hurt him— 1st Platoon was without a lieutenant, and he was learning as he went along, struggling until we reached Saudi Arabia.

Our platoon sergeant at the time was Sergeant Negron. The glue for our unit and a truly outstanding leader, Negron had rejoined the LAV community after being out of the Marine Corps for a few years. The marines of 1st Platoon loved this guy. He turned out to be my best friend in the company. We would sit for hours discussing tactics and ways to move our respective sections on the battlefield. What I had in technical and tactical knowledge, he had in common sense and natural leadership ability. In Saudi Arabia we found a way to play on each other's strengths for the benefit of the platoon.

Each of 1st Platoon's three sections consisted of two LAVs with accompanying crews and scouts. Sergeants Negron and Worth made up one section, with Negron as section leader. Sergeant Larson and I made up the second section, with Larson—who joined the unit from the other company—as section leader, the position I had held until his arrival. Within a month of our getting to Saudi Arabia, Sergeant Larson left (he received orders to recruiting duty), and I again assumed the duties of section leader.

We felt really good about our organization, and all of the NCOs in the platoon looked for some event to lead every minute of the day. Perhaps it was rather comical: five sergeants moving all about the company area looking for some responsibility. We invariably stepped on each other's toes, but nevertheless we had the right attitude. I don't think that at that time we had a clue of how ill-prepared we were to fight a war, though. Until Desert Shield none of us knew how much work we had to do. There was no negligence involved; we just hadn't had the opportunity to train as we needed to.

One thing about training: it is nearly impossible to duplicate the stresses of combat in a garrison environment. Any attempt to come close to that duplication falls short. And at that particular time, there were so many things going on within the battalion that training was secondary. No one would have spoken those words aloud, and certainly it wasn't what Captain Shupp thought, but it was true. Sandwiched in among maintenance stand-downs, dog and pony shows, inspections, parades, and the like, training had to be scheduled well in advance. When the training was conducted, there were so many things to do that you ended up doing everything halfway. Even with Captain Shupp's headstrong approach, we were limited by the situation as far as training went. Our saving grace was five months in the desert before the actual war began. Without interruption Captain Shupp was able to prepare us for war.

At the same time that Alpha was preparing for the deployment to the Persian Gulf, Corporal Buntin was welcoming aboard Captain Hammond, his new company commander. Buntin was assigned to Bravo Company, 3d LAI Battalion, which is located in the middle of the desert at Twentynine Palms, California.

Bravo and Delta Companies, 3d LAI Battalion, would join up with Alpha and Charlie Companies, 1st LAI, to create a complete four-company 1st LAI Battalion—Task Force Shepherd—in Saudi Arabia. About a month prior to the deployment to the Persian Gulf, Captain Hammond joined Bravo Company as the new commanding officer. His background was artillery, and he was joining a well-trained light armor unit. When I interviewed Corporal

Buntin, I asked him what he thought of his new commander at the time. Specifically, I wondered if he had any concerns about the change and if the company had changed the way it conducted business.

Artillery and armor are very different things. An artilleryman lives by the old French maxim "Artillery conquers; infantry occupies," whereas a light armored leader realizes the maxim refers to positional warfare and therefore has no place on the modern and fluid battlefield. What it boils down to is a school of thought. Leaders who successfully make the transition into the light armor community are exceptionally talented. Corporal Buntin recalls that he had been a little wary of Captain Hammond's assignment to the company, his particular concern being whether Captain Hammond would be able to make the transition into light armor rapidly enough to lead the company into battle.

Adding to Corporal Buntin's concern about his new leader was Captain Hammond's demeanor. Altogether, Captain Hammond gave the impression of being somewhat unintelligent. He was awkward in his handling of language, speaking very slowly and methodically as though he had to formulate every word in his mind before he could say it. But the real concern about Captain Hammond's abilities surfaced when you combined his vocal traits with his physical characteristics. He was given the call sign "Swamp Thing" by one of the marines in Bravo Company; it was painted onto the side of his turret in grotesque letters underneath a black smudge of a creature that represented the "Thing" itself. And Captain Hammond fit his call sign. He was built like a professional bodybuilder. When he walked, he glided. It was like watching a giant three-toed sloth move: his arms swung wide and smooth, and he traversed the ground with very little effort—there was no wasted motion in his legs as they skated over the ground. If he turned to you, it would remind you of some of the *Big Foot* footage shown on TV.

Captain Hammond's outward demeanor and mannerisms belied his talent and bravery, however—and the idea that he lacked intelligence could not have been further from the truth. Later action in training and in the war saw a sharp, charismatic, and confident leader of Bravo Company. Captain Hammond's courage and leadership during combat led not only to the defense of the 1st Marine Division Command Post (MarDiv CP) but to his being awarded the Navy Cross for valor.

Corporal Buntin was Captain Hammond's gunner. When I asked him what kind of changes in the company were made, he responded almost immediately, "No problems. We had the XO." Bravo Company's XO, Lieutenant Parkerson, was a very experienced LAV leader. The company had trained well together, had developed SOPs (standard operating procedures), and had had the XO to keep them together during this change in command. Buntin was very adamant about the fact that the XO helped Captain Hammond make the transition, and thus the company didn't go through any major changes as a result of a new command identity.

In an LAV company the XO is the commanding officer's right and left hands. The XO is usually the senior lieutenant in the company and in most cases has established experience as a platoon commander before assignment as XO. There are a lot of billets within a unit that you could do without. The company XO is not one of them; the unit cannot function without a good XO.

In a garrison environment the XO develops all of the training programs and handles all the intrabattalion coordination required to conduct training. Once the unit moves to the field for training, the XO puts on his second, third, and fourth hats. Riding in the C2, he heads the fire-support team of the company. Organic indirect fires, supporting fires, and air are all coordinated by the XO for the company through the bank of radios in the rear of the C2 vehicle.

Furthermore the XO works with the commanding officer and provides intelligence preparation of the battlefield, control measures, and in some cases, operation orders. Throughout the course of the exercise or battle, the XO will handle the flood of radio reports and allow the commanding officer the luxury of positioning himself at the decisive place on the battlefield to "fight" the company. The XO conducts the interunit coordination required to keep the company alive on the fast-moving field of war. Adding to all this responsibility is the fact that the XO is second in command and must thus be as familiar with the CO's plans as the CO is. Bravo Company was fortunate to have a marine XO the caliber of Lieutenant Parkerson. Under a new CO, the potential for major change in company procedures is always present, even likely. But with Parkerson's leadership, the command cell for the company was able to continue functioning without major upheaval.

Alpha's XO was Lieutenant Masters, who came to the company when we returned from the WestPac deployment. Lieutenant Masters was a good XO. He wasn't in the same position that Lieutenant Parkerson had been, since he joined the company close to the same time that the CO, Captain Shupp, did. Lieutenant Masters was forced to jump in and try to establish within the company tactical and training procedures that matched Captain Shupp's intent.

I was called into the XO's office one afternoon shortly after I had been appointed company master gunner. When I sat down in a chair across from his desk, I couldn't help but notice the stark contrast between the XO and Captain Shupp. Lieutenant Masters was a very personable leader: young, fit, and clean-cut, he was genuinely concerned with what was on your mind. When he asked me a question, I felt at ease.

"Sergeant Michaels, take a look at this and tell me what you think." He smiled and passed across a rough draft of a unit SOP he had been working on. Alpha Company didn't have such a document, and the captain had assigned him to complete portions of it. I looked at the printed pages in my hands and noticed that the particular section dealt with establishing security.

I spent a few minutes silently reading the text that was marked throughout in red and blue ink. The purpose of the pages was to outline a standard procedure for establishing and maintaining security while the LAV was in a static position. The XO's slant was directed toward the crew's actions. Procedures are similar just about anywhere in the LAV community. The infantry scouts in the back of the vehicle dismount and establish observation posts (OPs) and 360-degree local security. The LAV crew (driver, gunner, and vehicle commander) man the vehicle weapons and radios. The XO's draft revolved around the importance of having a marine man the pintle-mounted machine gun on the vehicle to aid in local security.[5]

"Sir, are you sure we want the pintle manned?" I was initially concerned about what the focus of manning the vehicle was. First of all, if the dismounted element does its job of providing local security, manning the pintle is a moot point. Second, in order to shoot the pintle mount, you have to be in the vehicle commander's hatch. The mount for the machine gun is positioned so that only the vehicle commander can fire it. The concern I had was that manning this hatch to operate the machine gun makes it harder to operate the 25-mm chain gun, which is the vehicle's primary weapon.

By design, the 25-mm chain gun can be fired from either the vehicle commander's or the gunner's station. However, ideal operation of the system requires a marine at the gunner's station. Loading, power-up procedures, and immediate action are done on the left side of the weapon—the gunner's side. What was the focus of the SOP? Was it to provide security or to allow us to move the vehicle, watch the radio, fire the primary weapons system, or fire the pintle mount—or a combination of these?

"What do you mean, Sergeant Michaels?" The XO always wanted to hear what you had to say. It was obvious that he was concerned about the quality of the product and not his own sense of importance.

"Well, Sir, what's the focus?" I went on to outline my concerns, and the XO listened intently. I finished up by saying, "And if we can't give the vehicle commanders a solid intent—i.e., to say, 'Gents, I want you to be able to move the vehicle to a position that supports the scouts within two minutes,'—then no matter what we put in the SOP, every vehicle will interpret the procedures differently."

I cannot describe how important it is to a unit for the NCOs to understand why something is being done. Any task can be accomplished eventually, but true accomplishment and success are a direct result of the NCOs' making decisions in accordance with the commander's intent. The XO listened patiently and asked me a few more questions before he had pumped everything out of me that he required to understand my position.

Charlie Company 1st LAI returned from a WestPac deployment on 11 July 1990. Charlie had relieved Alpha six months prior when Alpha returned from the Pacific cruise. Sergeant Hernandez had been in Charlie Company for six years when they returned from the WestPac. He started out as a private, driving an LAV-25, and six years later he had turned into a young, motivated sergeant who wanted to be trained. Hernandez was totally frustrated when he came back to the United States from the Pacific. He had absolutely no idea what the focus of effort was within the company: he saw the things at which the company failed but didn't acknowledge, and he wasn't being trained in his craft as a marine light armored leader.

Sergeant Hernandez expected that after six years of dedication to the company, he would be able to see some return on his investment. Unfortunately, the company had not advanced tactically or technically. For six months aboard a navy vessel, the company remained stagnant. Hernandez remembers talking to other NCOs about his greatest fear at the time: to go into harm's way with the current level of training.

Hernandez recalls that there was never a time when a tactical procedure or action was carried out the same way twice—in every instance it was done differently. Mistakes were never learned from, and marines reinvented the procedures each time around.

Three weeks after Charlie returned from deployment, Iraq invaded Kuwait. Sergeant Hernandez remembers the invasion as simultaneous with the company commander's departure. Charlie Company was scheduled to deploy to Saudi Arabia, and not only was the unit poorly trained but it had lost its commanding officer.

Charlie's XO, Lieutenant Sellers, stepped in to assume the responsibilities as the company commander. With his assignment, Charlie Company packed gear to go to war, and Sergeant Hernandez found confidence in the new situation. Lieutenant Sellers wanted the company to feel self-assured in its duties. He wanted every marine to be a key player and to have stock in his own future. The first thing he did was gather the NCOs with experience on MPS (maritime prepositioning ships) to ask them how to plan the deployment.[6]

Because Sergeant Hernandez had worked an MPS off-load twice before, he was immediately an integral part of the planning process that would move the company more than eight thousand miles across the globe. Lieutenant Sellers asked questions, and more importantly he listened to what the NCOs had to say. A comprehensive list of equipment required to get the MPS vehicles operational was generated by the group of experienced NCOs. Sergeant Hernandez saw focus in Lieutenant Sellers, and to him this was a good thing.

Lieutenant Sellers was also able to schedule some live-fire training during the busy month of August. Charlie spent almost a week out on the range shooting the 25-mm chain gun. They integrated the scouts into the firing evolutions so they would be used to working with the vehicles in a shooting scenario. Confidence was boosted tremendously within Charlie Company; the marines were finally getting the training they had been hungering for.

Lieutenant Sellers was only human, though, and he could not completely overhaul the unit in the short time before the desert deployment. But the lieutenant did know the direction the company had to go in. And he also knew that he would have to draw upon the NCO's experience and hunger if he was going to be successful in his venture to prepare the company for war. Lieutenant Sellers started on the correct path.

2

THROUGHOUT AUGUST we all knew that if things in Kuwait did not change, we would be heading over to the Persian Gulf. We looked forward to this. If there is one common thing I have observed about professional NCOs, it is that they want to do their job, and they want to do it correctly. I don't think that anyone in 1st LAI Battalion—which was untested in combat—wanted to go off and live through the horrors of armored warfare. But we did have a strong desire to conduct the actual missions that we had spent years training for. We also felt an almost romantic calling: to move about the modern battlefield in the high-speed LAV. We were like children who had not yet figured out that we weren't invincible; we had a reckless desire to perform heroic and chivalrous acts on the field of honor.

Activity peaked during August 1990. Only two companies from 1st LAI Battalion, Alpha and Charlie, were scheduled to go to the Persian Gulf. We received our complement of desert-war fighting gear, loaded our equipment, and waited on recall.[1] We spent every night sitting by the phone waiting for the word to go. My wife couldn't see why we were all so excited to go to the Gulf. I had tried to explain it to her, and had even received understanding nods from her, but I knew she didn't really grasp the idea.

It's hard to describe the feelings I had at the time. At this point I had about six years in the Marine Corps. There was always training for combat, but never had I been put into a situation where I had to use my training against a real enemy. I had questions inside my head that required answers, questions that involved my validating some things about myself: proving that I could do what I was trained to do and that I was really a marine. For me those issues were very important; they were the reasons that I joined the marines in the first place. Hence it was very frustrating for me to have to wait for the word to go, knowing that I would be given the chance to answer those questions soon. I know that others had similar feelings. They may not have been exactly the same as mine, but the desire to go was there.

I asked Sergeant Hernandez what his feelings were during the time that we waited at Camp Pendleton. I expected him to be apprehensive due to the poor training his company had received and the sudden change in leadership. He did have concerns, but they had nothing to do with what I had anticipated: his major focus was his section. He was a section leader, and he felt bound to be with his marines when the time came for war. He couldn't imagine that he might not be there for them when they needed him. He too had questions within him that had to be answered, but they were essentially irrelevant at the time. His primary focus was on what he was required to give his marines: solid leadership.

But there was one marine NCO who I know did not want to go. I didn't know it at the time, but when we got to Saudi and started training, I noticed that he really wasn't happy about what we were being asked to do. I don't think it was a matter of homesickness; I believe it was a conflict of ethics, values, and personal belief about war. I think he joined the marines for the education benefits and never really figured that he would have to fight in a war.

But whatever his motivation for joining the Marine Corps, I respect this NCO for one reason: Corporal Davison did his job and did it well, regardless of his personal views. Too many servicemen, NCOs included, used the war as an opportunity to express their grievances: to forget about their oath of enlistment and suddenly to claim that personal convictions prevented them from fulfilling their contracts. They didn't think that they should be required to fight—they joined only for the college benefits, or they just plain didn't believe in war. I have no respect for such individuals: those who didn't live up to their word as men, who joined a fighting force and then backed out, claiming personal objections. There is no place for servicemen of their ilk in the armed forces.

Corporal Davison, my wingman's gunner, lived up to his obligations without complaining or compromising his oath. I could see the personal struggle he went through as a result of his attention to duty. I have so much respect for this kind of service that I cannot describe it sufficiently on paper. Some may say that Corporal Davison compromised his integrity by succumbing to the pressure and failing to stand strong in his convictions. I would say that he displayed the utmost integrity by realizing that he had made a commitment and that he had to fulfill it.

Aside from waiting to fly off to Saudi Arabia, packing for the war was frustrating for us. The command seemed to be forcing us to take a lot of unnecessary gear—equipment we would have to carry on our persons. We grumbled as we placed our shelter halves, field jackets, and woolly-pullys into our seabags in preparation for a desert deployment.[2] As a marine, you get accustomed very early in your career to packing a great deal of gear whenever you go anywhere. You usually don't use half the things you take, but eventually you accept that fact and just learn to deal with it. The situation now was no different.

Every time the subject of gear packing comes up, Sergeant Ramirez tells the same story about a young, motivated lieutenant who has just read S. L. A. Marshall's *The Soldier's Load and the Mobility of a Nation,* which depicts the high price of overburdening combat troops.

The lieutenant, clearly excited by the revelations within the book, asked Sergeant Ramirez if they should give a copy of it to all of the marines in the platoon. Sergeant Ramirez replied, "No."

The lieutenant looked at the sergeant with confusion. Ramirez could tell he was at a loss for words. *This great piece of work, this learning tool—how can it not be disseminated to all marines?*

Ramirez looked at the lieutenant and asked him, "Sir, do we practice any of the lessons learned out of it here?"

The lieutenant paused before answering. "Well, no, but that's why everybody should read it."

"Great. All the marines read it, and then they all know that their leaders aren't practicing the lessons learned."

The lieutenant was still not clear about what Ramirez meant. Sergeant Ramirez is an intelligent and forthright leader, but he doesn't explain his thoughts very clearly. I have known him for about six years and am just now able to pick up on his ideas and understand his point. He rephrased his response: "Sir, the people who should read this are your bosses. When they have read it and practice it, then the rest of the marines can read it." Apparently, this was enough for the lieutenant, and the issue died.

I relate this story now because it tells so much about the type of leader

Sergeant Ramirez is. Always focused on the objective, he is very difficult to sidetrack. If any training is going to be done, he always considers what it will do for the marines before he does it.

Back to our packing: among the items were mission-oriented protective posture (MOPP) gear. These are charcoal-based suits that are designed to provide protection against a nuclear, biological, or chemical (NBC) threat. We were all happy about packing this particular gear because we had already been told about Iraq's flagrant use of chemical agents in the past. The downside was that the suits were very bulky. Each suit took up about the same amount of space as a medium-sized suitcase. On top of that, since a suit lasted for only a few hours in a contaminated environment, we had to take two of them.

For me, there was also a size issue. "What size suit do you wear, Sergeant Michaels?" the company supply NCO asked when I reached the head of the lineup for issue. Behind him, rows and rows of boxes of NBC suits filled the shelves of the cluttered warehouse.

"Medium-long," I answered. I am six-foot-four, so the "long" part of the size is very important.

"Sorry, Sergeant Michaels, don't have it." He reached behind him to a stack of boxes and produced two suits. "How about extra-large medium?"

I ran into the same problem with the desert utility sizes. In fact the only marines to get the correct size uniforms were the "medium-regulars." Since I've been in the Marine Corps, I have rarely gone to supply and been able to get properly sized for uniforms. Consequently I wore desert utilities and MOPP gear with plenty of room to grow—as long as I grew wider. But they were about six inches too short in the legs. I don't know what is worse: wearing a uniform equipped for flood conditions or watching some poor marine roll his pant legs up eighteen times so he doesn't trip over them. My hope is that someday the Marine Corps supply system figures out how to order properly sized uniforms.

After the uniform debacle, we finished packing our two seabags and field packs. We banded the seabags to pallets and kept our packs with us; the seabags would fly over as freight. We weren't taking our vehicles to the desert; we were going to use those that were on MPS. The problem was that we had to take our own tools because the MPS vehicles didn't have the full tool complement. Additionally we took pintle-mounted machine guns (also not aboard MPS), and we packed SINCGARS radios and mounts. If you can picture this—we were packing a lot of gear; all we wanted to do was get over to Saudi and get to work. But to this day I don't know how we would have operated in-country without those three weeks in August to prepare for it. In my mind I can picture us arriving without the proper vehicle equipment or uniforms to do the job.

The casual observer may think that you just call up the marines and ten minutes later they are flying off to war, but this couldn't be further from the truth. Units that aren't on alert have an immense task to complete before they can go and fight bad guys across the globe.

Finally the word came that we were flying to Saudi Arabia. We all kissed our wives and children good-bye, donned the desert uniform, and mustered for an accountability formation. I don't recall Alpha having any problems here; it's all kind of a blur now. We rode in buses to an air force base in Riverside, California. We had helmets, flak jackets, 782 gear (equipment belt and harness), M16A2 rifles, and field packs.

While the recall and trip to the airport is now hazy to me, what happened at the airport will stick in my mind forever. Though smaller and not as cushy, the air force terminal was set up in much the same way that a civilian terminal might be. All the marines from the battalion were staged at the airport waiting for the plane that would take us away from California. I found a vacant piece of floor and tried to get comfortable. I expected the wait to be incredibly long. There is one thing that marines do very well: we know how to wait for something, and we are very adept at figuring out a good way to do it. In this case, however, the wait was quite short. I was truly surprised: all of the practice we had in waiting, and we didn't have to wait at all. It was anticlimactic.

Just before our mode of transport—a United Airlines Boeing 747—arrived, the NCOs were called up to the company gunny, Gunnery Sergeant Chevice. We were given 5.56-mm rounds to issue to the marines. The rounds were still in the ammunition crates and boxes, and we had been instructed to issue 120 rounds per man. Further we were ordered to load the rounds into our six magazines on our equipment belts.

One way to really motivate marines is to give them live ammunition. Seldom will you find a marine whose eyes don't light up when you present it to him. Ammunition makes everything real; firing ammunition makes a bang; marines love ammunition. Everyone was motivated when we handed out the rounds. They were even happier when we told them to load twenty rounds per magazine. At the time, I remember thinking that it was kind of unusual for us to be doing this. I liked it, but I just couldn't see us hopping off a Boeing 747 in a hot LZ (landing zone) to engage the bad guys. It made a lot more sense to keep the ammunition crated until we got in-country. But hey, who was I to argue when ammunition was handed out?

As they ran to board the 747, the marines were smiling broadly. Those who were especially afraid of missing the plane ran to the head of the line and therefore wound up having to sit in the tail section. Those who either had the foresight to know that the plane would not leave without them or were too old to run to the plane ended up in first class. Myself, I was three rows from first class. I guess I had moved a little too fast in boarding the plane.

It was crowded aboard the 747. I don't know how many people generally fit into one of those birds, but I'm sure we had that many and more. And we were loaded down with war-fighting gear as though the plane were going to land in a hot LZ when it arrived in Saudi Arabia. Impatiently we waited like sardines for our mission to begin. Cries of *Are we there yet, Mom?* rattled through the 747's frame before we even took off.

United Airlines, however, had a surprise for us before we left. *What do you mean, every one of you has 120 rounds of rifle ammunition?* Apparently, there is some rule in air travel that prohibits the carrying of live ammunition aboard a commercial carrier. It didn't matter that we were United States Marines flying off to war. The specter that had aroused my initial concerns about loading the ammunition came back to haunt us all. Bad idea.

Before the plane left Riverside, every round had to be turned in. Kevlar helmets passed up and down the aisles of the plane, and marines stripped 120 rounds from their magazines into the overloaded helmets. I laughed so hard inside I will never forget it. I recall thinking *I wonder if someone has to count all of this stuff?* This event had the potential to really slow us down. Imagine the nightmare of accounting for a 747-load of ammunition. But as it turned out, the process was relatively painless. It took about an hour at most to accomplish the task, and no one ended up counting the loose bullets. I don't know what they did with the ammunition; maybe they just threw it out the open hatch and told the pilot to put the pedal to the floor. The marines for the most part were not too disappointed about losing their ammunition so rapidly. They had to give up the ammo, but at least they were still going to war. The smallest things make marines happy: ammunition, hot chow when it's raining, and flying into harm's way.

3

THE UNITED AIRLINES FLIGHT was for the most part uneventful. My seat three rows from first class ended up being third-row center for the in-flight movies. I remember wandering into the first-class area during the flight and giving the NCOs of my company a hard time. Most of 2d Platoon's NCOs ended up there, flying in style. Well, at least they had some room. Two NCOs from my platoon were there: Sergeants Griswald and Sweeny.

I had floated with Sergeant Griswald to the Western Pacific the year before and knew him well. A very mature and responsible NCO, Griswald had spent many years in the Fleet Marine Force (FMF) as an infantryman. At this point he had spent about eighteen months in the LAV community, and he had a deployment to the Western Pacific under his belt. I met him when we were both corporals and instantly liked him. He spoke with a slow, methodical, almost musical drawl, and he had a distinct Southern charm.

Griswald's tactical proficiency was what had led me to seek out his friendship when I met him. After we were both promoted to sergeant, he was the type of NCO that I didn't want to stand next to: anyone would surely pale in comparison to this dynamo. He was in 2d Platoon at the time, and I gave him a good-natured ribbing about the life in first class. He genuinely felt bad about it. He hadn't planned on sitting in first class, and he kept peering back through the curtain that separated his accommodations from coach, wondering whom he should trade seats with.

I remember telling him, "Hey, just kidding, man. Enjoy yourself. You don't want to sit back there." I pointed back to coach at the mélange of bodies sprawled awkwardly across the cramped seats in an effort to avoid each other and the adrift gear while trying to get some sleep. Sergeant Griswald smiled sheepishly from his first-class seat and nodded. He stayed in the seat, but I could tell he wanted to find the marine with the worst seat in coach and trade with him. That's just the way he was.

Sergeant Sweeny, on the other hand, was truly enjoying his flight to Saudi Arabia in first class. Sweeny was one of those people who looked like the marine in the recruiting posters: a clean-cut appearance, flattop haircut, unbelievably square jaw, and muscular frame—there was no mistaking this marine for anything but a marine. He was an infantryman by trade and our senior scout by billet. He was taking care of what would become the platoon commander's vehicle while we awaited the attachment of a lieutenant.

When I wandered to his area in first class, he had a crowd of the United Airlines flight crew around him. When I got closer, I saw that he was demonstrating all of his marine gear. His M16 was slung across his chest, and he worked the action of the attached M203 grenade launcher back and forth for the attentive crowd. As he explained how each item of equipment worked, they watched in awe. Soon they were snapping pictures with each other, and I think he left the plane with the address and phone number of every female member of the flight crew.

Sergeant Ramirez, being a member of the 1st LAI Battalion staff, probably could have finagled his way into first-class accommodations, but he didn't. Ramirez was still upset that he hadn't been able to get to Alpha Company when Captain Shupp took over. On the plane he wanted to sit with the marines—the marines, in Sergeant Ramirez's eyes, were the line-company men in coach.

Being the battalion master gunner was difficult at times. A lot of marines saw and knew Sergeant Ramirez—his was a high visibility billet —but he knew hardly any of the marines outside of the S-3 shop. He wanted so badly to be in Alpha that not knowing the marines of that company, not being part of the group, truly bothered him. So Ramirez left the confines of first class and found an uncomfortable spot among the marines of the line.

If I didn't mention the flight crew of the United Airlines flight, I would be negligent. It is a terribly long journey from Riverside, California, to Saudi Arabia. The flight crew made that journey bearable for us. They were resoundingly pro-American, and the attention they paid us really demonstrated their support for what was going on—even after they made us turn in our ammunition. They didn't disappear into the bowels of the aircraft when it took off; instead, they overfed us and gave us all the blankets, pillows, condiments, food, and drinks we could ask for. It was apparent that they were really going out of their way to be nice. I knew that the airline was required by law to fly us, and I didn't expect the crew to be very happy about it—they probably worked long enough hours without having the marines around. That was not the case, though, and I thank them for their hospitality.

Eventually the plane touched down in Saudi Arabia. I'm not sure exactly where it was; it was dark and I didn't have a map. I stepped off the plane and followed the rest of the company to an area behind the terminal where we were directed to muster. It was late at night, but it was hot. When I looked around, I could tell that the marines had taken over this little corner of the desert. General-purpose tents covered in camouflage, generators feeding dozens of powerful floodlights, and supply points had turned the small airport into a bona fide Marine Corps logistics base.

Once we mustered in the company area, the first sergeant appeared and passed the word. First Sergeant Guerrero was a fun guy to work with. When he talked, there was no mistaking that he hailed from Jamaica. We strained to understand his thick accent when he spoke, and we laughed when he tried to say a tricky word that came out as something different.

He gave the company orders: "I've got five cases of water up here. You make sure you drink. It's going to be hot. NCOs, I want you to make sure that everyone drinks." He went on for about five minutes about the importance of forcing water into your system and remaining hydrated. There was no doubt in anyone's mind that the five cases of water in front of the company were supposed to disappear quickly. From that point on, we drank water all the time. Anytime we went anywhere, we carried water. Forget your rifle when you go to the head, that's OK, but do not forget your water.

Buses eventually arrived to pick us up, and we began a two-hour bus trip to the port area where we would meet our vehicles. I had to urinate from the moment the buses left. I wasn't the only one, either. The entire company, taking the first sergeant literally, had pushed the water into their systems, and on the moving bus our systems had decided that not all of the water was required—some of it would have to go. Anyone who has ever had to use the bathroom when there is no bathroom in sight can understand how badly our bladders were hurting. We had absolutely no idea how long the bus trip was, so we didn't know whether to pee in our pants or hold it in anticipation of a stop. The bus driver could not speak English, and nary a one of us spoke Saudi. It was a nightmare: we sat on the buses and fidgeted like schoolchildren.

Eventually the bus stopped on the side of the road. We poured out of the bus, everyone searching for a piece of sand to urinate on. Imagine fifty people trying to get off a bus with the same thing in mind. To the observer it probably looked like a planned and rehearsed event. When I finished relieving myself, I noticed that we were in the middle of nowhere. The road was lit by orange lights perched atop metal poles every hundred yards, but there was nothing else. It looked as though we were in the middle of an oil field.

We climbed back on the buses, feeling very content, and continued our journey to the port of al-Jubail. I never felt better. My bladder was relieved, and the cool air-conditioning of the bus was very comforting. Then, five minutes into the trip, I had to urinate again. To this day I'm sure that if you ask anyone who took that bus trip what they remember about it, they would say they drank too much water at the airport.

Eventually we arrived at our destination: an open-bay warehouse on the pier. Inside the warehouse we set up rows of cots and slept. Those next few days were very busy ones. It was very hot, and we had to get accustomed to the heat. Initially we did nothing outdoors during the day; the high temperature would render you incapable of functioning in a matter of minutes. We did, however, get up early and conduct company PT (physical training) before the sun came up. We held classes in the warehouse and, almost to an individual, tried to find a phone.

Deployed marines have one thing in common: they all want to call home and talk to loved ones. Unfortunately I don't know if any of us ever found any phones. I spent most of my time putting together impromptu gunnery classes and conducting last minute reinforcement training. We were idle for the most part until our vehicles were off-loaded from the ships.

Once the vehicles were off-loaded, the pace picked up. We brought the LAV-25s into the open warehouse and got them ready to use. Before the vehicles could go anywhere, we had to inventory all of the gear, add radios and radio mounts, and load the vehicles with all of the basic necessities. I had no idea what to expect when I opened the back hatches of a vehicle. I knew that we had to install the SINCGARS radios that we had brought from stateside, and I knew we had to fill POL (petroleum oil lubricant) and water cans, but I didn't know we would start from scratch.

Every single item in the back of the vehicles was wrapped in heavy treated paper that was lined with a sticky preservative to protect its contents while aboard the MPS ship. Great principle. Unfortunately it was incredibly difficult to recover the contents from these parcels. As I stood with a 180-item checklist behind the vehicle, one of the crewmen would pull out a rectangular package, and we would all stare at each other. "I wonder what this one is?" my gunner would ask as he peered at the tiny letters on the label. We would open the package (not easy) and pull out what looked alien to us all. Fifteen minutes later, when the item was stripped of most of the Cosmoline, someone would shout, "Hey, it's a breaker bar!"

After looking down on my checklist to see if we already had the item, I would reply to the crew, "Shit! Toss it over there. We already have one," or "Bag it!" This process was repeated for each item, and it took the better part of an entire day to accomplish the task.

We spent the rest of the day cleaning the M60E3 machine gun that came with the vehicles. Most of the guns we received were preserved the same way the tools were preserved, and cleaning them required hours. My crew drained diesel fuel out of the vehicle's fuel/water separator and into the lid of the squad stove. The diesel fuel was used to strip the Cosmoline off the weapon, but it also dried out the weapon—which wasn't good. We then took the stripped weapon, and part by part, scrubbed weapons oil into the pores of all the metal surfaces. When each part was lubricated with the oil, it turned into a dust and sand magnet—this was not good either.

We wiped down each part of the weapon with a rag and Q-tips until the excess oil was completely removed. Each crew had one machine gun to clean, and by the time we were done, we were very proud of the work. Like everything else in the Marine Corps, the cleaning turned into a competition among crews. Who had the cleanest gun? Who could find a spot of excess oil in the workings of another crew's gun? An arduous task, but a lot of fun.

In the end the word was passed to turn in all the M60s: we were going to give them to an infantry unit to augment the machine guns they had.

Truthfully, we did not require the weapons. When the LAVs were originally placed in MPS, the M60 was the pintle-mounted machine gun for the vehicle. As the LAV community grew, the M240E1 replaced the M60. The M240 is a Belgian-made weapon and a truly reliable piece of gear. We already had one version of the M240 mounted coaxially to the cannon, and the replacement of the M60 with another version of the M240 made a lot of sense. So losing the M60s didn't hurt us as far as equipment was concerned—we had brought our M240E1s with us from the states. But losing the weapons did hurt us emotionally. Machine guns, especially the big one that Rambo uses in the movies, motivate marines. Taking away those guns that marines had cleaned and babied for half a day created a palpable disappointment. We all got over it, though.

The next few days went by rapidly. We moved the vehicles outside and started finalizing all the preparations for the field. We had no idea how long we would be at the pier, and we had received no solid word on our mission. Marines were still anxious to get to business, but now that we were in Saudi Arabia, the stark reality of the desert heat took a small bite out of our desire to get to the field.

One afternoon we received ammunition. I had never seen as much of the stuff in one place as the amount that was dropped off next to the warehouse for Alpha Company. If 120 rounds of 5.56-mm motivated these marines, you can imagine how they reacted to the sight of thousands of 25-mm armor-piercing and high-explosive rounds; crates of hand grenades, LAW (light anti-armor weapon) rockets, and incendiary smoke grenades; and hundreds of belts of 7.62-mm linked ammunition. We spent many happy hours unpacking this treasure, and then we spent more happy hours loading it aboard the vehicles.

What surprised me the most was the fact that we actually loaded the ready boxes of all the weapons and uploaded the cannon to the feeder (where the rounds are moved for firing). In the United States, the only place rounds are ever put into a vehicle is on a firing range. Even then, safety is so paramount that each phase of loading is tightly controlled and oversupervised. Now we were being told to load them up here. This was new to all of us. We weren't waiting until we left the pier to load, or even until we staged for movement: we were loading right then and there. As a result everyone was hyped-up for action. In addition to motivation, ammunition added reality to the equation, and the truth of our business was abruptly pounded into our senses.

One of the reasons we practice so much safety with ammunition in training is that marines get killed by other marines through negligence. Marines leave training areas with ammunition because they forget it is in their weapons. Invariably those weapons go off and hurt or kill other marines. Safety is therefore a serious business. In garrison, ammunition is generally not carried around unless you are going to fire it; weapons are checked and double-checked by SNCOs and NCOs, and the realism that characterizes almost all training is interrupted so that positive safety measures to avoid these accidents can be emphasized.

It is unfortunate that in the process of keeping marines safe from negligence, we forego the very realism that is necessary in teaching them what they need to know to keep themselves safe in combat. If marines walked around every day with rounds loaded into their rifles, there would be far fewer accidents and casualties. The constant familiarity with loaded weapons in itself would give them more respect for the weapons they carry. Desert Shield and Storm showed us all that marines were not accustomed to carrying loaded weapons or driving loaded weapons platforms. Marines were killed or wounded by other marines. We had at least three negligent discharges within our company during the deployment. No one was hurt, but that did not excuse the negligence. We need to carry loaded weapons, but unfortunately marines are still getting killed through carelessness and inattention.

This was my first leadership challenge: to keep the crew safe from incident while they were at the same time training and living with loaded weapons on a daily basis. I attacked the problem through familiarization and supervision. Every day, under a variety of conditions throughout the deployment, we loaded and unloaded the vehicle weapons systems. We established procedures for when to clear the weapons, when to clean them, and how to clear and clean them. I tasked the scout-team leader with supervision of the scout team, my gunner supervised the crew, and I watched everyone.

Supervision was important, but it was also very important to me that the marines were not overmanaged. I didn't want the marines to have to show the NCOs their chambers every time they cleared their weapons. I didn't want to do the routine by the numbers in unison as it might be done on a range. I wanted the marines to feel confident with their weapons, and I wanted them to trust their own abilities to carry out the procedures correctly. Most of all, I wanted my crew to know in their hearts and minds that I trusted them and that I didn't personally have to check their procedures in order to maintain that trust. For me, this worked. We never had a negligent discharge within the crew, and I honestly feel that the marines were very comfortable with their weapons systems. They had respect not only for their own abilities but for the weapons themselves. I think the reason they had confidence was that we worked so hard to establish a regular routine that involved clearing and cleaning the weapons.

After all the ammunition was loaded and distributed, we received word that we were leaving that night to go to screen for the rest of the division's off-load. We were wasting no time. We finally were going off to do our business. I thought we would be the first marine forces to leave the port. At a time when I should have managed to get a few hours of rest, I was unable to sleep because of anticipation. As a result, later that night I was exhausted.

As it turned out, we were not the first to leave the port. Corporal Buntin and Bravo Company, 3d LAI Battalion, arrived almost two weeks earlier than Alpha Company. The company flew from California on 17 August, and it was truly the tip of the spear for what would become Task Force Shepherd. When Bravo began its journey to Saudi Arabia, the advanced element of the 1st Marine Division was busy at the port of al-Jubail off-loading equipment from MPS. Among the equipment off-loaded were thirteen LAV-25s that Bravo Company would fall onto once they arrived.

Bravo went to work much faster than Alpha did, once we got in-country. The 7th Marine Expeditionary Brigade (MEB) commander was concerned about the continuation of the Iraqi offensive into Saudi Arabia just two weeks after their initial thrust into Kuwait. Thus the first combat elements to arrive in-country were required to man their equipment and quickly assume a defensive posture north of the port area so that the MEB, and later division off-load, could be completed without the threat of enemy action. But because of the coordination required with the Saudi forces, Bravo didn't actually leave the port until 21 August.

In the interim, as Corporal Buntin recalls, the marines of Bravo Company performed almost exactly the same tasks that Alpha had done almost two weeks later. The same tools and machine guns were wrapped in protective Cosmoline for protection and had to be recovered for use.

In the blistering 120-degree heat, Bravo stood by to go to the field. On the nineteenth, Captain Hammond took the company out for a run around the pier area before the sun was up. When the company returned from PT, the vehicles underwent final preparation for the field. The same amount of ammunition Alpha later received was issued to Bravo Company, and they uploaded the weapons systems to the safety stops.

Once the 7th MEB commander gained approval from the Saudi officials to send marines inland, the combat forces that had been waiting patiently at the overcrowded port of al-Jubail moved out into the open desert to establish defensive positions. If the Iraqis wanted to push into Saudi Arabia and disrupt the center of gravity—the off-load at al-Jubail—marine forces would be positioned north and northeast of the port at what would later be called the "speed bump." By the time the word got to my end of the chain of command, you didn't have much of an idea exactly what was out in front of you. In fact when Alpha left the port on 3 September, I thought we were all there as a line of defense.

On the evening of 21 August, when Corporal Buntin left the port of al-Jubail, he had about the same impression that I did. He was not aware that there were Saudi forces well forward in a position to provide the alert of an enemy offensive. When Bravo left the port that hot evening, Buntin was down in the gunner's seat with his eyes glued to the M36 passive night-sight. The company column took its business very seriously. If there were Iraqis out there, they had to be found before they saw the company.

And when Alpha left the port, we did the exact same thing that Bravo had done when they left. When the column stepped off from the holding facility, I remember passing the battalion executive officer standing there, arms across his chest, carefully watching each vehicle of the company as it rolled by. We took this movement seriously. We had no idea that Bravo had gone through this exercise and, further, no idea that the entire 7th MEB had off-loaded and was in a defensive posture north of the port. He who shoots first in an armored engagement usually wins, and winning is defined by the destruction of the opponent. So in Alpha Company, gunners' eyes were glued to sights, senses were honed, and vehicle commanders kept their eyes fixed to night-vision devices.

After almost a five-hour movement, the company conducted a security halt on the coastal highway adjacent to the area in which we were to operate, a nine-hundred-square-kilometer expanse of desert we later named the Triangle. Bordered by three hard-surface roads that intersected at three corners to form the legs of a triangle, the area was a mixed terrain: from rolling sand and rocks that were easily trafficable to pronounced hills—not so trafficable—that jutted skywards almost three hundred feet.

Immediately after that initial security halt here, we all fell asleep. I remember standing a watch and looking around the company area. Everyone had been so hyped the night before that they had totally depleted their well of energy. Little did I realize what I had yet to learn about adrenaline deprivation.

I talked to Corporal Buntin about that recent first movement into the field. I asked him, "When did it hit you that we were really far from the border [over 120 miles]?"

Corporal Buntin laughed in reply. "Probably about a day or two later when my vehicle broke down because a fuel-water separator was clogged, and I finally got ahold of a map, a large-scale map where I could see just how far out we were, and found out that all the other troops [from different countries] were up in front of us."

Fortunately the Iraqis did not attack. They missed a golden opportunity. We all knew that if they attacked in force and with armor in those initial days, we were ill-equipped to do anything other than serve as a "speed bump." LAI battalions traditionally trade space for time. This meant we make contact with the enemy well forward and maintain contact as the enemy advanced by falling back. Eventually we handed off an enemy that has been harassed, attrited, and exposed to a larger, more powerful killing force. North of the port, however, there were no fallback positions. If Iraq pushed, we held; there was no space to trade for time.

It is appropriate that the first vehicle in Bravo Company went down as a result of a fuel problem. Throughout the entire deployment to the Persian Gulf, the LAV had a terrible problem with fuel-related malfunctions. The fuel injectors of the six-cylinder diesel clogged up or burned out regularly. Fuel filters clogged almost constantly. The trouble was with the fuel itself —but not because it was of poor quality. The LAV can burn any of a number of grades of diesel. Usually the vehicles are filled with a standard commercial-grade diesel. In the Persian Gulf, however, that fuel was replaced with a higher-quality aircraft fuel—which actually cleaned the fuel cells, removed the sediments, and carried them through the system. Those sediments first clogged up fuel filters to the point that vehicles wouldn't run. If the crew didn't have a filter on hand (which is common when filters are being replaced for every vehicle almost weekly), the clogged filter was removed, and the fuel was mainlined to the engine. Then the unfiltered sediments eventually made their way to the fuel injectors and clogged them to the point that the cylinder housing the injector would not even fire.

We had left Camp Pendleton for the desert expecting to experience engine coolant and rubber-tire problems. In actual experience, however, the engines remained cool enough to operate even in mid-September afternoons, the tires lasted the whole deployment, and the clean fuel was killing us.

Alpha, Bravo, and Charlie all went into the desert to participate in the defense of the port at al-Jubail. Sergeant Ramirez was still upset that he wasn't with Alpha Company. When he got to Saudi Arabia, he took advantage of every opportunity with the colonel to sell himself *out* of the battalion. "Sir, I am really terrible as a master gunner," he would politic. "I really can't function in the three shop [operations]. I don't know how to set up tents, can't set up maps; in fact, I can't do anything."

By now the colonel was aware of Sergeant Ramirez's strong desire to join a line company. What happened next, though, sealed Ramirez's fate with the operations shop. When the battalion staff arrived in-country, they picked up their vehicles from the MPS and moved out to what was called the "Chicken Ranch." The battalion operations chief (the senior enlisted marine in the operations shop) was stuck in the United States waiting on a flight to Saudi Arabia. Through sheer fate, Ramirez was tasked with setting up the shop at the Chicken Ranch in the operations chief's absence.

Unfortunately for Ramirez, he did the standard professional job he always did: he got the shop up and running, including setting up tents and maps. To top that off, he assumed the additional task of establishing security for the battalion CP (command post). Sergeant Ramirez did a bang-up job; Sergeant Ramirez was not going to Alpha.

The Chicken Ranch was the base of operations for the entire battalion during those first months in the desert. In the middle of the desert, located immediately off the main north-south hard-surface road, the Chicken Ranch stood as the lone landmark in the area. The ranch proper was six single-level rectangular buildings lined up, side by side, perpendicular to the road. They were in awful shape. Completing the scene was an old trailer and a water tower at the northeast corner.

When Sergeant Ramirez pulled in the first time, he was overwhelmed by the acrid odor of chicken droppings. The buildings were vacant, but the odor was unmistakable. The water tower was filled with water from an underground well, but it leaked—and when it leaked, it released the pungent smell of sulfur, like rotten eggs. The combination of chicken droppings and sulfur created an intolerable odor. The marines of the battalion CP were not at all happy to be setting up office at the Chicken Ranch. After a couple of months, though, everyone was taking showers underneath the sulfur water tower. The smells no longer affected them. They had become nasally immune to the vile odors, and everything went well—until chicken season arrived again in Saudi Arabia.

Upon returning from a visit to one of the companies in the field, Sergeant Ramirez was surprised to see that they had visitors back at the ranch. Every one of the hundred-foot-long buildings was chock full of baby chickens. The tiny yellow biddies were not only laying droppings of their own but chirping all day long as well. The CP, who had learned to tolerate the smell, was now presented with an additional challenge: survival of an aural assault. In addition to his regular duties, Ramirez and his fellow marines now had the distinct pleasure of watching—and listening to—baby chickens grow into adult chickens. Like unwanted houseguests, the chickens outstayed their dubious welcome.

4

IF THERE WAS one particular area that every member of Alpha Company was ill-equipped to deal with when we arrived in-country, it was navigation. In fact we were so naive in the area of desert navigation that our learning process itself makes a worthwhile tale to tell.

Mounted navigation (that is, navigation from a ground-vehicle platform) is a very tricky procedure: the high-speed movement, the wind, the dust, and the elements all contribute to a rapid loss of orientation. When the intricacies of the open desert are combined with the basic problems of mounted navigation, the complexity of the situation doubles.

We had lived and trained in Southern California. Mounted navigation was conducted using a map scaled 1:35,000 that was divided into one-kilometer squares: each square depicted incredible detail vis-à-vis road surfaces, surface structures, and terrain. We trained in areas that we were very familiar with—we worked, operated, and lived in those areas. Finding your position on a map was never a concern; it was an afterthought. The distinctive terrain representation provided by the detailed maps made it very easy to fix your position down to a ten-meter box. Bottom line: at our home in Camp Pendleton we were never lost.

When we trained in the Southern California desert, navigation became a slight challenge. We weren't as familiar with the area, and navigation by IFR (I follow roads) was not possible; the limited road system within the desert bases prohibited the street-map approach. However, like Camp Pendleton's, the desert's topography was very distinctive. You could literally drive around for an hour, casually following your general trace on the 1:50,000-scale map. When you needed to know your exact location, you conducted terrain association; that is, you looked around, found the biggest hill in sight, and located your position on the map in relation to that hill. This was slightly more difficult than navigating at home station, but it still was not a formidable task.

Our first operation in the desert of Saudi Arabia showed us just how complex desert navigation was: the operation revealed, in an unkind manner, the immense chore we faced every minute of the day simply to keep from being lost. I had always fancied myself a very good navigator, and it took me about a heartbeat in the hot sun to admit that I had a lot of work to do to live up to my own expectations.

There are some basic problems associated with desert navigation in Saudi Arabia. For example, there are not a great many physical features to use as reference points. What few there are look like those of every other piece of terrain in the area. Right up front we found terrain association to be an unreliable method—a fact that didn't stop hardheaded marines from attempting it, however. And because there are virtually no road networks beyond the main highways, the second of our favorite methods, IFR, was also rudely withdrawn from our tool bags.

In the desert the night can be incredibly dark. You really have to go some place like it, where the familiar lights of civilization do not glow in the distance, to appreciate just how deep the darkness is. There were a few landmarks in the desert that we could use as a reference, but we could not see them at night, and even during the day we found it very difficult to see anything that didn't loom large on the horizon.

In addition to the basic problems inherent in desert navigation, we in Alpha Company started out with the deck stacked against us. Initially, only three maps were issued to the company—one map for the company commander, and one for each of the two platoon commanders—a situation that had something to do with division's policy for map distribution. Apparently there was a shortage of maps in-country, and to make the most effective use of the maps available, division established a plan for distribution: one map was to be issued to each infantry platoon, and then, as more maps became available, one would be issued to each squad. I don't know how this policy affected an infantry platoon, but it didn't work very well for an LAV platoon.

We had three sections of vehicles in each of our LAV platoons. Each section operated as a separate entity within the platoon. Sometimes the entire platoon might have been located within a one-kilometer square, but normally the platoon was spread out over two to three kilometers. Additionally, each section conducted independent tasks that might take them as far away as ten or twenty kilometers from the platoon. So having one map per platoon did us very little good at all, allowing only one of the three sections to navigate with such an aid. It was October before Sergeant Negron rectified the map situation.

But the three maps that had been issued to the company were themselves a cause for disgruntlement. They were air maps (designed for an aircraft to navigate with) and therefore did not include the detail required for ground navigation. The scale was 1:250,000. Where a kilometer would be displayed in about an inch on our normal map, the air map used that same space to show six kilometers. A 1:50,000 map is broken down into roughly half-mile squares, and the 1:250,000 map is broken down into six-mile squares. Basically it was like navigating with a road atlas where there weren't any roads.

With all the difficulties presented to us, it would have been easy to roll over and admit that the desert had beaten us. We didn't do that, though. The challenge was issued; it was a matter of professional pride.

One of our first nights of desert navigation went like this. We traveled in a company column down the main highway through the desert, and at a point that was defined by absolutely nothing, we departed the road, broke into platoon columns, and drove off into the open desert. The moon was almost full that night, and you could really see very well. Normally we would wear night-vision goggles, but under these conditions we didn't need them. The moonlight reflecting off the sand and the lack of terrain to create moon shadows resulted in a surreal brightness that provided enough illumination for us to be able to see for miles.

We drove under these conditions for five or ten minutes until we reached the top of a short rise where our new platoon commander had called for the vehicle commanders to assemble.

When I got there, I found out that one of the staff sergeants had followed an azimuth (a magnetic heading) on a compass from the hard-surface road to get to the position that the platoon commander had plotted on his map. A side note: the pen mark that indicated the position covered a one-kilometer area on the map—that's how small the features on the maps were.

Listening to the staff sergeant explain how he had gotten the platoon to the position, I made mental notes—any technique that would help me navigate in the harsh environment I heartily welcomed. The light was so good that I could see all the terrain on the horizon, 360 degrees around. Since I didn't have a map, I tried to memorize the scene as the staff sergeant talked so I would have some reference to go on for the nights ahead.

The next couple of days we didn't do much but try to get used to moving around the desert. Being without maps ourselves, we didn't learn a lot about desert navigation. We just stuck together in platoon formations and followed the guy who did have the map.

The first problem developed a few nights later. We moved back to our positions of the first night—the positions that the staff sergeant had led us to—along the same route as the first night, following the same marine as the first night. He was navigating as before: following an azimuth on the compass.

The mental picture I had created the first night alerted me to the problem. I wasn't a hundred percent sure, but it seemed to me that we drove a lot farther to find our positions than we had the first night. The moon was still casting enough light for me to see the desert around us, and when we stopped, I was almost positive we weren't in the same spot: my mental picture of the horizon did not correspond to the current picture of the horizon. We were on top of a slight rise within a depression, but the scene around us wasn't the same.

Lieutenant Tice called the vehicle commanders to assemble so he could pass the word. When I got to his position, the other leaders were already there. "Sir, are we supposed to be in the same position we used the other night?"

"Yeah, why?"

Before I could answer, the staff sergeant interrupted and started explaining how he had followed an azimuth to the position. He was immediately very confrontational. He acted as if I were questioning his abilities, and he responded with a defensive posture.

When he was done, I said, "I don't think that we are at the same position." I paused, looking around at the horizon before continuing. "No, this isn't the same spot at all." I did not intend to ruffle the staff sergeant's feathers, but I felt that we were in the wrong position.

The other NCOs started looking around at the ground, trying to spot vehicle tracks or any other sign of our previous presence. None of the

NCOs disagreed with my proclamation, but they didn't agree either. No one was sure one way or the other.

As we went back and forth with ideas, I interjected, "See that small hill over there?" The group looked to the left at a distinctive knob of earth on the horizon. When I was sure they were all looking at what I was pointing out, I continued, "That hill was exactly to our nine o'clock last time. Now it is closer to eleven o'clock. I think we moved farther to the south."

But the staff sergeant was sure of his navigation. "No, Sergeant Michaels, I followed a 148-degree azimuth, and here we are, same hill, same position."

"Hey, Staff Sergeant, I'm not saying you didn't follow the right azimuth, but I don't think we ended up in the same place. I mean, we drove for almost twenty minutes." I looked around to the others, who remained silent while the two of us traded comments. "Does anyone remember driving that long before?" No unified answer.

The map didn't provide any help either. You couldn't find your position on the air maps unless you were in the middle of a major road intersection. In the end we never figured out whether we were in the right position or not. Out of the whole experience, the platoon learned a few things. First, an azimuth was not good enough by itself to use to navigate over the desert. You had to navigate just like a ship on the sea would navigate: travel on a heading for a specific time or distance. From that moment on, we used our odometers to keep track of how far we had traveled. That way, at least we would know when we'd gone too far.

The second thing we learned was that while you could use a magnetic compass from the vehicle commander's position atop the LAV, you had to calibrate the compass to the vehicle. Each armored vehicle had a different effect on the compass. We had to shoot an azimuth to a distant point from the ground in front of each vehicle, and then we had to get into each vehicle commander's hatch and shoot an azimuth to the same distant point. The difference in the azimuths created by the armored hull of the vehicle was the declination. For example, if the azimuth to the distant point was 180 degrees on the ground and 192 degrees from the turret of the vehicle, the declination for that vehicle was twelve. But, as I said, each vehicle was different. My declination was six degrees—I had to add six degrees to my headings to use the compass on the vehicle.

Lieutenant Tice approached me later and told me he appreciated that I had the conviction to argue my point when I thought we were in the wrong position. He told me he personally thought I was wrong, but he admired the fact that I had stood up for what I believed and then dropped the subject when it was played out. I didn't think it was an issue, but I guess knowing he had strong-willed leaders was important to a new platoon commander.

From that point on, although we didn't always agree, Lieutenant Tice trusted me—and my judgment. That trust is a very important thing between a commander and his subordinates: without it, there is nothing. Proficiency and experience alone do not accomplish missions. Trust binds a unit, and trust is what allows a commander to select a course of action that uses the proficiency and experience of his subordinates.

We had by no means learned all of the lessons of navigation that night. In fact, until the day we left the desert and headed home to the United States, we were still learning how to navigate. There was a distinct evolution in our navigational abilities, however. We arrived in the desert as primates, and through the months, we walked on two feet, and eventually we ran.

The next lesson in the navigational learning process was this: finding individual vehicle fighting positions. We established these positions orienting north whenever we stopped moving. They were always adjacent to the closest available terrain. It might have only been a slight rise in the sand —if that was all that was in the area, that was your position. We used the same vehicle positions for days or even weeks at a stretch before moving on to new areas. Being able to find your position day or night was essential.

We were conducting security operations oriented north near what we called the "Crusher Road." The Crusher played a big part in the early days of Alpha Company here; almost all of our training missions were based on executing actions around it. A constant and familiar landmark, this manmade gravel road was what you searched for when you were lost. Named after the Crusher Brothers gravel quarry located at the southern end of the Triangle, the Crusher ran more than sixty kilometers from the base of the Triangle to the north, into what would be future training areas. There was another improved-surface road that we never named—I don't know why, but I guess it was because it wasn't the Crusher. Only the Crusher was the Crusher.

On this particular occasion we had just conducted a resupply of fuel, water, and chow. We carried out these resupplies at night—Captain Shupp would have it no other way for Alpha. When darkness fell upon the desert,

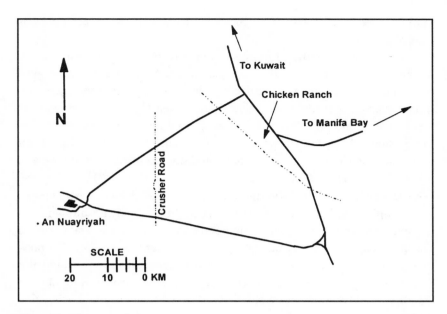

Figure 2. The triangle.

we met the trucks that brought us the supplies on the Crusher. It was always easy to find that road, so moving to resupply never presented any problems. We linked up with the trucks, conducted business, and went back to our vehicle positions. This is when the problems surfaced: finding your vehicle position at night. After all, the positions were nothing more than a set of tire tracks on the reverse slope of a piece of terrain—a spot that was totally indistinguishable from the rest of the terrain around it.

We learned the azimuth lesson, so we marked locations on the side of the Crusher with piles of rocks to give us references to plot headings from. When you saw the rocks—the pile that you had made for your own reference—you turned and followed an azimuth a distance until you came to the rise in the sand that was your piece of terrain. Then you looked around until you found the tire tracks that marked your fighting position. No problem. We were high-speed and proud of ourselves. No maps, but we were professionals: we improvised, we adapted, we overcame—we got lost!

The moonlight went away. The lack of civilization that allowed the moonlight to reflect unimpeded on the earth was the same lack of civilization that ensured the desert would be shrouded in utter darkness when the moon went away. In my life I had never experienced such complete darkness—a spongy kind of darkness that came without a warning. I was thoroughly unprepared.

The first time I returned from a resupply with no moon, I was lost for about an hour. I left the road where I had marked my turnoff and followed my azimuth—with the correct declination of six degrees—for the appropriate distance. But there was a flaw in my system: I was navigating to the general area, and once I was in that area, I thought I would be able to see my position. The problem was that the visibility was so low I could not make out the slight rises in terrain. I could not see my old tire tracks, and hence I could not find my position.

A few degrees of error throughout the route had thrown me off course by a couple of hundred meters. Though I could locate my position in such an area in the moonlight, it was impossible in true darkness. For an hour I backtracked, again and again trying to find my fighting position. I'm positive I passed within a few meters of it a number of times. I could not believe I had gotten lost. The entire crew was baffled. Just a few nights earlier, the slight rise was so obvious. I would never have imagined being able to miss it.

I finally found the spot and decided that there was a lesson to be learned: you can't find what you can't see. After that I always marked the reverse slope of my position with a water can or a pile of rocks. That way, if I were within a hundred meters of the position, moon or no moon, I could look out with the night-vision goggles and see the mark. It took each vehicle commander a different amount of time to learn this lesson, but this is a lesson we all did learn. There was no way around it; the compass in the turret was simply not accurate enough to guide you to within a meter of your destination.

Each vehicle commander had to live through his own ordeals as he solved his land navigation problems. You can pass information onto each other, things that you learned, but being lost has a certain way of driving the points home. It is always better to experience the problem if you are looking to learn something.

We understood that people had to learn navigation on their own, but that did not mean we granted those marines who got lost immunity from ridicule. After we learned the lessons, each of us had fun with anyone who hadn't yet learned them.

The one incident that sticks out in my head as the funniest happened a night or two after I had learned to mark my own vehicle position. It involved Captain Shupp. I had just finished resupply and had moved the section back to our positions. The night was inky dark, and the desert fog was rolling in—visibility was about fifty meters. I had just established the turret watch when a vehicle drove by. It was about fifty meters to the front of my position, but I couldn't tell who it was. My gunner and I exchanged bewildered glances, and I grabbed the night-vision goggles to check it out, but the vehicle was already gone. About five minutes later, the vehicle drove by again. This time it was to our right and heading behind us. Wearing my goggles, I could make out the vehicle commander's form peering forward into the darkness; he had his goggles on, too.

This went on for a while: the vehicle moved back and forth from all directions. Then the radio that had been silent sparked to life. "Black 5, this is 6, over." Captain Shupp was calling the XO.

"Go ahead, Black 6."

"Five, are you back from FARP yet?"

"Roger." At about that time, the vehicle drove by again, and through the goggles I watched as the captain keyed his helmet.

"Black 5, shine a red lens for me." Captain Shupp was probably no more than two hundred meters from his position, and he had driven in and around the company CP, the entire 1st Platoon, and the company trains, and never saw any of them. We all laughed so hard. I remember that no one came up on the net to help except the XO. Everyone had to figure out navigation: you learned from mistakes, and the CO was no different. The XO eventually got Captain Shupp home using the *Can you shine a light?* method. It was a procedure that would be used often—in fact, overused —during our stay in the desert.

The next step in the navigation evolution was drawing—in the absence of real maps we drew our own.

It started out when the platoon commander gave me the air map cluttered with checkpoints, phase lines, and other control measures at 1130 in the afternoon. "Sergeant Michaels, copy what you need, give the map to Sergeant Negron for his section to copy, and get it back to me by 1500." I looked at the map and chuckled. It would be impossible to reproduce the map in such a short amount of time.

I really couldn't get much from the map in the time he gave me, so I copied what I could onto an MRE (meal ready-to-eat) box and handed it off to Sergeant Negron at about 1300. The copied map didn't help much, but the idea did. After that, I tried drawing maps of areas as we traveled through them. Using a compass and the vehicle odometer, I drew moving range cards from the turret of my vehicle.

For example, when we did a zone reconnaissance to a screen, we would conduct a survey of a large area of the earth defined by phase lines on a map. At the end we assumed positions that allowed us to provide early warning of enemy approach. When we got to the phase line where we started from, I recorded the odometer reading. Then as we conducted the reconnaissance, I simply asked the driver for odometer readings and recorded them on a strip of duct tape in front of me. When I had to put something in the box, I did the math, converted to kilometers with the scale taped in front of me, and quickly drew the information, to scale, in the box. I showed my wingmen (I had three of them throughout the deployment) how to do it, and pretty soon we had refined the system to the point where the Defense Mapping Agency (DMA) might have considered hiring us. The information helped the platoon commander with his reporting and scheme of maneuver for fallback plans, and before long, he was requesting them from the whole platoon.

Eventually I reached a level of skill where I no longer required the scale and duct tape. It became second nature for me to do the math and conversions. I had predrawn boxes for all occasions, colored pencils and pens, tracing paper, and graph paper: all benefits of being married to a woman who would send me whatever I asked for.

We really had the process down, but eventually we tapered off on the drawings. A drawing was only good if you planned to use the area again. If you weren't going to stay there, it did no good to map the place. And as the months progressed, we didn't stay in any one place very long.

September marked the end of the platoon's operating without maps. Sergeant Negron had decided that if the battalion couldn't fix the map problem, he would. During one of our rest trips to the camp area, Sergeant Negron came to my room and said, "Michaels, let's go." He stood at my door with a smirk on his face, his slight frame at the ready.

"Where are we going? It's hot out." The rooms at the camp had the best air conditioning I have ever experienced. He would need a very good reason to drag me into the searing heat outside.

"We're gonna get some maps." He was nodding his head with confidence. The grin on his face then changed to a gritty scowl. I could tell he was bound and determined to be successful in this venture, but I was curious as to how he was going to get the maps when battalion had been unable to get them for us. I was also wondering what kind of trouble the two of us were going to get into. But Sergeant Negron was the type of guy that you wanted to follow. He was a true leader within our platoon; I don't know how we would have gotten along without him. I acquiesced.

We caught a ride with a marine in a HMMWV (high-mobility, multipurpose wheeled vehicle, a souped-up jeep made by A. M. General). After about ten minutes of driving, we ended up at a building on the other side of the camp area. Apparently Negron had figured out where the division rear was; he assumed that if we just showed up at the G-2 (intelligence office/officer), we could con someone out of some maps. He was right.

We walked into the fenced area surrounding the building and cleared our rifles in the clearing barrel at the hatch. I laughed about this. Clearing barrels are an extra safety measure to ensure that no one gets hurt. A fifty-five-gallon drum is placed at a forty-five-degree angle to the ground and filled with sand. Then a sign is posted with the exact, as per the technical manual, procedures for clearing each type of weapon that a marine might carry.

As we locked our bolts forward, placed the end of our weapons into the barrel, and pulled the trigger on the empty chambers of our rifles, I felt very proud of my crew. The types of things I wanted to avoid were the mindless, automaton-like responses to safety. Marines actually fired rounds into clearing barrels all the time. With all of the safety procedures posted, it seems hard to believe, but it is true. When my crew cleared their weapons, they were really clear; we didn't have the safety net of a clearing barrel in case a mistake was made. The marines were responsible for their weapons; they didn't follow a list of procedures that could eventually lead to complacency—*Oh, shit, I'm glad that round I fired into the barrel didn't go off into a marine!*

We finally found the G-2 after explaining to one of the dozens of majors within the building what our situation was and what we were after. This was when I first saw how screwed up the system for pushing gear to the marines was. There were so many maps inside that building it was unreal. I think every driver, clerk, and gear guard had his own map—in case they got lost going to the Post Exchange, I assume.

When we asked why the maps were not being pushed out to the marines, we were told that the policy of one map per platoon was still in existence. The officer in charge of the maps listened to our story and eventually gave Negron enough maps for the six vehicles in the platoon.

I don't think the officer believed that a section of LAVs actually operated by themselves. Moreover, this officer really believed that the platoon commander was the only one who needed a map. Sitting in the building, forty miles from where Alpha operated, I understood how he could have thought such a thing—but that didn't reduce the amount of disgust I had for a leader who from his soft chair questioned what we needed. I considered us very fortunate to receive a half-dozen maps from this marine, but Negron was after more; he asked to use the prized lamination machine.

My goodness! I was shocked, and I remember thinking that this officer was probably going to take back the maps he had begrudgingly parted with and lock us up in the brig for even suggesting the use of the laminator. You see, laminating machines, copiers, fax machines, printers, and the like, are the prized possessions of the people in whose office they reside. Once a piece of high-speed equipment is placed at someone's disposal, they become very protective of that piece of gear. It is as if they have a personal philosophy to ensure that the machine never breaks—that is, the gear will not break if it is never used. If a laminating machine is in any intelligence office at the battalion level that I've ever seen, you would have a very hard time getting permission to use it. Here we were in the desert asking a marine to let us use his personal lamination machine—I just didn't see it happening, and I wanted to drag Negron out of there by the collar before we lost what we had already gained.

I expected that the officer would say *Well, that machine is for limited use, we don't have maintenance support, and we're really short on lamination paper. . . . Sorry, can't help you.* I was not disappointed on that score. The officer was not going to help us any further—and for exactly these reasons. Negron didn't give up, though. Like a frugal old man, he bargained with the lieutenant until the marine could stand it no longer. In the end Negron received one laminated map, the lieutenant's personal map— *I hope you two sergeants understand that*—in return for not bothering him anymore.

The platoon's map problem solved, we couldn't wait to get back out to the field and put the new 1:250,000-scale maps to use. We quickly learned that as long as you knew where you were when you started, you could always know where you were on the map when you stopped: using the methods we had already learned, azimuth and distance.

We thought the scale would still be a problem, but in reality it wasn't. We were never required to navigate to a precise ten-meter box on the ground. The only time we had to be precise was when we were moving back to our position; when we did that, we relied on azimuth, distance, and marking our positions. Because of the open desert terrain, navigating to within one kilometer of the objective was good enough. We became very proficient at using the maps to move around in the desert.

The maps were a precious asset. I have to admit that just having one made us feel much more comfortable. Being lost without a map leaves you just one option: you drive around until you find someone you know. Being lost with a map lets you believe you might actually be able to use deductive reasoning to find your location yourself; that, at least, gives you a lot of confidence.

One night I was returning from a trip to the battalion CP along the main highway that headed north. At about sixty miles per hour, my map blew off the turret and out into the desert. It wasn't until the next morning that I noticed it was gone. I knew immediately what had happened to it: it was common to lose things that were lightweight when driving down the road. I knew that somewhere in that ten-mile stretch of desert between my position and the CP, my map had liberated itself. I figured that it was gone for good and that I would be without a map indefinitely. The company checkpoints had been scrawled on it, and when I told Lieutenant Tice that I had lost it, he was concerned about compromising the control measures. He wanted to find the map. I thought he was crazy—there was no way we would ever find it.

Sergeant Sweeny, on the other hand, was motivated. "We'll find it. I've got good eyes." I thought he was crazy too. When he proposed a plan that included driving up and down the highway using the vehicle optics and binoculars to search the sides of the road, I was sure he was kidding. But when I looked at his face for a hint of sarcasm, all I found was an energetic grin. We drove off looking for the proverbial needle in the haystack.

After about the third time we had driven down the route, I began to grow tired of the search. Sweeny, positioned in the scout hatch of Lieutenant Tice's vehicle, was sharp, though: he actually spotted the map and retrieved it. I could not believe it. How lucky could the guy be? On a ten-mile stretch of road, he finds an object all of one square foot in size.

It took me a couple of days to get the map back from Sergeant Sweeny. Since I had written the thing off as gone, and he was the one who had found it, it was his—after all, what claim did I have to the map after the lack of faith I had displayed regarding Sweeny's optical powers? I was, however, finally able to thank Sergeant Sweeny enough, praising his skill to such a degree that he gave me back the map. Indeed, Sweeny had not been operating out of sheer luck that day—his extraordinarily keen vision later led to his saving a wounded marine's life at OP 4.

Eventually the whole company got the air maps. You could see the challenge coming a mile away when Captain Shupp developed a night land-navigation course. The captain's consistency in training continued; he pushed us hard. And with land navigation he made no exception. By this time I think we all realized how fortunate we were to have his leadership in Alpha Company, so the course did not cause any discontent. We enjoyed testing our land navigation skills against the other platoon in Alpha and relished testing our skills against the captain. We wanted to impress him.

After Captain Shupp got lost coming back from the resupply, he had been issued a GPS (global positioning system) from the battalion. GPS uses satellites to track your position to a ten-meter box, and it gives headings and distances when you want to go somewhere.

So, armed with the GPS, Captain Shupp went out to set up checkpoints. At each checkpoint he placed vehicles from the command group and maintenance section for us to link up with. The whole course was about thirty miles long if you finished without backtracking. It was longer if you ended up getting lost in the middle of it.

We were conducting the exercise by section, and my wingman and I sat down and plotted out navigation legs for the course. We drilled the azimuths and distances into our heads. We really wanted to do well. I let my wingman lead the section through half of the evolution so we could both get some practice.

Everything went well until we got to about the third checkpoint. My wingman had been leading, and I was following him, checking the azimuth and distance to each checkpoint myself. He stopped on the west side of a very large hill. I pulled up next to him and, after getting the driver's odometer reading, concurred that we had arrived at the checkpoint. There was no vehicle in sight to link up with, though. The moon was fair, and as far around us as I could see, there was no sign of life.

I remembered from the preparation we had done that the checkpoint was adjacent to a dot on the map that represented a hill—the same hill I thought we had stopped at. I double-checked the map inside my turret and was sure we were there. I called on the radio to the XO who was coordinating the exercise, "Black 5, this is Blue 5, over"

"Go ahead, Blue 5."

"Black 5, do you have a vehicle manning checkpoint three, over?"

The XO responded that he did, and after I explained that I was on top of checkpoint three and there was no vehicle here, he added that the vehicle was placed by GPS, and GPS didn't lie. I was perplexed.

After a few minutes I figured that since the closest I could get with the

1:250,000 map was a kilometer and that the pen mark designating the checkpoint was as large as a kilometer, I had probably interpreted or copied the checkpoint slightly off and thus had ended up the width of the pen mark (a kilometer) off. I took the lead, and we conducted a one-kilometer search around the area. After about an hour I saw some light to the southeast and drove toward it. After driving three kilometers I found checkpoint three in the middle of a vast expanse of flat sand.

I got off my vehicle and went to the vehicle at the checkpoint, where I found Sergeant Walker, a mechanic. He and Staff Sergeant Free, the company maintenance chief, were manning the checkpoint.

"Hey, Walker, what checkpoint is this?"

Walker laughed, "Lost, Greg?"

"Well, I don't know, Doug. I've been looking for checkpoint three for about an hour." I presented my map to show him where I had it plotted. It turned out that he was manning checkpoint three. I didn't know at the time why Walker was so far from where I perceived the checkpoint to be. I do remember I didn't trust the GPS reading that the captain had used to plot the checkpoint. But what could I say? The GPS doesn't lie.

Recently I figured out what had probably happened in the desert near checkpoint three. I was reading a manual on global positioning with satellites when I discovered that the satellites send an erroneous signal. Further, that erroneous signal is sent on purpose: the government does not want the bad guys to use our satellites to their advantage. During military operations you can receive the signal without error, but you must have specific electronic data (a fill) loaded into the GPS receiver to decipher the erroneous signal. Without the fill the position reported on the GPS is not accurate. It's pretty darn close, but we all know when close counts.

Checkpoint three was most likely plotted at the edge of the built-in signal error. Further, my plotting was not accurate on the air map. Combine that fact with the natural error of following an azimuth in an armored vehicle, and the result is the disparity between locations. The lesson to learn is this: never allow anything to replace map reading and manual navigation. Use all technology to your advantage, but avoid overreliance on that technology. The less work your mind has to do, the less work it will want to do; and when it is required to work, the less it will be able to do. I didn't learn this lesson in the desert, but fortunately I didn't have to: I never had a GPS to rely on.

As the months progressed in late 1990, our navigational prowess increased. With our newfound skill came cockiness. We were good, and we knew it. We stopped marking spots on the road that indicated where we turned off to find our positions. Instead we used road intersections as reference points and drove a set distance from the road intersection—using the vehicle odometer—to find our turnoff points. In order to avoid creating trails that would give away our locations, we plotted a number of turnoff points at various intervals for each vehicle position. Because we spent so much time in the desert training, we were better navigators than those who supported us.

One fall day I was returning to my position when I noticed that someone had placed a huge, used rubber tire on the side of the road. Leading away from the tire was a distinct and well-worn trail that five-ton trucks, our support, had made through frequent use. I decided to follow the trail and quickly realized that it led to our positions. This was the trail the FARP team had used at night when they came to resupply our company.

I was not very happy that our positions were so distinctly marked by the supply folks: I probably should have had sympathy for them, but at the time I didn't. I drove back to the tire and found that they had marked an additional turnoff with another tire. After a brief conference my wingman and I decided to remedy the situation. We loaded the tires onto our vehicles and drove off. We drove north a kilometer or so and reset one tire next to the road. We took the second tire back to the platoon area and dropped it off at the platoon commander's position.

The lieutenant wondered what we were doing, and when I explained the situation to him, he rolled his eyes and chuckled. I don't know if he was pleased by the confusion we must have caused the supply trains, but he let it go. He knew that we were very proud of our skills and that we didn't appreciate those who hadn't learned the lessons yet. To us it was a matter of professionalism: either you knew how to do something right, or you went to great lengths to learn. Looking back, however, I believe we may have been a little harsh on the poor souls who drove through the desert every night to support us.

I think our resupply team was late that night. And after that, we started getting assigned the task of linking up and escorting the resupply convoys to our positions every night. Our counterploy had resulted in an increased workload for us; we had hurt ourselves, but it was good training.

Another time, farther north, we harassed our lifeline to the rear again. It was getting very late, and our scheduled resupply had not shown up yet. After hours of waiting, finally we could hear the five-tons rolling across the desert behind us. Sergeant Negron went out to meet the trains as they approached us from the rear. He stopped the lead truck, and the driver stuck his head out the window. "Hey, is this Charlie Company?"

Negron responded, "What do you need Charlie for? You've found Alpha. You don't know how lucky you are; now you can resupply us."

"No. We're scheduled for Charlie." They went back and forth for a few minutes, with Negron trying to convince the marine to resupply our company: it was obvious that someone had forgotten about us. The driver didn't care, and he drove off into the desert looking for Charlie. With the last truck gone Sergeant Negron noticed that the rear truck in the train was dropping off chemlights every couple of hundred meters, like bread crumbs to guide them back to the road.

I'm not sure whether Negron was just angry at not getting resupplied or if he was appalled at their lack of professional navigation skills, but he decided to retaliate. He took his vehicle and went out to rearrange the lights. When he was done, they formed a very large circle in the desert— a circle that led nowhere.

We were still waiting for our resupply an hour later when those trucks returned—following the lights—from resupplying Charlie Company. Later, when the trucks passed behind us the second time, I approached Negron. "What's going on, man?"

He was standing behind his vehicle with his clenched jaw set in a scowl. He bobbed his head in satisfaction and said, "I fixed their chemlights for 'em, man."

I laughed. We all laughed. That night we watched the unsuspecting drivers loop around and around the desert floor wondering why it was taking so long to get home. Eventually they must have figured out what was going on because we didn't see them anymore. I would have paid big bucks to be a fly on the wall in one of the trucks.

Perhaps the most memorable navigation moment occurred sometime in November when I asked the lieutenant if I could lead a section patrol forward of our lines. I was hungry to train. If we weren't conducting night operations, I always went and asked the platoon commander if we could go on a patrol. There were two big reasons for us to seek out training. First, it was very good training—truly a challenge—to move about and navigate at night, and I wanted all the practice I could get. Second, it made the watch schedule easier. If we went out at night and trained, it cut four to five hours off your watch schedule. After three or four months of nightly turret watch, every minute that you didn't have to do it was invaluable.

Just before dark the platoon commander got back to me and called me to his position. Usually when he approved my training, he let me do what I had planned, but this time he had gone to the captain and gotten a bona fide training mission. I was tasked with a reconnaissance of a number of key areas spread out more than fifteen or twenty miles. The areas were known or suspected Saudi and Kuwaiti positions, and the captain wanted to know exactly where they were and what their disposition was.

I was only trying to conduct navigation and section movement training, but I started champing at the bit when I was given the mission. This would really be a challenge. I would have to navigate to a number of locations where there would be something to see. The distance was incredible. After I received the order, the platoon commander told me to brief him with my plan before I left.

My wingman, Corporal Matlain, and I talked about the mission and plotted out our course. In this particular area I navigated during the day by using the few distinct desert trails as references. It was very easy because there was only one major lateral trail, and just a few trails perpendicular to it. And all major trails were depicted on the air map. I assumed that I could use the same procedures at night. I decided to use the major trails and intersections as references to plot odometer legs for movement to each of the areas of interest. It was very complex, but Corporal Matlain and I worked it out and drilled it into our heads before I briefed Lieutenant Tice on the plan. When I briefed the platoon commander, he simply nodded and told me I had about four hours to conduct the mission.

From the minute we stepped off, small navigational errors accumulated, and in the end I got lost. I found the major trail I was looking for to base my movement off of, but I entered the trail at a different point than I had intended. As a result my odometer planning was out the window. I improvised and tried to terrain associate using the small dots on the map that represented the hills in the area.

Eventually I found the first and second areas of interest. There was nothing at either location. We continued the rest of the reconnaissance, and I felt I had recovered nicely from my original mistakes. I continued to feel good until we entered the Crusher Road; according to my calculations, I had gone about five miles farther than I should have to reach it.

This being the case, my reconnaissance of the first two areas was suspect. I was probably in the wrong two places. We stopped on the road, and I looked over to my wingman's vehicle. I could see Corporal Davis standing up in the gunner's hatch shaking his head. He was not a very happy camper. Corporal Matlain, however, was still motivated, and we tried to determine exactly where we were.

I figured that I was about four or five kilometers away from where I should have been, so the best course of action would be to move up and down the Crusher until we found a familiar intersection for reference: without a good start point you could not navigate at all using the air map. The next hour or so proved that it was extremely difficult to find a reference point here.

Finally I found a road intersection that I was quite sure I recognized. I did some quick math in the turret and plotted a new course, and we finished checking out the last two areas we were supposed to check. By now I was late in returning, so I tried to call the platoon commander on the radio but couldn't reach him. Since we were almost done, I would just have to explain our tardiness when I got back.

The return trip was very confusing: I had found Saudi and/or Kuwaiti positions in both of the last two locations and therefore assumed that I had really recovered from the navigational errors. However, on the way back, distinct terrain features and auxiliary routes appeared where they shouldn't have been. I didn't dwell on it, though. I couldn't afford to second guess myself this late in the game. I was getting tired, and I was susceptible to making a bad decision in a heartbeat. I stuck to my plan and continued home.

Just as my odometer reached the appropriate numbers (about fifteen miles), we drove into a position occupied by a number of vehicles. *Bingo!* I figured for sure that we had adapted to the situation and had nailed the navigation dead-on. That would have been an extraordinary ending to a long evening, but I couldn't have been more wrong.

"Blue 1, this is Blue 5. I'm late but am returning to friendly lines at this time, over."

There was a very noticeable pause before Lieutenant Tice answered. It was late at night, but you could always count on Lieutenant Tice to stay up when we were out training. "Blue 5, are you sure? I don't have any signs of your movement."

Just as I started to reply, something dawned on me. Suddenly the position didn't look that familiar at all. The terrain wasn't the same, and the vehicles were much bigger than our LAVs. I told the platoon commander to "wait one," and almost immediately we had to stop because there were people running out into the road in front of our vehicles.

Finally I realized my folly. On all sides Saudi M60 tanks had turned their turrets toward our vehicles. An LAV is not a match for a tank in the first place, and as close as they were (fifty meters), we couldn't even move to seek cover.

I called my wingman. "Blue 6, I don't think we're in Kansas anymore."

"Yeah, Blue 5, I was starting to think the same thing."

"Blue 6, are those tanks?"

"I think so, Blue 5."

"OK, let's not do anything overt right now until we can sort this out." In front of me a dozen Saudi soldiers pointing AK-47s in my direction halted the vehicle and looked for a place to come aboard.

"Blue 1, this is Blue 5. I think we've driven into a Saudi tank position. There are a bunch of Saudis moving around pointing rifles at us."

We had never been allowed to work with the Saudis, and contact with our allies was guarded. A moment later the platoon commander returned, "Blue 5, solid copy." A pause. Then, "What do you want to do?" I guess I was waiting for advice from the platoon commander.

I thought about it a second and realized I had to figure this one out myself. At that time a soldier climbed aboard and began screaming at me to get down from the vehicle. Having his rifle pointed at me did help his case. I told the crew to stay calm and not to shoot anyone. At the same time Corporal Matlain was being convinced to get down from his vehicle as well.

"Blue 1, they want us to come with them. Let me. . . ." I was going to explain to him what I was going to do but decided against it because I wanted to ensure no one did anything crazy with the soldiers on the vehicles. "Wait out, Blue 1. I'll get back to you. Break. Blue 6, let's see what they want."

I grabbed my M16 and slung it over my shoulder, muzzle down, and got off the vehicle. I met Corporal Matlain on the deck, and we were escorted by very nervous guards to the middle of the position. A couple of minutes later, we were guided toward a large tent.

From the outside the tent appeared to be a normal military general-purpose tent: green, canvas, and unattractive. When we stooped under the two door flaps, a warm blast of air greeted us. So sharp a contrast existed between the cool outside temperature and the warm inside environment that I gasped sharply upon entering the tent. When my eyes adjusted to the lit interior, my jaw dropped to the floor.

It was a scene from *Lawrence of Arabia*. The floor of the shelter was carpeted with deep pile rugs that extended all the way to the walls of the tent.

The tent itself had a white winterization liner, draped from the ceiling to the floor, that provided insulation from the crisp night air. Two kerosene space heaters burned silently, casting golden, flickering shadows on the four walls. The distinct odor of the burning kerosene was overpowering.

Directly in front of the door a very elegant, well-groomed gentleman sat in flowing white pajamas on top of what looked like three or four full-size mattresses. The mattresses were covered with thick, elaborate blankets and exquisitely ornamented Persian throw pillows. My first impression was that the man was very clean. In contrast to Matlain and me, our bodies covered in road grime and dust, he seemed to have recently showered and shaved. The hint of puffiness around his eyes made it appear that he had been woken from a peaceful sleep by our arrival.

I didn't say anything right away, and as I looked around, it became apparent that this was the unit commander. The men who had escorted us into the tent stood at attention behind us until the gentleman mumbled some words I did not understand, at which the nervous guards stood hesitantly at ease. He looked at me and asked a question. Though I do not speak Saudi, I was pretty sure he was asking me what I was doing driving into the middle of his position at four in the morning. In fact he said only one word that I understood: captain. He addressed me as "captain" each time he spoke.

I remember he was very calm. He sat perched on the edge of his bed straightening the fabric of his flowing pajamas as I tried to explain what we were doing there. I had an impressive explanation, but it was very obvious from his expression that he did not understand English. So there we were, staring at each other and wondering what to do. He turned and spoke to what I figured was his XO, and the XO replied and went away. After that, there were several very awkward and silent minutes in the tent.

I tried one more thing. I bent down and drew a circle in the deep pile of the carpet. I gestured to the man and then to the area around us before I pointed back to the circle I had drawn. Then I drew another circle in the carpet and pointed first to Corporal Matlain and then to myself. I then pointed back down to the second circle. Finally I drew a long and meandering path around the circles with my index finger. The path began at the circle representing our position and ended at the circle marking the Saudi position. I closed my silent oration with the international gesture for *I'm lost:* I shrugged my shoulders with the palms of my hands upwards.

After a moment I saw a light bulb suddenly appear above the gentleman's head. He started nodding and stood up from the bed. A smile appeared on his face, and he extended his arm to shake my hand. I accepted his proffered hand with my own; he smiled even more warmly and said, "No problem, Captain," in heavily garbled English. And just like that, the tense atmosphere in the tent changed—the guards noticeably relaxed and moved quickly to escort Matlain and me from their commander's presence.

When Matlain and I walked back to the vehicles, I turned to him. "How about that?"

He was smiling from ear to ear. "Fun time. What are you going to tell the lieutenant?"

"I don't know yet." We laughed, and he continued smiling. Corporal Matlain was always a happy character. Here it was, in the middle of the morning, we were at least three hours late, I had just committed a major navigation faux pas, and Matlain was still energetic and cheerful. I was very fortunate to have him as a wingman during the deployment. I could always count on his support and an easygoing approach to problems.

When we mounted the vehicles, I immediately turned the section around and took off. I didn't shoot an azimuth, look at the map, or take an odometer reading: I wanted so badly to just get away from that position. I looked up to the sky, found the North Star, and headed south. I had a feeling I was close to the company and a really strong suspicion that I was too far north.

Once underway I keyed my helmet to activate the radio. "Blue 1, this is Blue 5, over."

Right away, the platoon commander answered back, "Go ahead Blue 5."

"Roger. I'm en route to your pos [position] right now, over."

"Roger, Blue 5, be advised, the six [the captain] wants to see you at his pos when you return."

I paused for a moment wondering what kind of discontent I had caused. "Roger, Blue 5, out." Whenever I did section night operations, I could always count on Lieutenant Tice to be up and waiting like the mother of a teenager on prom night. Not that he worried; rather, he felt obligated to share the hardships with the marines. If I was out with my section training, then he was up participating as the platoon commander. He never did my job, but he always did his job.

I did not, however, expect the six to be up every time I came back from training. The simple fact that he wanted to see me meant that he had been woken and notified that one of his NCOs was causing trouble. Unpleasant visions of his piercing eyes and scathing voice were running through my head. I decided I would stop at the platoon commander's position to try and get a little heads-up before I went to see the captain.

Remarkably we left the Saudi position and rolled almost directly back to the platoon commander's position. Five minutes of driving and looking at the stars, and I drove the section directly to my intended destination.

The evening had one bright spot: after all the navigation problems, I had missed the company position by only about two kilometers. With a 1:250,000 map, that was well within the acceptable tolerance. Unfortunately this bright spot was clouded by the fact that within that area of tolerance was a Saudi tank battalion.

The lieutenant looked tired when I got off the vehicle and approached him. He met me halfway between our vehicles, and we had a short conversation over the noise of my running engine.

"Welcome back, Sergeant Michaels." There was a slight hint of sarcasm in his voice.

"Thanks, Sir. Sorry I'm late. I ran into some navigation problems out there." He nodded. I gave him the sketch of the reconnaissance. "I got everything required, though."

He took the sketch and looked at it. "I figured you'd have some problems."

I wasn't sure what he was getting at. "What do you mean, Sir?"

He was still studying the sketch of the reconnaissance when he replied, "You planned your route off of the trails. I didn't think that was the best course of action. Should have navigated to terrain features; planned the route off of that." He looked up from the map.

I pondered what he said for a second and knew he was right—my problems had stemmed from the plan. "Why didn't you tell me, Sir?"

He handed the sketch back. "You probably wouldn't have believed me, and besides, it's better that you learned it yourself."

He was right. I was drawn a little further into the mind of my platoon commander. I responded seriously, "Thanks, Sir. You're probably right."

He laughed ever so slightly, as energetically as he could laugh after waiting for me all night. "Take the sketch to the CO, and then get to bed."

Just like that, the lesson was learned; just like that, the lieutenant sent me on my way without dwelling on the navigation error. He knew I had cataloged the experience. As I look back today, I realize it was a great piece of leadership. I don't even recall if we talked much about the tank position: it wasn't an issue. In his own way the lieutenant was developing me into a better leader. He knew how I learned things, he knew I wanted to learn things, and he knew what buttons to push to affect that learning.

Before I turned to leave, I said, "Sir, the CO probably is going to chew my ass, huh?"

"Probably."

"Roger that, Sir. Hey, I'm going to send Matlain and his crew home, OK?"

"No problem. Now, get out of here."

It was a fifteen-hundred-meter drive to the CO's position. It was very dark, and I wondered what was in store for me. As I peered into the black murkiness beyond my vehicle, hoping I was going the right way, I wondered what he would say if I got lost again on the way to his position. Fortunately I didn't. I trusted the azimuth and distance, and in a few minutes his vehicle materialized in the darkness ahead. Having parked my own vehicle, I soon recognized the CO's shadowy form moving toward me, and as he approached, I popped to attention. "Sergeant Michaels reporting as ordered, Sir."

He had the biggest smile I'd ever seen on his face as he reached out and patted me vigorously on the shoulder. "Stand at ease, Marine." I was so shocked I couldn't begin to formulate words. His demeanor was so uncharacteristic of him. This was not what I had expected. I expected an ass chewing to end all ass chewings. Instead he was happy and very curious. "So what was he like?"

I didn't know whom he was talking about. "Sir?"

Still smiling, he said, "The colonel, the Saudi colonel, what was he like? What happened?"

During the next five minutes I explained the entire situation to the captain. He was very much interested, and he listened intently, laughing throughout the whole story. I was truly relieved.

"So, did you have fun, Sergeant Michaels?"

"Well, Sir, I wouldn't trade the experience. I learned a lot." As an afterthought I remembered the sketch in my pocket and rapidly withdrew it. "Oh, here, Sir. Mission accomplished."

He took the sketch and examined it before putting it into his pocket. "Good work, Sergeant Michaels. Good work."

As I drove home (about a ten-mile drive), I couldn't help but realize how fortunate I was to work for a marine of his caliber. He was multifaceted and very talented, and he had a knack for solving problems. I already knew he could be a hard-ass in ensuring that we were well trained, but that night I learned that Captain Shupp had compassion and that he would tolerate the learning process of a young NCO.

Years later I asked Captain Shupp—by then, Major Shupp—why he didn't chew me out that evening. I explained to him that I'd really been shocked by his departure from character and that I still did not understand his treatment of me.

Captain Shupp simply said, "Sergeant Michaels, you did the right thing." And that was all. I thought I would be enlightened, but the reply was cryptic to me. I may never understand his character completely, but I revel in the fact that he and I can talk for hours about that incident and others. There is an invisible cord that binds the former members of Alpha Company together. Every inch of that cord leads back to Captain Shupp, and that tie will remain strong and unbroken because of the captain's character.

On 5 November, Lieutenant Tice received a warning order for a raid on the battalion forward command post. The raid to assault the CP was going on the night of the sixth and involved moving the platoon about thirty miles to a position we were not familiar with. Lieutenant Tice decided to send Sergeant Negron and me out on a reconnaissance to map and plan the route.

It wasn't often that Negron and I got to work together. We were both section leaders and hence had our own sections to train. We relished any opportunity that Lieutenant Tice gave us to work together, though. It was a running joke between Negron and me that whenever the situation got really bad in Iraq or Kuwait, the president of the United States would make the call to stand up "Hell Section" to take care of business—that's what we were when we worked together.

Negron and I were both so cocky about our abilities and respected each other to such a degree that when we got together, magical things happened. We truly believed in the Hell Section concept. Lieutenant Tice would never put us in the same section, but at times he would let us work with one another. This was one of those times.

The navigation of the route for the raid was particularly challenging. The actual straight-line distance from our positions to the battalion CP was probably no more than three or four miles, but Lieutenant Tice wanted to move well south—to mask our engine noises—and attack from the CP's opposite flank. Further, there was specific terrain that he wanted to use to hide the vehicles and dismount the scouts to observe the CP. We only had time to conduct the reconnaissance during the day, and the raid was going to take place the next night. There was no room for mistakes;

the navigation had to be dead-on to meet the time line.

Negron and I were up to the challenge. We left on the reconnaissance, and for the next four hours we mapped, plotted, and reconnoitered every aspect of the route. It was at this time that I realized exactly how much we had really learned about navigation. We were combining every aspect of that science into a well-functioning system. There was no room to dwell on one particular facet such as sketching: it had to be second nature because simultaneously we were navigating to the next piece of terrain—and the next, and the next, and the next. At one time I would have hovered over my compass as we moved to keep on the appropriate azimuth, but now I took only casual glances. We noted odometer readings and converted the miles as part of the larger picture. We had really come into our own.

We finished the navigation and returned to the platoon where we briefed everyone on the route. Lieutenant Tice tasked me with leading the route to the raid site on the next evening. Even with all the confidence that I had in my abilities at the time, I would be lying if I said I wasn't a bit apprehensive. Using a route during broad daylight is entirely different from using that route at night. I looked forward to the challenge but felt light in the stomach knowing that the entire platoon would be behind me and that any mistakes I made would translate into a problem for all of us.

The next evening came, and we started the raid. We left in a staggered column formation and traversed the ground that Negron and I had detailed the day before. I was in a heightened state of awareness for the entire movement, but my thoughts wavered between confidence and worry as I passed each key feature on the route: *Was that the right turn? I don't remember that hill.*

Two hours later, I pulled up behind a gentle rise and broadcast on the platoon radio net, "Blue 5, set." I felt comfortable with the navigation, but the real satisfaction came when the scouts dismounted the vehicle and immediately observed the battalion CP to the front.

We surprised the CP with the raid and *killed or captured* the key battalion staff officers. I think that this one mission was where the platoon truly realized how effective we were. Where there had been confidence before, there was now proof to back it up. I have to credit it to leadership again. Negron and I loved a challenge, and we loved to train, but without development, that kind of desire manifests into nothing more than heightened ability. With development it leads to excellence.

After the raid we moved back to our platoon positions, and Lieutenant Tice called Sergeant Negron and me over to his position. Briefly he explained to us that there was an opportunity for us to get in some training with the reconnaissance marines located at Manifa Bay. The reconnaissance marines had requested a section of LAVs to operate at night in the area southeast of Manifa so that the marines manning observation posts could practice reporting techniques against a motorized element operating at night. Simply put, they wanted a training aid, and we were chosen.

Lieutenant Tice was allowing Negron and me to work together again, and he was pretty much leaving it up to us as to what type of training we could get out of it. I was very tired but saw a golden opportunity to navigate and move in a new area at night. As worn as we were, Negron and I looked forward to this new venture.

We arrived at the recon CP with Hell Section well after dark and linked up with the reconnaissance platoon on the road about three kilometers southwest of Manifa proper. The platoon had established its CP just off the hard-surface road, and our vehicles were ushered into the center of the platoon's positions by ground guides.

We were greeted by a weathered staff sergeant who explained what he wanted us to do: periodically, throughout the night, to drive up and down a stretch of the road to the southeast. In the hills to either side of the road, he had established observation posts and patrols. He wanted to keep his marines on their toes by giving them something to report—that something was us. After looking at the route Negron and I determined that the entire movement would take about forty-five minutes each time we conducted it, which left us a considerable amount of time throughout the evening to find training.

The staff sergeant did not object to our wanting to train in his area, and we began a period of collective bargaining. Within a half hour we had a training plan that would allow us not only to accomplish his primary task but also to experiment in navigation and reconnaissance techniques.

The first training event took place almost immediately. When we arrived, the reconnaissance platoon was preparing to insert a four-man patrol twenty kilometers to the southeast. Normally the staff sergeant would have used his HMMWV to insert the team, but when we explained that we inserted our own scout teams upon occasion and that we knew a thing or two about insertion techniques, he agreed to allow us to conduct the insert of his team.

The staff sergeant gave us the location of the insert point, which I plotted on my air map. As Sergeant Negron and I planned our route— about half of the forty kilometers, round-trip, would be off-road—the staff sergeant looked over our shoulders and laughed. He couldn't believe we were going to try to navigate with the map we had. We knew where he was coming from—we had thought that way once, too—and laughed with him. I explained to him that this was part of the reason we wanted to conduct the insert—we needed all the navigation training we could get.

He didn't mind that we were going to practice navigation, but he wanted to make sure his team got to where they were supposed to be. He produced a LORAN (long-range aid to navigation) positioning device from his field pack. He intended to ride in my turret with the LORAN, so regardless of our success or failure, he could navigate to the insert point without incident.

We left, following the hard-surface road to the turnoff point as indicated by the odometer reading. Leaving the road at that point, we turned left and began the thirteen-kilometer trip, due east, to the insert point. I kept glancing over at the staff sergeant, who had his head buried in the screen of the LORAN, wondering if he was going to stop me because I made a mistake.

Almost immediately we ran into problems. Operating within five kilometers of the Persian Gulf, we were in an area littered with *sabkhas*—low areas of boggy land, like a tidal basin, where the water table is just beneath the earth's surface. Driving through a sabkha would result in our getting stuck in the mud, and it was impossible to travel due east without driving through a sabkha. I was forced to bypass immense fields of them as we moved.

It was like being in a maze. I couldn't possibly conduct a ninety-degree bypass—the normal, as per the technical manual, method of bypass—because there was always another sabkha forcing me to go either farther to the right or the left or to backtrack. I was maneuvering on a thin island of elevated sand between the low sabkhas. I just kept moving, taking odometer readings, jotting notes, and trying to continue east. When I bypassed a sabkha, I watched the stars to the east and tried to weave until I was back to an easterly heading.

The only way I was able to determine my location was the odometer readings, but I had two odometer problems to deal with. First, I had to manage the distance I was traveling to the east. Each time I bypassed, I had to stop that count until I was heading east again. Second, if I backtracked, I had to subtract the distance, and if I bypassed running north-south and east, I had to add a portion of the distance based on the geometry I learned eight or nine years earlier.

The other odometer reading I had to manage was the distance north-south that I was off from my primary heading—the distance, in other words, I was off from the centerline of my route. Each time I bypassed right, I had to come back the same distance left, to the center of my route, and vice versa. When getting back to the centerline was not possible, I had to keep track of how far off I was and try at some point to reconcile.

About halfway through the route I saw something move in front of the vehicle, and I stopped. I could have sworn that the bush ten meters to the front had just shrunk in size; I asked if the staff sergeant saw it too. As I peered in the darkness at what looked like tumble weeds, I was beginning to think that I was just tired and seeing things. Then four bushes stood up and walked to the vehicle. The four marines, who belonged to the reconnaissance platoon, were on patrol. They were wearing desert jackets, made of a dark green and black crosshatch-patterned material, and when they had heard our vehicle, they made like bushes. Had not one of the marines made like a bush a little late, I would never have seen them in their almost perfect camouflage.

The staff sergeant talked to the marines, and we moved off again. He was very impressed that we had found his team the way we did. I accepted the compliments but neglected to tell him that it was pure luck. Why spoil a good thing? If the staff sergeant was willing to think we were a highly impressive bunch of marines, why should I destroy his expectations? Besides, if we missed the insert point later, it might be a good consolation that we had found his patrol.

Eventually I crunched all the numbers, and by my calculations I was at the end of the journey to the insert point. I looked up and pointed to a piece of terrain about a kilometer to the front. "I think we're there, Staff Sergeant."

I looked to him and watched as he took a few moments to consult the LORAN. After what seemed like forever, he patted the LORAN, looked up to me, and said, "Good to go. Let's insert them on the east side."

After we dropped off his team, we moved south to a hard-surface road and headed back—the trip back was much easier than the trip out. I was relieved that we had found the insert point. It was very important to me not only to validate the training we had done but to make a good first impression on any marines we worked with. In this situation fortune had smiled down upon me, and we had accomplished both.

Later that evening the staff sergeant wanted to see if we could find another one of his patrols: he was still talking about how we had found his first one, and I still didn't let on that it had been nothing but luck. He outlined a twenty-four-square-kilometer area on the map and told us he had a team operating within the box. Could we find this team as we had done the other? I knew how we'd managed it before, but I couldn't resist the opportunity to get back out and challenge the navigation gods again.

Negron and I sat down over the map and studied the box we had copied onto it. It was four kilometers wide and six kilometers long. For an LAV platoon this would be a reconnaissance challenge; for an LAV section this would be a reconnaissance nightmare. Negron and I knew that the frontage was way too wide to reconnoiter if we were looking for dismounted elements. If we were looking at routes within that zone, the size was acceptable, but looking for people in the same zone would be like looking for needles in a haystack. The possibility of failure did not sway our desire to train, though.

The outlined zone was in the same sabkha area that we had already traversed. We decided that since we only had about three hours to accomplish the mission, we would maximize the use of hard-surface roads to get to the zone. This worked well, and within thirty minutes we were at the western edge of the zone, ready to conduct the reconnaissance.

For the next two hours we navigated individually through the zone searching for the reconnaissance patrol. We moved forward through the center, fanned out laterally, and made huge loops to the outside edges of the zone. Those loops allowed us to traverse the most ground possible in the least amount of time. We didn't mutually support each other at all times, but for the mission it was an acceptable technique.

In the end we didn't find the marines. I didn't think we would, but it didn't matter. I considered it a successful evolution. Negron and I put together the navigation tools using an unorthodox approach, and we completed the reconnaissance as planned. Instead of being the primary focus of training, navigation was just one of the tools we used. The evolution of navigation in 1st Platoon had reached its zenith. I cannot overstate the importance of that fact. In war, navigation can never be the focus of effort. And it is vital that in training, the same thing be the case. In 1st Platoon, it was.

The tool worked flawlessly, and I think that at this point—8 November in the early, early morning—I felt we had mastered desert navigation. Certainly after this point there were challenges and problems concerning navigation, but never again was it the overriding concern. Navigation took its rightful place in every operation; it became just one of the many elements that enabled us to complete the operation successfully.

Just when we mastered desert navigation, the division distributed the very 1:50,000-scale maps we had requested since early September. In January the section leaders were called to the company CP to pick up the maps. On my way to the CP, I was motivated: finally we were getting the proper tools to do the job we had been asked to do. When I got to the CP, I was shocked. Into my hand was thrust at least fifty individual maps. Each 1:50,000-scale map had to be properly matched and aligned to the eight maps that surrounded it. I had so many maps I didn't know where I was going to keep them all. Further, as I started putting the maps together, I found out that many of them were simply blank—white paper with grid squares on them.

The maps had been drafted and issued hastily to meet the needs of the deployed units. For whatever reasons many of the areas of the desert were labeled "uncharted." I quickly found out that not only was I much more comfortable using my 1:250,000 air map (imagine that) but that the smaller-scale maps were almost impossible to use: I found that I had no reason to know my six- or ten-digit grid location, that the map covered too small an area for most of the movements we conducted, and that when I needed the small-scale map for terrain association, these maps were inaccurate because of their hasty construction. For the most part the maps went unused.

As a direct result of our five months of navigation exercises, we built up a level of confidence that was incredible. Throughout both the air and the ground war I could move around at night with never a worry about getting lost. That type of confidence, which allowed me to concentrate on more important things during the course of Desert Storm, is the result of training. It does not happen automatically.

5

ALPHA COMPANY'S first operation in the desert went from 3 to 18 September 1990. In addition to training in navigation we were acclimatizing to the harsh desert environment—and to operating as an LAV company under Captain Shupp's tutelage. This was the longest field-training exercise we had participated in since Captain Shupp had joined the unit. In fact in today's Marine Corps a field operation of this length would be unusual for any LAV unit. The mundane requirements of garrison life do not allow commanders the luxury of packing up a company for two weeks and going off to train. The only exceptions are large operations or specific training exercises where the unit is required to go to another base to conduct the exercise. This stagnant training environment is truly unfortunate. In order to get a real feel for the unit and the commander, you must go out into the *bush* for an extended period of time, and in a garrison environment, bush is tough to find.

The company operated during this first field exercise in the area we called the Triangle, which we first entered from the southern end on the Crusher Road. In order to get there, we moved east-west along the hard-surface road that was the bottom leg of the Triangle. It was in the extreme heat of the desert on that day that I was introduced to the Saudi rules of highway driving. The east-west road was about the same width as a three-lane highway, but it lacked the distinct yellow and white lines that characterize American roadways. Instead of having a shoulder, the black surface of the road blended into the sand of the desert on either side. At times the sand would form huge dunes at the point where nature began. After an afternoon sandstorm, the dunes spilled down onto and across the road surface, obstructing traffic. When you drove on the road, you never knew what to expect—it was like a living being; it changed every day.

The southern road of the Triangle was the major route for commercial and civilian traffic west from al-Nu Ayriyah to al-Jubail and east. Being a commercial route the road was always busy with traffic moving in both directions. When we drove down the highway that first morning, I noticed that the rules of the road were very different from what I had expected. First a truck passed me on the left at a high rate of speed. I was surprised. It wasn't the fact that the truck was moving so quickly but that it had no room to pass. To the front another truck was barreling toward me in the eastbound lane. I was positive I was going to witness a horrific collision between the two vehicles. I told the driver, Lance Corporal Robertson, to slow down and drift to the right. I didn't have time to help the truck drivers, but I thought I may have time to save our own vehicle from the mess that would result when they collided.

I winced as the trucks sped toward each other. Remarkably they didn't crash. The oncoming truck moved to the right and barely avoided the head-on accident. Apparently the first rule of the road was this: you pass whenever you want; the responsibility of avoiding a collision is relegated to the oncoming traffic. I cataloged this rule, thinking it might come in handy at a later time.

Before we got to the Crusher, I was able to confirm this rule. Additionally I confirmed that if a vehicle was passing to the left but was moving too slowly, the vehicle waiting to pass could do so on the right. That way it would not have to wait. Then the onus of avoiding an accident fell not only on the oncoming traffic but on the vehicle being passed. We didn't use the hard-surface roads after that if we didn't have to.

Wrecked cars littered both sides of nearly every hard-surface road in the area—a testament to the rules of the road—and what was funny is that these cars had just been left there, right where they had crashed. I remember thinking *If you crash your car, leave it on the road and go buy a new one.*

We eventually did get to the Crusher, and during the next two days we got used to the heat. During the day the heat would exceed 120 degrees, and touching the metallic hull of the vehicle would literally burn your hands if you didn't wear gloves. Alpha Company played with camouflage nets at this time. Everywhere we moved, we put them up over the vehicles—as much for shade as for camouflage. As one of my scouts said, "We buy shade, make shade, steal shade . . . whatever it takes."

That first week we learned some things as a company, too—for example, you had to drink a lot of water to survive in the desert. At that time the Marine Corps had a bottled-water contract with Al Wadi, so we received a ration of bottled water for each marine on a daily basis. Additionally, on the vehicle we had seven five-gallon jugs filled with purified water—perfectly safe, but it didn't taste very good. We were told that each marine needed to drink five gallons of water per day. Well, it takes a lot of one-liter Al Wadi bottles to make five gallons, so we had to drink a lot of the purified water.

I can remember walking around under the net, telling the marines to pick up their canteens and drink. I watched them, monitoring how much water they were consuming. It was a particular challenge to ensure that they all drank enough water to stay hydrated, which really meant they had to force themselves to drink more than they actually wanted. They had to drink even when they weren't thirsty.

We tried to make the purified water taste better by cooling it. We saved our Al Wadi bottles, filled them with purified water, and put each bottle in a green sock. If you wet the socks with water and then drove around with the sock-encased bottles hanging on the vehicle, the water on the wet socks evaporated, drawing heat from the bottled water. The result was a bottle of water that was cool, refreshing, and drinkable. Because I have always been a coffee fanatic, I would put a black five-gallon water jug on the mount above the vehicle muffler. The black jug heated nicely in the desert sun, so I had hot water for instant coffee twenty-four hours a day. I was in heaven.

Sergeant Negron buried his water jugs four feet underground, wet the sides of the hole, covered it with a tarp and sand, and then parked his vehicle over the improvised cellar. It was a lot of work, but I believe Negron had the coldest water in Alpha Company. Sergeant Ramirez's water at the Chicken Ranch was the coldest water in town, though.

At the Chicken Ranch, construction had been completed on Montiago's Wine Cellar. Adjacent to one of the chicken houses, the battalion staff had dug a huge pit in the desert sand. The cellar was so deep that it had stairs. The water bottles and jugs were placed in the cellar; the entrance was insulated with a tarp and then covered. The end result was that no matter how hot it was during the day, a trip to Montiago's Wine Cellar would result in the finest vintage: a bottle of cool, refreshing Al Wadi.

Our effort to make the platoon drink water, and to make it better tasting, largely failed in its goal, however: we still had marines go down because of the heat. On 6 September, I was tasked by my platoon commander to go to the company command post and pick up an NBC news crew who had spent the night with us. I was to give them a ride back to the Chicken Ranch. It was early—0530 or 0600—so the temperature hadn't peaked yet.

After we dropped off the news crew at the Chicken Ranch, Captain Shupp gave an order: he wanted to start moving the company around more during the heat of the day. We were to cross the open desert about twelve kilometers from the northwest end of the triangle to the southern end of the Crusher.

We were in a platoon line formation on the company's left flank, and it was hot—over 120 degrees of blistering, dry heat. I looked at my driver and saw that he had rolled up his CVC (combat vehicle crewman) suit around his knees and zipped it down to the waist—the driver's compartment is probably twenty degrees hotter than the outside temperature, and Robertson was battling the heat. He told me he was getting hot, and I told him to keep drinking water. I turned around, and one of the scouts was being continuously doused with water from the other scouts' canteens. Apparently he was feeling nauseous, and the rest of the team was trying to cool him down.

I called the platoon commander and told him I was having acclimatization problems, and he told me to push water and to keep him informed. It was a very tough situation for me. I knew that my crew was having problems, but aside from forcing more water I could do nothing about it. I only hoped that the mission would end soon so we could find some shade.

We made it to the Crusher, and all we had to do was swing around the hardball of the legs of the Triangle back to where we had started from. Almost as soon as we got on the hard-surface road, though, my vehicle started to weave. Before I knew it, I saw Robertson's head bobbing, and the vehicle swerved to the right into a sand dune at fifty miles per hour. The sand slowed us down immediately, and I climbed out of my hatch and over the top of the turret to the driver's hatch. Before I could get to Robertson, the vehicle came to a sudden stop, and I had to grab the pintle-mounted machine gun to keep from tumbling off the vehicle. Once we were settled, I reached through the open hatch and killed the engine because I knew the vehicle was still in gear.

It took us a few minutes to pull Robertson out of the hatch. He had a clear-cut case of heat exhaustion, bordering on heat stroke. The company column continued on the mission, but my wingman stayed with me. We moved Robertson to the shady side of the vehicle, loosened his clothing, and started pouring water on him while someone got an IV bag from the back of the vehicle. Robertson was really worried: he was crying and muttering about being afraid to die. It was pretty clear to me that he was not in control of his emotions. His cooling system was in danger of shutting down completely, and he felt like he was going to die.

Try as we might, we could not find a vein to put the needle in for the IV. The veins in his arms had dilated to the point that they weren't accessible from his skin. I wasn't sure what to do at that point, so I went to the turret to call the corpsman on the radio. The rest of the section was still pouring water over him and trying to calm him down, when I saw a helicopter flying over to the south—just by chance, an Army medevac chopper.

I told one of the marines to grab a red-star pyrotechnic and launch it skyward. But it seemed to take forever for him to launch it. Pyrotechnics are shipped in narrow metal tubes that open with a key, like a sardine can, and the marine was extremely slow in completing the process. By the time he finally did get the pyrotechnic launched, the helicopter had passed by us, and I was certain there was no way he could have seen the flare.

A few minutes later, though, the helicopter returned and landed on the road behind us. A bona fide army medic came out of the chopper and was able to find a vein in Robertson's hand to give him the IV. The medics took Robertson away on a stretcher, and when they saw Lance Corporal Folker (the scout who felt ill), they took him too. I watched as the helicopter took off, carrying two of my crewmen away.

Both marines turned out to be fine, and I got Folker back in a week or so. Robertson was worse off, and when he finally came back, he went to the company trains to drive for Sergeant Walker.

I felt pretty bad about the whole incident. Heat casualties are always scary because even with all the training, it's hard to distinguish how bad off the marine is. Captain Shupp was furious. At a company meeting that night, he alluded to marine leaders not following his guidance about pushing water. His intensity and eye contact were in vintage form. After the meeting I talked to him, and in no uncertain terms he let me know that I was at fault and that I had better start following his guidance.

I was crushed. I had always considered myself a professional, and I didn't like the accusations. I knew that I had done what the captain had asked and that I cared for the marines' well-being. The worst part about the situation, after I knew the marines were OK, was that the captain had lost faith in me: you could have done anything hideous or demeaning to me at that time, and I would have rolled with it, but I was hurt when I failed Captain Shupp. He was steamed at me for about a month after that incident.

Captain Shupp did not accept weakness in any form. I don't think he was expecting anything out of his marines that he wouldn't expect from himself, though. He believed that no marine—including Captain Shupp —should lack intestinal fortitude.

It was common to wake up in the morning to find that a scorpion had sneaked underneath your sleeping bag to share your body heat. Captain Shupp was unfortunate enough to get stung by one of these creatures— the large, black, ugly variety. Any normal person would have sought medical attention immediately, but the captain refused to believe that the tiny scorpion could harm him. The corpsman found out about it and told the captain that he needed to get an IV into him. He went on to tell him that he also needed to get some rest, that he was going to get hit pretty hard with diarrhea and uncontrollable vomiting.

Captain Shupp would have none of that. "No. Not me. I'm too busy." The captain went to the LAV-C2 and started doing his work. He didn't last thirty minutes. In the middle of a radio conversation, he calmly handed Lieutenant Masters the handset, walked out of the C2, and doubled over. Captain Shupp was in bad shape for two or three days. The scorpion had induced the diarrhea and vomiting, just as the corpsman predicted. Still, though, Captain Shupp didn't accept weakness. He didn't go to the rear; he didn't run off to seek better accommodations. He gutted out the sickness in the field with the company. How could you get mad at a man who only asked the same of you?

We had deployed to the Gulf without a platoon commander. Based on my letters, notes, and tapes, I believe it was the afternoon of 4 September that Lieutenant Tice joined on. He was an infantryman and had never been attached to an LAV unit. Whereas Corporal Buntin had been a bit apprehensive when Captain Hammond, an artillery officer, joined Bravo, I don't believe I had a single misgiving about Lieutenant Tice. I think my immediate confidence in this marine leader was the result of first impressions.

Lieutenant Tice stood all of five-feet-four and weighed in at about 140 pounds. The first time I saw him walking toward our group, I thought that Audie Murphy himself had returned from the dead and had deployed to

Saudi Arabia with the marines. Most noticeable was his 9-mm pistol: it was attached to his body in a high-speed nylon holster that hung almost to his knee, where it was tied to his leg. His deuce gear was salty and well used but immaculate in appearance and condition. He wasn't wearing the standard desert cover: his headgear was a light-colored tan (almost white), and the wide brim shielded his entire face, neck, and shoulders from the sun. I found out later that this cover—which was so big it made him look like a kid in his father's clothes—was an Australian bush cover given to him by his girlfriend.

He walked up to us, lifted his head, and smiled. His boyish grin was belied by the seriousness in his expression. He immediately took charge and executed the difficult task of commanding the 1st Platoon of Alpha Company. What he didn't know, he asked about; what he did know, he made you figure out on your own. Throughout the next six months I watched a very complex man guide our platoon. He was the epitome of ethics and morality in a leader: no matter what he did, it was always the right or correct thing to do.

In September Lieutenant Tice started allowing us to develop as leaders, and he continued throughout the ground war to bear on his own shoulders the burden of each life in the platoon. In fact I believe he was so concerned with the lives of the marines in his charge that he put himself at great risk personally many times. He never failed to make a decision, but he always tempered his decisions with the same risks required of everyone else.

In addition to my first impression of Lieutenant Tice, what helped me accept him was that he replaced an inexperienced platoon commander. This NCO could have overcome his lack of experience—Lieutenant Tice did. But nothing could have ever given him skill in leadership.

My section leader, Sergeant Larson, left for recruiting duty sometime near the beginning of September. One night before he left, the company had no operations scheduled, so our section was allowed to conduct a section-route reconnaissance of the improved-surface trail that ran south to the Chicken Ranch. That night we were reintroduced to the sabkha, the low areas of the desert that litter the entire eastern coast of Saudi Arabia. We had already driven over the sabkhas numerous times during the day. It was like maneuvering over a dry lake bed that has large muddy areas. Sometimes the roads went through the center of them. We had been given the standard gouge about the vehicles' getting stuck in the muddy soil, but we had to learn about it ourselves for the lesson to be effective.

In the heat of the day, the vehicle was actually able to gain considerable speed over a sabkha due to the reduced friction on the tires. But we had never tried it when the tide was in and the sun hadn't dried the top layer of the surface to a thick crust. Toward the end of the night-route reconnaissance I remember plotting a lateral route on my crude strip map when the vehicle stopped. I looked up, and I didn't have to ask the driver why he'd stopped. I knew. We had crested a slight rise in the road and started moving slightly downhill. The temperature of eighty degrees dropped to what felt like sixty degrees in the space of fifty meters. It was very cool, and the dry air had suddenly turned very moist.

The moon was out, and I peered forward into the darkness and swallowed hard. All around me, the moon shone onto the desert floor and reflected upwards brilliantly. I could make out rocks, sand dunes, and bushes out to almost a kilometer. In front of me, however, the road continued into a black, wet, and spongy darkness—as though it disappeared into a black hole. It was no wonder that the driver stopped. The scene was so surreal, the most fantastic feature of nature I had ever seen in my life.

I talked to Sergeant Larson on the radio, and he agreed that we should continue the reconnaissance on the remaining leg. I had the driver move forward into the dark void. Over the next two hundred meters of road, we dropped about ten meters in elevation. For the first time since I had been in-country, I suddenly felt very cold. In front of the vehicle the road turned from ash white to midnight black along a distinct perpendicular line. The black extended a hundred meters to either side of the road and as far as I could see to the front. Palm trees had grown in small copses on the perimeter of the sabkha.

I continued on the road and into the sabkha. After we had gone about twenty-five meters, I felt the weight of the vehicle suddenly plunge downward as if I were in an elevator going from the tenth floor to the basement. We were stuck.

I looked behind me, and fortunately my section leader hadn't yet entered the sabkha. I got off the vehicle, and the whole crew came out to look. To a man, they were impressed: this was a good stick. The mud was thick and dank—rich and full of a pungent odor. It was disgusting.

All LAVs are equipped with at least 150 feet of steel cable wrapped on a winch drum with a pulling capacity of fifteen thousand pounds. We spent the next hour and a half pulling the vehicle backwards out of the sabkha with Sergeant Larson's winch. We figured we probably had a little bit over thirty thousand pounds of resistance in the mired vehicle. We couldn't get close enough initially to connect the appropriate rigging to overcome the resistance, and so we ended up doing a lot of digging and expedient work beneath the tires in an attempt to gain some traction before we finally got my vehicle out.

We must have traveled down that road fifty times after that, and I never got stuck again. Out of all the units in that area I don't ever recall seeing anyone get stuck on that road. That was the weird thing about sabkhas: they were living things that changed daily.

In November we were operating on the east side of the coastal highway near Manifa. By this time, almost the entire company had some experience with the sabkhas—we all had been stuck. The captain scheduled some vehicle recovery training in the afternoon. Staff Sergeant Free, the maintenance chief, was going to show the company how to use the allied kinetic-energy rope to recover a mired vehicle. To date, almost all recoveries had been conducted using the vehicle winches. It took a lot of time for a crew to play out a length of cable, erect rigging, and recover the vehicle. Additionally, when the vehicle was recovered, the crew had to wrap the 150-foot cable back onto the drum.

What Free wanted to do was teach us how to use a piece of equipment we already had to recover vehicles that met certain criteria. If the vehicle wasn't stuck over the top of the wheels and you could drive within five or ten feet of it without getting stuck yourself, the rope could be used to affect the recovery. This would save a considerable amount of time for vehicles that weren't stuck too badly.

The rope itself was a piece of gear that we had always had, a nylon white rope about two inches in diameter. The LAV community had used it almost exclusively for a safety rope when swimming. Using the rope for its designed purpose—which we weren't familiar with—left us all a bit skeptical.

I was tasked with finding a sabkha and getting stuck for the company demonstration. After about an hour I had driven through probably six or eight different sabkhas when I finally found one that allowed me to get stuck. The driver picked the speed up to about forty miles per hour and, in the middle of the sabkha, turned hard to the left. We immediately broke the crust and got stuck. I guarantee that if I had come out there any night, I would have gotten stuck at every sabkha. This day, though, it was almost impossible to get stuck.

The company formed around my vehicle, and Staff Sergeant Free conducted his class. He backed the LAV-R up to about five feet in front of my vehicle and attached one end of the white rope to his towing pintle and the other to one of my front towing points. After coiling the excess rope neatly between the two vehicles, he stepped back.

We all stood back about 150 feet—except for the driver, who remained in the vehicle with the engine on and the vehicle in neutral. Free then got into the LAV-R, put the vehicle in first gear, and drove off. He wasn't moving rapidly. He had floored the accelerator pedal, but in first gear the LAV doesn't go very fast. The white rope stretched and stretched, storing an enormous amount of energy. It was incredible: the stored energy caused the rope to collapse like a giant rubber band, and my 28,000-pound LAV literally leaped out of the hole it was in and rolled away, free of the mire.

What would have required forty-five minutes of winch work, and thirty thousand pounds of pull, had taken all of five minutes. From that point on, vehicle commanders attached the white ropes permanently to the front towing points and coiled the ropes under the trim vanes for rapid deployment. Staff Sergeant Free was smiling ear to ear when the demonstration was over. He was always a cocky, confident mechanic, and on this day he added to his reputation. Anytime a mechanic can show a crewman something, it is a moment to be relished—for the mechanic, anyway. Since then I've used the technique whenever I could.

Throughout the entire deployment I tried to figure out the mighty sabkha. I was sure I would see them in Kuwait and/or Iraq, and I wanted to know under exactly what conditions I could traverse them.

I got stuck many times throughout the deployment, but Lieutenant Tice was very tolerant of it. He understood what I was trying to do. He stilled ribbed me when I got stuck, but as long as I exercised judgment and didn't go experimenting during a battalion operation, he supported me. The end result was that 1st Platoon moved over sabkhas on a regular basis, whereas 2d Platoon and other units avoided them. We got stuck on occasion, but in the end we were able to make a calculated risk based on experience when a sabkha blocked our path.

Lieutenant Sellers—he would later be promoted to Captain Sellers—discovered glaring problems in Charlie Company during its first outing into the Saudi Arabian desert: the marines did not know what they were doing. Their lack of tactical expertise had resulted in a company that wanted to do the right things but didn't know how.

The first night in the desert Lieutenant Sellers ordered the company to assume a screen orienting to the north. The marines of Charlie Company went to the ordered positions and did what they thought they were supposed to do. Sergeant Hernandez recalls the events of that evening as the point when Charlie Company got back on track as a well-trained LAV unit.

Hernandez was sleeping beside his vehicle, and he was woken by Lieutenant Sellers's angry voice. The lieutenant had driven out to each vehicle's position to check on the company's status. He was not happy with what he found. Hernandez woke up when Lieutenant Sellers was asking Hernandez's crew, in a very harsh tone, what they thought they were doing.

The turret watch in Hernandez's vehicle had fallen asleep, and the crew was sleeping on top of the vehicle in front of the turret. Lieutenant Sellers had found the same situation at each of the vehicles he had checked, and he was appalled at the company's lack of tactical awareness.

Sergeant Hernandez approached Lieutenant Sellers and asked if he could talk to him. They walked off away from the vehicle, and Hernandez tried to explain the situation. Out of earshot from his marines, the sergeant told the lieutenant that he understood his concern over the fact that the turret watch was asleep. He accepted full responsibility and assured the lieutenant that he would take care of the situation.

As for the lack of tactical awareness and marines sleeping on top of the vehicles, Sergeant Hernandez said to his commander, "What do you want, Sir? We have never done anything the same way twice, and to be truthful, we don't know what to do. Tell us what you want, and we will make it happen."

Lieutenant Sellers must have realized what Sergeant Hernandez was getting at. The lieutenant knew what the company had gone through in the past year, and he knew that Hernandez was right—the marines did only what they were trained to do. After that part of the conversation, Sergeant Hernandez recalls, his commander left without saying much more.

The next morning Lieutenant Sellers began a detailed training program. They were in Saudi Arabia. They didn't know when they would have to fight, and they didn't have much time to prepare. Charlie Company had to be trained—and trained fast. Sergeant Hernandez was elated when the training program began.

From that day until the war began, Charlie trained every day. They started from ground zero. Every morning the vehicle commanders met at Lieutenant Sellers's position and received classes on reconnaissance, security, navigation, attacks, delays, raids, and so on. Following every class the group of marines leaders conducted sand table exercises in order to practice the training. After the exercises the vehicle commanders went back to their platoons and taught their crews what they had learned. After the crews had been taught, the sections and then the platoons went out and drilled the lessons using the vehicles. Finally Lieutenant Sellers drilled the company as a unit.

When he was satisfied that sufficient progress was made on each tactical subject, Lieutenant Sellers introduced a new subject, and the training process continued. Charlie Company finally received the training that they not only required but longed for.

When I talked to Sergeant Hernandez about all of this, I realized an unfortunate side effect from this training program. Since Charlie had to start from scratch with training, they didn't get an opportunity to learn a lot of the lessons we were learning in Alpha. Hernandez didn't get an opportunity to conduct any section training beyond what was required for platoon operations. He didn't get to learn all of the navigation lessons that we had learned. Charlie Company was limited to company and platoon operations, and it traveled on the roads to get to where it was going.

So it was good that Charlie was finally being trained, but it was also regrettable that these marines didn't get the opportunity to learn the same lessons we had learned—lessons I feel were invaluable to my development as an LAV leader.

While Alpha and Charlie were traveling the company training path, Sergeant Ramirez was at the Chicken Ranch learning about supply acquisition. It became readily apparent to him during those first months in Saudi Arabia that supplies were not being pushed forward adequately from the pier to the marines in the field. Chow was scarce at times, water was hard to come by, and fresh fruits were virtually nonexistent.

Ramirez knew that the supplies were in-country, but the S-4 (logistics office/officer) was not making the acquisition of those supplies happen through the regular channels. When the battalion CP went without MREs (meals ready-to-eat) for an entire day, Sergeant Ramirez decided to take matters into his own hands.

It started out with a HMMWV trip from the Chicken Ranch to the pier at al-Jubail. Once the fifty-five-mile trip to the pier was complete, Ramirez wandered about the rear area scavenging supplies. He acquired bottled water, chow, fresh fruits, and anything else he could scrounge. Working outside the proper channels, he was forced to sign rosters with a number of pseudonyms in order to get the supplies.

Sergeant Ramirez brought that first HMMWV-load of supplies back to the Chicken Ranch, and the following day the sergeant major trucked them out to the marines in the line companies, where I was. I was just happy to see the stuff. I was not aware of the effort Ramirez had put forth to acquire it.

The trips to the pier grew in frequency. Pretty soon Ramirez was taking two vehicles down to al-Jubail three nights a week in order to increase the bounty. But eventually, like all good things, the trips came to an abrupt halt. During a staff meeting, accolades were given to the S-4 for doing such a great job supplying the battalion. Ramirez had heard enough of this balderdash, and so he spoke up. "No," he said. "They aren't getting the chow. Me and Harris are. Nobody is going down there to pick it up; we're picking it up ourselves."

The S-4 was responsible for getting through proper channels the very supplies that Sergeant Ramirez was forced to get through improper ones. In defense of the S-4, the system was overtaxed. This was the largest deployment of troops in decades, and the supply system wasn't yet geared to handle the severe logistic strain. So while the S-4 tried to work the system correctly, Sergeant Ramirez worked the system effectively—albeit incorrectly.

Ramirez caught flak for his method of working and was told not to do it anymore. He was frustrated, but he did stop the nightly trips to the pier. For two or three days after that, the battalion didn't get any supplies.

In Alpha we didn't have to worry about the supply issue. The battalion was always really good at getting us chow and water. In fact, from what I have learned, the battalion staff probably went without things in order to ensure that we were taken care of. We just continued to train, unaware of the struggles of Sergeant Ramirez at the Chicken Ranch.

Even with the wonderful shade they provided, camouflage nets proved to be a major thorn in our sides. We put up the nets religiously during that first outing in the Triangle. It was tough work. And on the tactical side of the matter, the nets were questionable. When you looked across the open desert, a camouflage net looked like a camouflage net; LAVs under camouflage nets looked like LAVs under camouflage nets.

We used the light side of the net in open terrain and the darker side if we were fortunate enough to nestle up next to rocks. But the result was the same: nets drew attention to your position. We conducted net drill after net drill, day and night, all with the same result: Alpha Company was very proficient at putting up nets, but they stood out like sore thumbs.

An additional concern was that once the nets had been erected, operating the turret was very tricky. In order to support the net and ensure it was up and off the vehicle's hull, you had to place poles and spreaders on the turret itself. Once these were supported by the turret, you couldn't move it without causing the net to collapse.

We didn't have a better method of camouflaging the vehicles than the nets, though. The LAVs were green at the time, and the desert was not. We drove to the nearest sabkha, made desert paint with mud and water, and painted the vehicles with the mixture, but we needed more than the slate-gray paint could give us. The net provided at least a limited bit of camou-flage. I think Captain Shupp was leaning toward not using the nets, but what really killed the net in Alpha was a force-on-force operation we did against another LAV company.

That company was tasked with attacking our positions. Captain Shupp ordered us to erect four camouflage nets nestled in some good terrain on the slope of a slight rise. They were to be erected in the exact same man-ner as we would erect them to camouflage our vehicles. Captain Shupp then maneuvered our company to hide positions, where our vehicles could not be seen. When the attacking company advanced, they picked up the nets immediately and moved to flank our "positions." By the time they knew what was going on, Captain Shupp had moved the hidden platoons around to the flank and rear of the attackers. As the bad guys moved to engage the nets, Alpha Company appeared from nowhere and, at point-blank range, destroyed the attackers.

What is amazing is that months later Captain Shupp used this decep-tion in another force-on-force exercise with the same results. We weren't idiots; when we saw the attacking vehicles advance and turn immediately to attack our nets, we knew we had to find a better way than the camou-flage nets to remain undetected.

What we did was sound tactical judgment. We used the terrain to our advantage: we minimized dust signatures, refreshed our sabkha paint on a regular basis, and avoided giving our positions away on obvious pieces of key terrain. These were not new principles, but we truly took them to heart. Survival in open terrain depends solely on your patience and your attention to detail. Without either, you will make mistakes that can get you killed.

When I interviewed Corporal Buntin, I found that Bravo Company used nets all the way up until the morning of 29 January. They would have used them longer, but on the evening of the twenty-eighth they had left their nets standing in the desert and went off to respond to the enemy contact at OP 4. For one reason or another they never recovered their nets.

I found that Charlie Company used their camouflage nets during the entire deployment as well. After my experience in Alpha with the nets I was surprised to hear that the other companies hadn't reached the same conclusion that we had about their usefulness.

In retrospect, though, it is easy to see why not everybody abandoned the use of camouflage netting: it is a written doctrine in the Marine Corps, and certainly there is valid reasoning behind it. For example, aircraft have a much more difficult task finding a vehicle hidden under nets than they do an exposed vehicle. Additionally, in certain terrain, the nets blend almost perfectly into the existing foliage, creating an excellent camouflage.

It is therefore difficult to argue against using the nets. I will, however, offer a few points in that direction. First, in open terrain a camouflage net may actually draw attention to your position rather than mask your position. Second, any disparity between terrain color and the two colors (sides) of the net may make the net ineffective in certain situations. Third, thermal and radar scattering/transparent nets work only under two conditions—that is, they must not touch any portion of the vehicle being camouflaged, and they must extend fully to the ground without any gaps. This is very difficult to accomplish and often results in a very obvious dome-shaped structure. So while the doctrinal use of camouflage netting cannot be refuted, its practical usefulness can and should be questioned. The ultimate decision on when to use the nets should be made on practicality and not on traditional dogma.

Even with all the company and platoon training going on, we never forgot our primary mission: to screen to the north and to provide early warning of enemy approach. A screen mission is one that provides the commander the opportunity to trade maneuver space for time. The commander designates the screening force and places it well forward to watch likely avenues of enemy approach. That screening force struggles to remain undetected while it gains information about the main body of the enemy. The screening force maintains contact with the enemy by falling back to subsequent positions, and it attempts to harass the main body and to eliminate the enemy's eyes, his reconnaissance assets.

This was standard stuff to Alpha. Ever since the company had been formed, if there was one thing we did a lot of, it was screening. Unfortunately screening is a tiring and thankless task. Twenty-four hours a day the sector to your front must be observed. Every night, watches must be established in each vehicle to maintain continuous observation of the assigned sectors. After about five months this process becomes very old. Not many nights went by that I didn't find myself standing alone in the turret, peering into the darkness in front of the vehicle wondering when I would be able either to fight the Iraqis or to go home.

Initially—before we realized exactly how far we were from Kuwait and before I got ahold of maps that showed the positions of Saudi and Kuwaiti units near the border—we expected to discover Iraqi armor moving toward us in the wee hours of the morning. After about a month in-country, though, it was obvious to us all that we would have ample warning from the Allies to prepare for the advance of that Iraqi armor—that knowledge made standing the watches even more difficult.

Standing watch for two hours at 0200 was incredibly difficult after that first month. But there was nothing we could do to eliminate the necessity of such watches. Captain Shupp, to his credit, kept Alpha in a tactical mode for the duration of the deployment. Early on, he told the officers that it was very important to make it as hard as possible for the marines of Alpha Company. Captain Shupp banked on the fact that hard training would help prepare us for war. Of course he was correct.

We could not avoid the watches, but what we could do was shorten the length of the evenings by training at night. Nature worked against us in this endeavor, however. The sun set late in the summer and early fall; and as the months went by, the days got shorter, and the nights got longer. Soon it was our standard practice to hound Lieutenant Tice for permission to conduct section training at night. The longer you were out training, the shorter your watches were when you returned. The noticeable increase in our level of night training came as the direct result of our need for a break from long nights on watch.

6

THERE WAS ONLY one event that completely eliminated the requirement for someone to stand turret watch at night: every eight to fifteen days, the company was pulled out of the desert and rotated to the rear for three days of R&R (rest and relaxation). This cycle started for Alpha Company on 19 September and continued through 25 November. During that time we spent our three-day R&R periods in two-man, air-conditioned rooms at Camp 3, a place we called "Stalag 3." Camp 3 was part of a large area consisting of a number of encampment areas. Each camp was designed around temporary trailer-type buildings. Each building was partitioned into rooms with common head facilities, hot and cold running water, sit-down toilets, and showers. Each camp had a mess hall, exchange facilities, and, eventually, phones—the desire to call home is imperishable.

Even with all the amenities the nicest thing about the camps was simply the air-conditioned break from turret watch. On 19 September the company was ready for a change. We mounted up on the vehicles and drove the entire company back to the parking lot outside of the camp area. We spent that three-day period of R&R conducting classes and maintenance on the vehicles. We received some time off to exercise, use the exchange, and sleep, but since the vehicles were right out in the parking lot, it was easy for us to be drawn to our "horses" to take care of them.

We eventually stopped taking the vehicles to Camp 3, parking them in the battalion area at Manifa Bay and riding five-tons or buses instead. It was a better arrangement for us because the vehicles weren't there beckoning to us. I don't know if it was the captain's call or battalion's, but parking the vehicles sixty miles away did make the time in Camp 3 much more enjoyable.

One trip to Camp 3 was particularly memorable. We parked our vehicles at Manifa and marched out to the dirt trail adjacent to the parking lot to wait for the buses. The date was 9 November. Alpha Company was milling about the side of the road in platoon formations, sitting on top of our gear required for proper R&R. We were waiting awhile when, over the horizon, a huge cloud of dust started to grow.

Soon a dozen yellow school buses with tacky trim and reflectors appeared out of the dust and drove toward us at a rapid rate. When the buses approached, we knew which one was ours because it made a savage U-turn, almost running over Lieutenant Tice, and rocked to a halt adjacent to our platoon formation. I had never seen the lieutenant move as fast as he did when he grabbed his gear and scampered from in front of the careening bus.

We loaded onto the bus with all of our gear, and I sat in the seat behind Lieutenant Tice, who was behind the driver. The bus itself was in horrible condition—the driver seemed barely ahead of the rust in the effort to control the vehicle's soul. As we were loading, the driver had produced a screwdriver from a pile of junk on his dash and started to tighten all of the screws within his reach. There was a cassette player bungee corded to the dash; exposed speaker wires that had been spliced and taped on numerous occasions trailed off in a tangled mess down the entire length of the bus.

The driver was an honest-to-goodness character who looked like a reincarnated John Belushi in Arab guise. He wore a flowing white robe, sandals, and Ray-Ban Wayfarers, and he had a burning cigarette dangling from the corner of the mouth. A smile was permanently plastered on his face, and when one of the marines gave him a Metallica cassette, he popped it into the tape player, turned up the volume, and started bouncing in his seat to the distorted sound that blasted forth from the makeshift audio system.

We all started laughing—it was hard not to. And the driver loved it. The more we laughed, the goofier the driver acted. I remember looking at Lieutenant Tice to gauge his response to the episode: he ran his hand back through his hair and shook his head in disbelief.

Captain Shupp walked up to the open window of the bus and spoke to the driver. "Now, don't pass anyone. Drive safe, OK?"

The driver had no complaints with the captain's request; he simply nodded his head vigorously and smiled. "Yeah, yeah. OK, no problem."

Nick—that is the name we had given the driver—had obviously been through the Saudi Arabian school for driving. When the captain left, Nick immediately took off. Barreling through the sand, he careened the bus around the one in front of us. As we lurched past a group of marines waiting to board another bus, they looked at us with gaping mouths and disbelieving eyes. In the staging area alone, Nick passed six buses, some stationary and some moving. All the while he was bobbing his head to the heavy-metal music.

The other buses had started passing as well. Apparently every driver's objective was to get to the front of the convoy heading back to Camp 3. Everyone on the buses was laughing and cheering the drivers on. As we rocked back and forth, the drivers were yelling at each other out of open windows, blasting their horns, and cutting each other off. Lieutenant Tice leaned forward to Nick and just loud enough for me to hear he said, "Slow down. Take it easy."

Nick, again, had no quarrel with this order. "Yeah. OK, no problem." He then jerked hard to the left, cutting off a bus that was trying to pass him. I looked ahead and saw that the road narrowed considerably. Nick had already committed himself to beating the bus adjacent to us to the point where the road narrowed to a single lane. He didn't have the power to overtake the bus to the right, though, and he lacked the common sense to pull back behind. I wasn't sure what he was going to do. Nick opened the folding doors of the bus and yelled to the driver next to him. Apparently that didn't help, so when the road narrowed, Nick simply swerved to the right, repeatedly bumping the bus next to us until it let him have the lane. I couldn't believe it. There we were, moving thirty miles per hour, and Nick was crashing into the bus on his right in a desperate attempt to merge.

We were all still laughing about the whole thing, but Lieutenant Tice had had enough. Leaning forward, he spoke to Nick in a low, menacing tone: "If you hurt any of my marines, I'll hurt you." Nick understood our commander's intent perfectly this time, and the rest of the journey was uneventful.

Most of the marines, including me, fell asleep on the way to Camp 3. But whenever I opened my eyes, I saw that Lieutenant Tice, obviously tired, was awake and watching Nick. That was the type of leader he was: he was very serious about his responsibilities.

During an earlier hiatus at Camp 3, I had one of many conflicts with a staff sergeant. Battalion supply had an issue point near our barracks there. Being in the rear gave us the opportunity to replace any unserviceable gear we might have. At this particular time one of the scouts on my vehicle had a pair of boots that had become unusable. Generally a marine could simply go to supply and exchange an unserviceable item on a one-for-one basis. But for some reason, a marine had to be accompanied by a SNCO to exchange a pair of boots.

The marine came to me with the problem, showing me the pair of boots. I figured I would go over to supply with him and convince the guys at supply that there was no reason to involve a staff sergeant in exchanging a clearly useless pair of boots. After about five minutes at supply, however, it became painfully clear that the rules were not designed with flexibility in mind. Further, supply had decided that they would now have business hours. It was ridiculous, but this supply tent had established hours of operation that forced marines to exchange gear during a couple of two-hour blocks during the day—and only during those blocks of time. I wondered where these guys had to go that wouldn't let them take care of a marine's requirements no matter what time it was.

At any rate, we were going back to the field the next morning, so I went to find a staff sergeant. There was one on the court playing basketball, not fifty feet away. I interrupted the game and let him know what I needed. Barely acknowledging my request, he continued his game. Looking at my watch, I knew that supply was closing soon—if he didn't move those fifty feet in the next few minutes, the marine would not be taken care of.

I reminded the staff sergeant again, but I only made him angry. He told me, in a confrontational tone, that he had heard me. I asked him when he was going to find the time to take care of the marine, and everything came to a head. The end result was this: the marine got his boots exchanged, the staff sergeant and I argued, and Lieutenant Tice pulled me aside later that afternoon to counsel me.

Lieutenant Tice took me around to the back of the camp area and stopped behind a building. I stood in front of him at a modified parade rest, unsure of what he planned to do. Then he pulled something out of his pocket, a small card, and read from it. "Sergeant Michaels, you have the right to remain silent." As he continued advising me of my rights, I really got steamed. I couldn't believe I was the only one who saw what was going on with the staff sergeant. Finally Lieutenant Tice finished reading the card— "You have the right to an attorney. Would you like to exercise that right?"

He looked up to me, and I answered immediately. "Yes, Sir. I would like a lawyer." I stared down at him, and I'm sure he could see the fire in my eyes as I struggled to hold my temper.

He looked at me, and neither of us spoke for what seemed like a full minute. Finally he put the card back into his pocket and asked me, "What's going on, Sergeant Michaels?"

I didn't waste any time revealing my thoughts to Lieutenant Tice. "Sir, that staff sergeant has no business being in a leadership position. Sergeant Negron is the one who does all the work." Negron consistently had taken care of the things that this staff sergeant was supposed to be doing. Negron wasn't trying to steal his thunder; he was doing what was necessary. It was a lot easier just to take care of something than to try to convince someone else to do it. Getting the maps was just one example of this fact.

Lieutenant Tice was going to let me speak my piece, so I continued: "Unfortunately, Sir, neither Sergeant Negron nor I could take care of this issue." I went on to bring up other issues that concerned me, such as the staff sergeant's lack of tactical proficiency and the confrontational way he responded when he thought someone was questioning his abilities.

Lieutenant Tice heard me out before responding. "Sergeant Michaels, I understand you're pissed off, but you've got to stay out of arguments with this staff sergeant, especially in front of people."

I knew he was right, and I had tried to avoid the confrontation from the start. "I know, Sir. Like I said, I didn't want to argue with him; I just wanted to get him to help the marine."

He paused for a moment. I think he was trying to figure out the best way to relate his concerns to me. "Look, you're right about the tactical stuff. It takes time for people not familiar with the LAV to make the transition to the point that you and Negron are at." But he stressed this point: "He's still a staff sergeant, and you're still a sergeant, and this is still the Marine Corps."

Right at that moment my spirits dropped. What he had just said was something very familiar to me. The bottom line was not ability, nor was it leadership. In the Marine Corps the bottom line was rank. The promotion process is designed not around promoting leaders but around promoting those individuals who stay out of trouble and serve their requisite time in grade. I had accepted this fact, but I truly felt that once we were in a real-time situation, the real concern would be putting the right people in the right position to accomplish the mission—regardless of rank.

Lieutenant Tice wasn't through yet, though. I think he saw the disappointment in my face. "Sergeant Michaels, I haven't been here long, and you have to understand my position. I have to give the staff sergeant the benefit of the doubt. He deserves that. I just don't think that I have enough time here to do anything but trust his abilities."

I didn't agree, but at that point it was futile to argue any further. The counseling session ended with Lieutenant Tice telling me to avoid confrontations with the staff sergeant and to trust him. I said, "Aye, aye, Sir"—and carried on.

Other NCOs in the company were not as fortunate as I had been in that encounter. My first wingman, Corporal Stanley, was fired by the lieutenant after a single incident in late September. Alpha had been operating on the north end of the Crusher inside the Triangle.

Every night a resupply convoy would come out to our positions to give us chow, water, and fuel. Lieutenant Tice started out, in earlier operations, moving the entire platoon back to refuel. But over the course of a few weeks he had changed his policy. At the time of this incident the minimum requirement was that one or more of the vehicles move to the resupply to pick up water and chow for the platoon. If you needed fuel, you took your vehicle to the resupply to get fuel. I remember that I went to the resupply almost every night. It wasn't that I needed fuel; I needed the movement, the navigation training. Others in the platoon did the same things. The bottom line, though, was that Lieutenant Tice trusted the vehicle commander's judgment: he expected each vehicle commander to resupply when it was necessary.

Corporal Stanley was Larson's gunner when Larson left Saudi Arabia to go on recruiting duty. With the vehicle commander's departure, Stanley moved up to that position. He was a young NCO and didn't have a lot of experience, but he was learning fast. This was his first outing as vehicle commander, and Corporal Stanley and I spent a considerable amount of time working on section movement, navigation, and communication. In the last week of September, I was escorting a bulldozer to my firing position in order to improve the position when Corporal Stanley called me on the radio to let me know he had run out of gas. My first instinct was to ask my driver what our fuel status was. It turned out that I had nearly a full tank, and I couldn't understand how Stanley had run out of gas. Before I knew what was going on, Lieutenant Tice, who had picked up the radio traffic, had moved to his position and fired him.

It wasn't a snap decision: Corporal Stanley had avoided resupply by claiming he didn't need fuel. Lieutenant Tice saw it as a clear issue of dereliction of duty and a violation of his trust. I felt sympathy for Stanley and even talked to Lieutenant Tice about it, but the lieutenant had made up his mind. It was hard to disagree with his logic. He had given us the freedom to make decisions based on sound professional judgment, and Corporal Stanley had taken advantage of that. It was ironic, though, that it didn't take much for a corporal to be relieved.

An NCO replaced Corporal Stanley and became the second of my three wingmen. The NCO, who was donated to the platoon by the company headquarters, had been with the company for as long as I could remember, but there wasn't much need for his particular specialty in the desert. As an NCO, he was given the opportunity to command a vehicle.

I was totally disgruntled with the idea that the NCO was going to be my wingman. His strength was computers; his weakness was leadership. He was one of those marines who had slipped through the cracks and been promoted to his current rank by serving his time in grade and staying out of trouble. The fact that he was a very weak leader had been recognized the year before. His subordinates did not respect him because he lacked technical and tactical knowledge, and he was completely devoid of any ability to make a decision and carry it out to completion.

When he was assigned as my wingman, I began again with the section training, trying to develop him into a competent vehicle commander. On the one hand, it was very easy for me because he tried to do whatever I asked him to do, and he always had a smile on his face. On the other hand, no matter how hard he tried, he failed on execution. I think what disturbed Lieutenant Tice the most, though, was the NCO's inability to grasp the lieutenant's intent when we conducted various platoon missions.

After a couple of weeks as vehicle commander, and a negligent discharge of a pintle-mounted machine gun on his vehicle, the NCO was relieved of his duties. The discharge happened when all vehicle commanders, including this particular NCO, went to Captain Shupp's position to receive an order. While we were at the order—eight hundred meters away from the platoon positions—the corpsman on the NCO's vehicle was playing with the machine gun and fired a round off into the desert.

Lieutenant Tice made his decision to fire the NCO fairly quickly—

which leads me to believe that the NCO hadn't impressed him at all by this point. Even though the NCO was eight hundred meters away when it happened, he had failed to provide the leadership required to enforce the most basic tenant of weapons safety: don't play with guns.

The NCO's dismissal turned out to be my windfall. My third and final wingman, Corporal Matlain, was moved from another platoon to assume responsibility of Blue 6. I started the process of training a wingman all over again, expecting the same long process I had already gone through twice. But to my surprise and delight, not only was Matlain a competent vehicle commander and leader, but he assumed the role as my wingman as if he had been there the whole time.

Corporal Matlain was, and still is, a fine leader and marine. He was so proficient that when I spent a week in the hospital, he served as section leader and not merely held his own at the job but excelled. When I returned to the platoon after that week, Lieutenant Tice welcomed me back and then raved about how impressed he was with Corporal Matlain's leadership of the section in my absence. I could tell that the lieutenant was tickled: with all the problems he had getting a competent vehicle commander for that vehicle, he had finally struck gold. I felt good, and I was happy for Matlain. The bottom line was this: I couldn't have asked for a better wingman to fight with than Matlain.

On 28 September our daily routine of training was postponed. Gen. Alfred M. Gray Jr., the commandant of the Marine Corps, came out to the desert to visit us and talk to the troops. The night before his visit marked the first noticeable change in the weather since we had been in-country. Up until that night you could have almost set your clock by the weather patterns. It was seventy to eighty degrees when we woke up in the morning, and it stayed comfortable until about 0900, when one of two things would happen. Either the heat would rise to over a hundred degrees or a sandstorm would materialize out of the desert.

I don't know which was worse. In the heat we were miserable because of the lack of adequate shade. In the sandstorms, we would be literally blinded for hours. The sand rolled in fast like a fog bank, reduced the visibility to about two feet, and forced us to seek shelter in the vehicle—and it wreaked havoc on our weapons and equipment.

When the commandant came to the desert, he brought autumn with him. A thick, wet fog rolled in on the evening of 28 September. Condensed water blanketed all weapons, clothing, and exposed equipment. For the first time I was actually cold at night on watch. We had gotten up early that morning and driven as a company to where the commandant would speak. Al Gray is a hero to a lot of marines. A real marine's marine, he didn't disappoint anyone with his visit.

He stood on top of an M60 tank and addressed the multitude. General Gray was tough. Using his characteristic gruff and frank tone, he explained to us what was going on. Looking salty and weathered, and swaggering about on the top of the tank with an air of confidence, he motivated the hell out of us.

When he had finished speaking, he opened the floor for questions. Our company was standing about two hundred feet away from the tank, and I remember Long (of 2d Platoon) standing up to ask a question: "Sir, my name is Sergeant Long, and I'm an LAV crewman. I've tried to reenlist and can't because there are no boat spaces for 0313s. I tried to move to another field, but I can't because we're short in our community. I don't understand. I want to make a career here, but the Marine Corps won't let me stay and they won't let me go."

Al Gray didn't pause for a moment when he boomed out across the crowd to respond to Sergeant Long. "Do you want to reenlist, Marine?"

Sergeant Long boomed back across the crowd, "Yes, Sir!" He had been upset with the system for quite a while. I knew he wanted the option to reenlist, but I think that was all he wanted: the option. At that time I think he was just voicing his disappointment, and I don't believe he was ready for the commandant's reply.

"Outstanding, Marine! Do you want to reenlist for four or six years?" *Be careful what you wish for; you just might get it.*

I started to laugh as I watched Long squirm. There he was, standing tall in front of hundreds of marines, and Al Gray was going to take care of him. I watched the sergeant swallow hard when he replied, "Uh, four, Sir." He wasn't speaking very loudly this time.

"Outstanding, Marine!" The commandant appeared very much inspired. "Raise your right hand, and repeat after me." Then and there, from two hundred feet, on top of an M60 tank, Al Gray gave the oath that bound Sergeant Long to another four years of military service in the United States Marine Corps. Cries of "Ooh-rah!" from dozens of marines broke through the moist morning air when the sergeant got what he had wished for— only I don't think it was a wish he really wanted to come true.

After Sergeant Long had taken his oath, dozens of marines jumped on the bandwagon. *Sir, I've been a lance corporal for two years and a squad leader for eight months. I've been recommended for promotion, but my MOS* [military occupational specialty] *is frozen.* Probably half a dozen marines had a story like this to tell the commandant.

"Come up here, Marine!" Al Gray commanded. "Someone give me some corporal insignia so we can get this marine promoted." On the spot the commandant was taking care of every marine's problem the only way that he knew how: *by doing as much as he could, for as many as he could, for as long as he could.* He took care of his marines.

The general situation was pandemonium. Soon the battalion commanders were trying to stop what was going on. Battalion commanders had specific concerns about a lot of the requests. Some marines who had encountered problems in their effort to be promoted had experienced those difficulties because they weren't qualified or recommended for promotion. Others had been denied reenlistment for solid reasons. And here was the commandant taking care of the marines anyway.

I think that one of the battalion commanders finally whispered into the commandant's ear because he stopped promoting and reenlisting marines. He stood tall on the tank and boomed, "I think I'm causing your battalion commanders some problems. Take your cases through the chain, and my aide will take care of what needs to be taken care of." With that, the commandant was gone: he got into his helicopter and flew away.

On Christmas Day, I saw the commandant and sergeant major of the Marine Corps again. That time the battalion commander was ever-present to run interference. It was a memorable day. Someone had received a Christmas tree in a box from home, complete with decorations. We set up the tree and had a very relaxing Christmas morning sitting around the vehicles eating goodies from home. The first sergeant had secured some fresh chickens—I have no idea where they came from—and the company staff cooked them on a makeshift grill for everyone.

There was a great degree of camaraderie in the company at that time. We all knew each other very well. Normal garrison routine does not allow marines access to the very personal elements of their brothers in arms, but living with them every day creates strong interpersonal bonds. At 1630 the work day in garrison is over, and marines head home to their respective families, taking their personalities with them. In the desert, there was no going home. We became attuned to each others' needs and problems. I was surprised there wasn't a lot more fighting among the marines than there was. There were arguments over the things that brothers and sisters might fight over, but they ended almost as quickly as they started—and there were no grudges. I don't know how a group of men could become any closer than we were throughout the deployment.

The marine who did most of the cooking on that Christmas Day was Gunnery Sergeant Chevice, our company gunny. I can honestly say he was the type of man you looked forward to seeing. I would go out of my way to stop by the company trains when we were out just to say, "How's it going, Gunny?"

He would always respond in the same manner, using the same gravely voice, with the same smile and twinkle in his eye: "Easy money. Ha, ha, ha! Easy money!" Gunny Chevice looked like Santa Claus. He was a dark green marine, and if Santa Claus was dark green, he resided with Alpha Company on that Christmas Day.

Chevice had been in the Marine Corps since Vietnam and was looking forward to retirement when he got back to the United States. He had seen combat in Vietnam, Beirut, and Granada, surviving all of these conflicts with nothing more than minor flesh wounds. And he survived with a positive attitude, an addiction to mentholated cigarettes, and a deep love of fishing.

In Saudi Arabia, though, Gunny Chevice had to survive Private First Class (PFC) Penguin, the young, clean-cut marine who had been assigned to drive for him. Unfortunately for Gunny Chevice, Penguin was accident-prone. Not clumsy accident-prone, but bad luck accident-prone. I felt sorry for Gunny Chevice—a three-war survivor looking forward to retirement—every time I heard about something new that Penguin had done to him.

It started out when we were operating in the Triangle. Combat engineers had worked in earnest digging tank ditches and obstacles to thwart a possible Iraqi armor assault. It is simply ill luck that the only thing these ditches thwarted was Gunny Chevice. Penguin was driving the LAV-L cross-country one dark evening and drove right into a tank ditch. The vehicle nosed in, bounced Gunny's tired body around, and sat there until he could get word to someone that he was stuck. It was a miracle no one was hurt. Still, we all thought *Ouch, bad luck for Gunny!*

Then the next incident happened. About a month later Penguin was driving the gunny around in the company HMMWV. They were moving north on the hard-surface road that marked the eastern border of the Triangle and were turning to the left to head down the hard-surface road that marked the northern border of the Triangle. Apparently Penguin wasn't familiar with the laws of the road, and as he turned, a vehicle tried to pass him and crashed into his HMMWV. Again nobody was hurt. Gunny was shaken up—and was looking forward to an early retirement.

We were now beginning to suspect that either the gunny or Penguin had bad luck in his blood. Gunny had been through three conflicts and survived, so how could his luck be so bad? Then again, he had been wounded in Vietnam when he didn't move far enough from a friendly hand grenade that was thrown into a bunker. Penguin, on the other hand, was new to the Marine Corps. We just didn't have enough on him to make the final decision as to whom the bad luck actually belonged—we needed more information.

And later on, we got it. Penguin was cleaning his rifle behind the Gunny's LAV-L while Gunny relaxed in the back of the vehicle. Penguin's rifle went off, the bullet narrowly missing Gunny and slamming into the radiator from the inside of the vehicle. Poor Gunny. We finally had determined who it was that bad luck plagued. Penguin was given nonjudicial punishment, and I think Captain Shupp decided to move him so that Gunny might come home from his fourth and final conflict alive and in one piece.

Everyone liked Gunny. We really felt for him and the problems he endured while trying to make it home alive. After that final incident I didn't believe for a moment that Gunny was accident-prone. With Penguin gone, the mystery of that bit of karma was solved.

7

DESPITE THE DEGREE of commitment and motivation that energized us throughout the deployment, all the marines on my crew suffered from homesickness. It was very frustrating for us to be in the desert so long away from our families. My wife and I had just had our first son the previous spring; my gunner's wife was due to have their first child the coming spring; one of my scouts wanted to be with his little girl. We just wanted to go home.

Another frustration was the fact that no distinct time line had been set for our going home. We had heard rumors we might be home by Christmas, but that hope faded quickly as the year progressed. When President Bush issued the 15 January deadline to Sadaam Hussein, we finally had a dim light to look forward to. I remember writing my wife on 3 November that it would really be depressing if they told us we wouldn't be going home until 31 March (which, ironically, turned out to be the very date I did leave for home). Of course the way we all wanted to go home was by having done the job we were sent to do—quickly.

In addition to the overall positive attitude we had about our mission and our reason for existence in the theater, we shared a strong dislike for Sadaam Hussein. We heard news of his exploits, including his having patients' life-sustaining equipment unplugged at hospitals and babies taken out of incubators in order to preserve resources for his war machine—babies who were left to die on the cold hospital floors. Hussein was destroying lives and futures; and as far as we were concerned, he deserved to die painfully. I can still remember vividly the distaste we felt for what he and his army were doing. There was no love lost between the Iraqis and us, the crew of Blue 5.

Perhaps the most pivotal moment in Blue 5's quest for understanding of our purpose happened during one of the battalion operations in November: the crew was privy to a sight that would live indelibly in our minds. There was nothing particularly dramatic about the sight, but the circumstance, and the meaning behind what we saw, strengthened the resolve we had already started to develop. We were on the left wing of the company formation when we passed a Kuwaiti position in the middle of the Saudi desert. I looked over from my turret hatch and saw tiny Kuwaiti flags flying proudly from every antenna of every BMP (an armored amphibious infantry combat vehicle). Some of the flags were makeshift, constructed by the BMP crews in memory of the freedom they had lost.

I told the crew to look, and as we passed the position, we all stared in silence. There were no words required: each of us reflected solemnly on the pain that the Kuwaiti soldiers must have been feeling. Yes, we all wanted to go home, but when we spoke those thoughts aloud, we realized they were selfish. These warriors before us did not have a home to go to! I think at that very moment I realized that no matter what the official position was, I could never believe that the war was about oil. Later, as a crew, we talked about that moment often. We all agreed. We all saw and felt the same things: the war was about freedom lost, a freedom that had to be regained. Our desire to go home was tempered by that brief passing in the sand.

We were getting American newspapers and magazines sporadically throughout the deployment. Each time we read the articles the presses were publishing, we got mad. We saw protesters in America who believed the war was about oil—they chanted slogans like *No blood for oil!* We read the letters to the editors in the newspapers and found the protesters there, too. We talked about these articles and these people on the home front, and we were disgusted. These Americans simply did not know what it was like over here; they did not understand. We were able to remind ourselves, however, that America is a free society and that freedom of speech, and of personal opinion, is part of our national birthright. So with all of our disgust the only thing we could do was continue to believe in ourselves— and in our actions.

The one element of the publicity that we could not tolerate, however, was the letters from service personnel in the *Stars and Stripes*. We had to accept civilians who didn't understand as we did and who chose to exercise their opinion, but we didn't have to accept the same from service members. I read letter after letter written by those in-country who were complaining about the conditions of the deployment, about fighting for Kuwait, about being away from home, and about little things like showers and food. I was shocked. It was one thing to hear such things from a civilian, but hearing them from a military member, who has sworn to carry out the orders given, was appalling.

I began to wonder why these people joined the service at all if they were going to complain at the first hardship to hit them. And I could not believe that NCOs could not control their feelings but had instead decided to air their grievances in a forum that all service personnel could read— including their subordinates, the ones they were setting the example for. Adding to the whole problem were the scores of service men and women back in the United States who elected to exercise their right to object to the whole war for one reason or another—and those were the ones who claimed conscientious-objector status.

I am very serious about my business as a marine, and I could not understand any of this. I wrote a letter to my wife on 10 November in frustration and disgust— "I don't understand the total, utter selfishness and lack of compassion . . . who has lost their rights? Let's think about the thousands who've lost their *country!* It's not about oil; it can't be! I won't believe it! It's about my comrade, and his tiny Kuwaiti flag flying high above his vehicle—that's what it's about!"

As I did my research for this book, I realized that this issue itself was an undertone in all my letters home. I had wanted to come home, but it was very important to me and to my crew that Kuwait was freed. We didn't appreciate the protesters, and we especially didn't appreciate the service people who had elected to exercise their free speech in the open forum they had chosen. It wasn't about free speech; it was about setting the example. Military leaders are obligated to set the example, and we must trust that our country's leadership will make the correct decisions. In this particular instance I felt that those who were protesting and complaining had absolutely no idea what it was like for the Kuwaiti soldier; they could not feel the pain of displacement or the hope of regained freedom.

The unprofessional behavior of the complaining servicemen just strengthened our resolve, however. We started out training in the Triangle in September, and as the months progressed we continued to train, moving farther north toward Kuwait. We started more than a hundred miles from the border, and when January arrived we had moved to within thirty miles of the tiny country. Each time we moved forward, we occupied new territory, established positions that allowed us to provide observation to the north, and became familiar with our new surroundings. We got by day to day knowing that our cause was a just one.

In November, battalion-level training picked up significantly. It started with combined NBC training that had us fighting the simulated war in MOPP 4 (the highest level of NBC protection), and culminated in a division operation that took place in late December.

We didn't do a lot of dedicated company training as we had done in the early months; we were relegated to moving about in huge company formations attacking and maneuvering on a simulated enemy. All training was based on the initial breach of an enemy minefield. The LAI battalion is not designated as the breaching force during this type of operation. The battalion is used as a highly mobile and versatile asset that can quickly exploit the gaps created in an obstacle belt, rush to the enemy's flank or rear to reach a higher objective, or take advantage of observation abilities to provide security for follow-on units.

Our battalion XO created a playbook using the names of actual football plays, such as "dive," "trap," and "sweep." These plays were the means used to maneuver the battalion during the operations. Weekly we would move around on a "sweep" to link up with friendly elements, where we would "block" so that another element could "dive" through us. I got a laugh out of using these names for the plays, but in reality they fit the operations.

At the end of December we participated in a division-level operation that did not begin to test the abilities Captain Shupp had developed within Alpha Company. For the most part we simply moved through the simulated breach lanes to a point in the desert where we provided security. Shupp had moved us so often as a company under so many conditions—day, night, NBC—that we probably could have conducted the division operation in our sleep.

We in 1st LAI Battalion had been training like this in the desert for three months when the advanced elements from 2d LAI Battalion arrived in theater. The marines from Camp Lejeune had watched the coverage of Desert Shield from their living rooms in North Carolina and had waited impatiently for the call to deploy to Saudi Arabia. In August, Bravo and Delta Companies (2d LAI) were told to prepare for a deployment. Subsequently they boarded amphibious ships and sailed for the Persian Gulf. Members of Alpha and Charlie Companies, considering themselves to be better trained as units to deploy to the theater, were frustrated as they watched their sister companies leave.

They didn't stay frustrated for long, however. When "Stop Loss" (an act designed to preserve the fighting force) went into effect, the battalion commander told the two remaining companies to prepare for deployment. Thus it was not the members of Bravo or Delta—they were still aboard ships in the Gulf—that stepped off the 747s in Saudi Arabia to represent 2d LAI Battalion as the advanced party. One of the marines of Charlie Company who arrived in Saudi in early December was Sergeant Smith.

Sergeant Smith and his contingent linked up with the MPS and, in a span of four days, moved the vehicles designated for Alpha and Charlie from the pier at al-Jubail to Camp 15. When the remaining marines arrived, they began to prepare the staged vehicles for operations in the Saudi desert.

Each Marine Corps vehicle is serialized. LAVs are designated by a six-digit number. One of the vehicles that Charlie had been issued from MPS was vehicle number 521666. It became readily apparent to Sergeant Smith that there were no volunteers to assume responsibility for it. Smith was feeling especially daring, and when he found out that no one else would take the vehicle, he said, "What the hell," and took it for his own.

Vehicle 666 developed problems immediately. After an incredible length of time on-ship, the vehicle arrived in Saudi Arabia with sand inside of its fuel tank. Sergeant Smith and his crew had to drain the tank and clean it out. The sand had already damaged the engine's fuel injectors, which had to be reworked and replaced. After all this, Smith still said, "Yeah, 666—that was a good vehicle!"

On Christmas Day, the crew of 666 decided that they needed to get the vehicle blessed by a priest. Sergeant Smith searched the area for a Catholic priest and learned that he would have to drive to the nearest artillery battery to find one. On the morning of the twenty-sixth as the company was preparing to move out into the desert to train, Smith and the crew of 666 drove to the artillery battery's position.

When Sergeant Smith located the priest and asked him if he would bless the vehicle, the priest laughed at first. When the priest joined the marines at 666, though, he became immediately interested in the vehicle. Not the tack mark, 666, but the armament and capabilities. After the sergeant answered all the priest's questions, the priest took the task seriously and blessed the LAV—after all, it was the day after Christmas, the vehicle was numbered 666, and the marines were going off to war. After a liberal use of holy water on the vehicle, the priest led the marines in two prayers. With that, Sergeant Smith thanked the priest, mounted up, and rejoined Charlie Company.

For the next few weeks Charlie Company attempted to accomplish all the training that 1st LAI had accomplished in three months. It was an arduous task—the days were long, and the nights were longer—but they nonetheless accepted it with vigor.

Our training in Alpha was complete. During the time before the new year arrived, I was preoccupied with getting mentally prepared to meet the enemy. I was very concerned about being able to do the right thing and to make the right decisions. I wanted my section to survive to go home to their families. I talked to my wife about it in letters; I talked to Negron about it. With the 15 January deadline set, we were no longer training for an unspecified time line. Every day now marked a day closer to our meeting the enemy, however ready we were as a company.

Lieutenant Tice was consistent and true to form. With all that we had learned, he still expected us to learn more; he still expected us to profit from our own mistakes. He never pushed any lessons on us but always assured us that there was something more we could learn. I was beginning to understand more and more about the man that led our platoon.

He was very serious about leadership. It would have been very simple for him to let things develop without guidance: to allow the proficiency of his section leaders—Negron and me—to guide the training of the platoon. That wasn't his style, though. He would always stay one step ahead of us, providing us morsels of knowledge through the lessons he himself had learned.

On 29 December the entire company moved south to Manifa Bay. Battalion had an assembly line of sorts to inspect and paint all the vehicles. In the course of one day, each and every vehicle in the company was painted desert tan—gone was the sabkha tan—and each vehicle had been inspected for serviceability. The feverish pace at which the battalion was working brought the reality of what we were doing closer to the heart.

As the battalion master gunner Sergeant Ramirez was responsible for establishing live-fire ranges for the line companies to shoot their weapons on. His first endeavor in this field resulted in the Ramirez Range Complex.

Initially Sergeant Ramirez was told that we required a range to shoot the 25-mm cannons on. He responded, "That's it, just the cannons?" That was it. He was given an area about a mile north of the Chicken Ranch that faced west into the open desert. Ramirez was not a school-trained master gunner at the time, and when they asked him for a surface-area danger diagram, he was nonplused. He had never heard of one, much less done one, but as a professional he was game to figuring it out.

A surface-area danger diagram is nothing more than an overlay that, when placed over a map, will illustrate where the rounds of a weapon will land when fired from a specific location. After careful searching Ramirez found an example in the gunnery manual and began the difficult task of learning how to draw the diagram in a day's time. The armor-piercing round of the LAV-25 will travel more than fourteen kilometers when fired at a certain angle—in the LAV community we like to say that it will fire just over two country counties. The diagram was very important to higher headquarters—nomadic Bedouins lived in theater, and we needed to avoid shooting them. When Ramirez produced the diagram to division, he was tasked with going out into the impact area and marking the boundaries of the range fan. Fortunately the battalion air officer was able to get a helicopter to assist Ramirez in this task. Once the area had been marked, Ramirez had to fly through the entire impact area to warn the Bedouins that there were going to be bullets flying toward them.

On three or four separate occasions Sergeant Ramirez spotted a Bedouin encampment from the air and was forced to land to convey his message. The Bedouins did not speak English, and Ramirez did not speak Bedouin. When he tried to explain to the nomads that they needed to move, they just smiled and invited him into their tents. Once inside a tent the Bedouins gave him fresh bread, tea, and camel milk. It was a ritual. The Bedouins were unconditionally open to Americans, and at every tent Sergeant Ramirez stopped in, the same ritual was performed.

Eventually he gave the international sign for bullets coming downrange—hands posed as if holding and firing a rifle—and received affirmative nods from the Bedouins. Whether they had really understood him or not, they were gone the next day.

The next task, acquiring targets for the cannons to shoot at, involved a scavenging tour throughout the open desert. Wood, metal, and scrap iron were collected, transported, and deposited at the range. The first time Ramirez left the targets out in the desert overnight, he returned the next morning to find them gone. The marines who worked for him were upset. All of the other units in the area had apparently gone scavenging themselves and had found Sergeant Ramirez's haul. Ramirez himself was not upset, though. He told the marines that he didn't know how badly the other units needed the materials; he couldn't blame them for looking out for themselves. After that, however, Ramirez spent the night in the desert with his targets. He was sympathetic but not stupid.

Battalion reneged on their initial request for a 25-mm cannon range only. Soon Ramirez had constructed a small-arms zero range, a 9-mm familiarization range, and four hand-grenade pits. The tiny firing line for the LAV-25s was quickly joined by a multitude of firing lines, protective berms, and bunkers. The range was a success, and the marines honored Sergeant Ramirez's efforts with the christening of the Ramirez Range Complex.

At the end of December, Ramirez was tasked with a more difficult range-making assignment. The company commanders had convinced battalion to build a range that would allow the companies the opportunity to fire the weapons while maneuvering at the same time. It only made sense —we had been training for quite a while, and the static range we had been using did not provide a good evaluation of our skills.

The original idea was that the companies would conduct an operation (movement to contact) that would culminate in a live-fire assault on a real-istic-threat target area. The company commanders wanted the latitude of planning the advance and the attack, so Ramirez was faced with a very challenging situation. He had to configure a safety fan that would allow the commanders the flexibility they desired but would also prevent our bullets from flying in all directions.

Additionally, Saudi Arabian officials had to come out and approve the final plan. Sergeant Ramirez, now proficient at surface-area danger diagrams, was able to pick a piece of terrain that married up with the existing safety fan for the Ramirez Range Complex. He gave the company commanders a wide swath of desert for maneuver, and then for safety purposes he slightly restricted the firing angle at the objective.

For the targets Ramirez made another trip to al-Jubail to work his acquisition skills again. There he was able to solidify a deal with a combat-support element that included the use of logistic support variants (LVSs, or "Dragon Wagons"—flatbed, off-road semitrailer vehicles) and a crane. Once the sergeant had the equipment, he simply drove down the road, stopped at each wrecked and abandoned car along the side, and loaded it onto an LVS with the crane. The targets were transported to the piece of terrain that would soon be the enemy position, and then they were dropped off in the most realistic target array possible. Ramirez stuck

wooden poles on the cars to represent the muzzles of the armored vehicles they simulated. But he had not forgotten what would happen to his
targets if he left them alone at night. When everyone else left, he curled up
in his HMMWV by the radio and attempted to get some sleep.

That first night on the range, around the first week of January, Ramirez
could not sleep, though. Over the radio crackled the news that an Iraqi
tank and helicopter had crossed the border to the north. It turned out that
these vehicles had defected, but to Ramirez, alone in the dark desert, the
simple fact was that the Iraqis were in Saudi Arabia. His 9-mm pistol found
its way to the palm of his hand. Every noise, every animal moving in the
desert, and every gust of wind rustling through the weeds was an Iraqi soldier sneaking up to kill him in his HMMWV.

He was so scared about the whole thing that he moved three hundred
meters away from his HMMWV and hid behind a group of rocks. He figured the Iraqis would go to his HMMWV first and then he could ambush
them with his pistol. That didn't work out as well as he had planned, however. In the rocks he could not hear the vehicle radio, he wouldn't know if
the Iraqis had started a full-scale assault, and he was out of touch with the
world. Periodically he scampered back to the vehicle to monitor the radio
and then scurried back out to the protection of the rocks.

I laughed hard when Ramirez told me this story. In retrospect it was
easy for me to tell him he should have left the targets and sought safety.
But Sergeant Ramirez was not about to lose his targets—he had worked
too hard to get them, and the first company was due on the range the following day.

When we in Alpha got our turn at the range, the setup was simply outstanding. The movement up to the range was simple—all movement for
Alpha was simple by then. When I got an opportunity to control my section's fires in a realistic environment, I was motivated. Everything worked
as I envisioned. I practiced a number of techniques that day.

First I dismounted scouts while my section remained in the hide position. The scouts radioed back a report and called us up to fire. I moved
Matlain and my vehicle simultaneously, issued a section fire command,
destroyed the intended targets, and then pulled the section back into a
hide. Next I gave an alternating fire command. The scouts were still up,
and this time the scouts guided each vehicle into a different position each
time we pulled up to fire. First Matlain pulled up, engaged a target, and
slid back down. While he repositioned, I pulled up, fired, and then dropped
back.

It was really satisfying to see the whole section working as one. The scouts did an excellent job of acquiring and reporting targets. The gunners went in blind and immediately picked up the required targets. My wingman executed perfectly, making my job easier.

So I laughed when Sergeant Ramirez told me about his evening with the ghost Iraqis, but I also thanked him for his enormous effort and outstanding job on the live-fire assault course. It was far more elaborate than I think anyone would have expected with his resources, and it did wonders in boosting our confidence as the 15 January deadline approached.

The crew of Blue 5, from the top: Uke, Spencer (our driver for a short time whom Dudley replaced), Tanner, the author, Fulton, and Allison.

Uke and the author discussing the best way to attack the bad guys and hamming it up for the camera a bit.

The author with the camel who joined us for about four days in December.

As it turned out, the camel that visited us was pregnant. In the background you can see our company kitchen.

Our company cook, helping the staff grill chicken at Christmas.

Christmas Day at the battalion CP. On the left with his hands in front of him is General Gray, our commandant, just off the helicopter that brought him in.

This is what a Kuwaiti BMP looks like in the sights at about 1,500 meters.

Delta Burke and the author on Christmas Day.

"Major Dad" (Gerald McCrainey) and the author on Christmas Day.

These photos were taken during a battalion exercise. Notice how crowded the
desert can get when a large unit of armored vehicles moves through.

The author with his vehicle the first night after the ground war at Manifa Bay. Notice the damage to the vehicle's hull and lights caused by the road signs on the cloverleaf and the fence at the Kuwait airport; the lights had to be tied with communication wire so the driver could see to make the trip out of Kuwait.

The author (foreground), Tanner (center), and Allison (right) relax in the back of the vehicle the first night after the cease-fire was announced at Manifa Bay. Notice the rounds of 25-mm ammunition draped over the seats (above author's boot), the LAAW rocket above the author's head, and the decorations adorning the bulkheads of the vehicle.

The author's vehicle at the start of a sandstorm.

8

THE END of December and the arrival of the new year brought a most miserable two weeks of weather. Thirty miles from the Kuwait border our new year began with temperatures peaking at twenty-eight degrees in the early morning. It rained off and on every day—big, cold drops of rain driven by hearty gusts of wind from the north. So much water burst forth from above that grass was starting to grow in the desert sand. When and if—and this was a big *if*—the sun came out, the temperature was high enough to strip down to your skivvies to dry off, but only if you stayed out of the shade.

We were in our farthest north positions to date, and we continued screening to the north, running around training day and night. The training itself was no particular challenge by this time; it was simply a rehash of everything we had done up to this point. Alpha Company had peaked in proficiency.

When we weren't training during the day, we were digging. We dug vehicle fighting positions on reverse slopes of hills with shovels, we dug huge holes to sleep in at night, and we dug holes just to dig holes—digging was therapy for the crew of Blue 5. Soon it had become more than just something we did to improve vehicle and observation-post positions: it was the one single act that relieved the pent-up anxiety of five months of waiting.

In particular I remember my amusement at watching my crew digging what they called the "bunker," an elaborate earthen complex that would end up housing the entire crew. They were happy and really "into" the construction. When my gunner came to me and asked if we all could go scavenge some roofing material for our soon-to-be home, all I could say was "OK."

We constructed a trailer out of scrap metal and wood, which we attached to the tow pintle of the vehicle. We drove around for hours picking up stray materials that had been left abandoned in the desert. Standing back and looking at the vehicle after the makeshift trailer was loaded, I couldn't help but think that we had been transformed into a band of gypsies. We had become nomadic, assimilating into the culture of the Bedouin tribes in the region. Everything we needed to survive was in the desert, and over the desert we roamed to find the things we needed.

Nomads as we were, construction on the bunker was coming along spectacularly. Then the rain came again. On 10 January winter fully arrived in the desert. What I thought had been simply awful weather got worse. Though the crew was nearing completion of the bunker, rain delayed construction on the roof.

For three days the skies over the desert opened up, and a torrential downpour soaked Saudi Arabia. It rained so hard, and it was so very cold, that it was impossible for us to do anything aside from seeking shelter. To have done otherwise would have surely caused us some extreme cases of hypothermia. Certainly I had been through rain and cold weather before, but I had always had the luxury of going inside to dry off and change clothes. In this case we simply were not equipped to deal with the weather.

Everything got wet. Even when we huddled inside the sealed hull of our LAV, it was raining in there as well: huge drops of condensation gathered on the internal hull of the vehicle and began to drop rapidly on top of us. Opening the hatch to relieve the condensation only allowed the cold and bitter wind to find us again as we nestled against each other for warmth.

There was not a single dry item left on the vehicle. Concerned about the weapons mounted on top of it, I periodically cracked open my hatch to spray oil onto the guns to combat the rust that was sure to accompany the moisture. The ammunition can that held the two-hundred-round belt of 7.62-mm linked ammunition for the pintle-mounted machine gun filled with water and started overflowing. I braved the elements periodically to dump out the can, only to see it immediately fill to the top again.

In addition to soaking us with moisture the condensation from the warm bodies inside the vehicle wreaked havoc on the communication and intercom system. When I had to make a resupply run in the rain, I could not talk to my driver. The water had seeped into the intercom connections, and whenever the system was activated, a loud squeal of feedback came over all the CVC helmet speakers. It did no good to dry out the connections; the moisture came right back.

On the third day, in the late afternoon, the rain stopped. It was about forty-five degrees, and I looked up into the sky and saw a tiny slice of blue slicing through the ominous gray clouds. Through that sliver a small portion of the sun shone: its warmth pierced the overcast and reached out to my cold and prune-skinned body. Unable to resist the opportunity, I immediately stripped and took a shower with a five-gallon water jug. I found the driest set of clothes I had, and in five minutes I was freezing cold but refreshed and ready for another three days of rain.

Perhaps the biggest problem the rain caused was damage to the ammunition. The weapons were wet, but after a couple of hours of scrubbing with oil they were free of rust and ready for action. The ammunition was severely damaged, though. The two hundred rounds of 7.62 mm for the pintle-mounted machine gun were corroded from one end to the other. Each and every one of the tiny black metal links that held the rounds together was stained a deep orange. The belt was starting to freeze at the joints, and I knew I would have problems firing the ammunition in its present state.

It took a long time for us to take the belt apart and scrub every single round and link with CLP (cleaner lubricant protectant) and an all-purpose brush. In the end the belt moved freely, but the damage caused by five months of exposure to the elements was still visible. I didn't trust the ammunition and vowed to test it at the first available opportunity.

On 15 January the deadline for Iraqi withdrawal from Kuwait passed, just as every other day in the desert passed. After an uneventful evening of turret watch we rose from the bunker on the morning of the sixteenth and walked around in frustration. Everything was the same; nothing had changed. We had been in-country for so long with only the deadline to look forward to, and now it had passed.

It is hard to describe the anxiety we felt. With normal Marine Corps deployments you always knew the exact date you were going home. Calendars with exaggerated red Xs counting down to the final day adorned the walls of every living area. But in the Saudi desert we couldn't maintain a calendar: we didn't know when we were coming home—we didn't know where to draw the final red X. I think that was probably the hardest part of the deployment. The physical strain on the body, the prospects of danger, and the burdens of constant leadership were nothing compared to not knowing when it would end.

With the 15 January deadline come and gone, the marines found levity in the running joke of the day—*Gee, it's hard to see the sky with it black from all the aircraft running north to enforce the deadline.* The weather was still nasty, and sarcastic humor was the one thing that allowed us to maintain sanity on the morning of the sixteenth.

In the afternoon Captain Shupp called all vehicle commanders to his position. When we arrived, he sat us down in a dugout hole in the sand and gave us an operations order that would take us to the border.[1] There was no word of the air war, but the scheduled trip to the border between Kuwait and Saudi Arabia brought a new purpose to the company: we were finally going to where the action was.

The order was no more special than any other order we had received. We were going to move in company formation along the western border of Kuwait in order to see if our presence caused a reaction. Captain Shupp was a phenomenal communicator of combat orders. There were no wasted words; everything was important. The captain passed the order as he did every order—with intensity in his actions and mannerisms.

We were informed that we might encounter surrendering Iraqi soldiers during the mission and that we were to treat them as enemy prisoners of war (EPWs). The captain spoke uninterrupted for about five minutes, but when he mentioned how the EPWs were to be treated, Corporal Houghton of 2d platoon muttered lightly, "Fuck that."

In midsentence Captain Shupp stopped and faced Houghton. His penetrating eyes became sharper, his solid jaw clenched tighter, and he let loose on Houghton. "Bullshit! I'm not going to hear talk like that. We're professional warriors, and we will treat the enemy that surrenders with honor, dignity, and professionalism." He then told Houghton to begin. For the next five minutes Houghton did pushups while the captain went on about the ethics and morals required of a United States Marine.

I smiled inside as I watched the encounter. I was proud to have Captain Shupp as my commanding officer, and at that point I knew I would follow him anywhere. *Intestinal fortitude* was one of his favorite terms, and he was always consistent—he lived by his principles himself. It would have been easy for Shupp to let the incident pass and pretend he didn't hear Houghton's remark. That wouldn't be in his character, though. He squashed the comment almost as fast as it had been made, and the subject never arose again. If I had to describe Captain Shupp in two words, those words would be *pure leader.*

We all knew that everyone was angry at the Iraqis. The crew had discussed among ourselves about where we should direct that anger. I basically let them know that I would have no beef with an Iraqi who surrendered—just one fewer Iraqi to fight, in my opinion. Besides, if we mistreated prisoners, they would stop surrendering. It was good to hear the captain reaffirm my beliefs to everyone in the company.

Insofar as prisoners were concerned, Alpha went through a metamorphosis throughout the air war. We started out with Captain Shupp's blood-and-guts counseling of Corporal Houghton, and we ended with a very possessive attitude toward the prisoners we captured: if we felt that prisoners we transported to the rear were being mistreated, there was hell to pay. Appropriately the last prisoners collected before the ground war were detained under very agreeable circumstances.

On 12 February I moved over to the company trains to pick up some prisoners from Gunny Chevice. My section was assigned to transport the prisoners to the EPW holding area about thirty miles to the south. When we got to the trains, we found out that one of the prisoners had walked since dusk across the desert to reach our positions. He had sneaked away from his unit because he did not want to fight—he was tired of the whole situation. And he had walked without a weapon, ever aware that he would be summarily executed if he were caught. He was completely unaware of what he might find at our positions, and remarkably he had walked without boots on his feet!

It was a brave thing that this soldier had done. There really was a great risk involved in it. We learned a lot from the interpreter attached to our company. Officers of the Iraqi Army were holding pistols to the troops' heads to keep them from fleeing. Further the Iraqi troops had been informed that the Americans were savages and that they would kill or torture them if they gave up. I could not imagine what was going through this soldier's head when he began his barefoot journey across the desert.

Lance Corporal Moore, one of my scouts, was touched by the prisoner's plight. He dug into his pack to fetch the extra pair of boots he had and walked up to the prisoner with the boots held out in front of him. Accepting them, the Iraqi soldier smiled. Moore smiled as well, and I could tell that then and there Moore had experienced a moment he would never forget. I know it was a moment of compassion that I myself will never forget, either.

While we were moving the prisoners to my vehicle for transport, one of the other prisoners turned to me with excited eyes and an energetic smile. In heavily accented English he asked me, "What's your name?"

I was startled, and it took a moment for me to answer. "Ah, Greg." The soldier smiled and nodded his head. It was very moving. I could almost read the soldier's mind. He was joyfully anticipating the future—he was being repatriated from the brutality of the Iraqi Army—and he was looking for his first friend in his new life.

When I dropped the prisoners off at the holding area, the same soldier turned to me, smiled, and waved. "See you in America," he said. I suddenly became very warm inside. Before we mounted up on the vehicles and left, I waited. I stood in the turret and watched the unit handle the prisoners we had just turned over. I was very concerned about the treatment they would receive, and I wanted to ensure they were properly cared for.

In the company order on the afternoon of 16 January, Captain Shupp let us know that a LAAD (low-altitude air defense) team had been attached to the company. The team rode in a HMMWV with dual stinger launchers fixed on either side of the vehicle's flatbed. I think we all felt better with the attachment. LAVs have absolutely no means to ward off an enemy air attack besides the main gun and M240 machine guns. With the stinger team, we had a viable, concrete method to destroy any enemy aircraft that chose to attack us.

We were motivated. Mission completion was one step closer. We had been wondering what had happened with the 15 January deadline, but as it turned out, we didn't have to wait long to find that answer. At 0400 on 17 January, PFC Dudley, my driver, was on watch in the turret listening to armed forces radio: he received verification that not only had the deadline been enforced but that U.S. aircraft were conducting offensive strikes against targets in Iraq and Kuwait at that very moment. PFC Dudley woke the entire crew and told us what was going on.

As the sun rose over the Saudi desert, the company coil was active with excited marines looking skyward.[2] Not only were we about to head north to the border, but the United States had begun its air attack in earnest. When we looked up into the sky, we saw aircraft heading north in pairs. We saw other aircraft coming south in pairs, too.

The morning took an inordinate amount of time to pass. We were scheduled to leave early, but Captain Shupp put us on standby while he sorted out the new information vis-à-vis the air war. At about 0815 Shupp came over the company net on the SINCGARS radio and passed a FRAGO (fragmentary order). As I have said, Captain Shupp was extremely effective at relaying orders. The FRAGO was nothing more than clarification of the present order for the movement north with the new information regarding the Allied air offensive.

The captain updated the current situation by explaining that the city of al-Kafji was under artillery attack and that there was a lot of traffic, both Allied and enemy, in our area of operations. Allied forces were moving north, and the enemy was starting to surrender in certain places. The result of the increased activity was confusion, and Shupp wanted to clear everything up before we left. He described the new locations of EPW collection sites and the procedures for evacuating EPWs to those sites, and he emphasized that all weapons were to be loaded and kept on manual and electric safe.

The reality of the situation started to set in when Captain Shupp spelled out the rules of engagement. He told us what he expected us to do: (1) if you receive artillery fire, break contact; (2) avoid decisive engagements and company firefights; (3) if you gain positive ID on enemy forces, you are clear to fire.

With the last rule of engagement came a loud roar from the company area. There was nothing the company wanted more than to engage the enemy. That one single statement ended five and a half months of waiting and moved the company in a new direction. No longer would we wait for things to develop politically; now, we could—or at least we thought we could—control our own destiny.

In the span of two or three minutes Captain Shupp passed, in an organized fashion, the marching orders for the company. He put us at stand-to (ready to move on order with all weapons and stations manned) at 0830. We were heading north.

We moved out and spent what seemed like forever getting to the border. We reached it at a point just west of the border's "elbow," and then we turned due north in a company formation about three hundred meters from the berm, the ten- to fifteen-foot-high mound of dirt that ran the entire length of the border between Kuwait and Saudi Arabia. The berm —which was located about two kilometers from the border and not on the actual border itself—functioned as something of a neutral zone.

On the Saudi side of the border, the berm was broken periodically by the construction of Saudi Arabian police outposts, which were the only

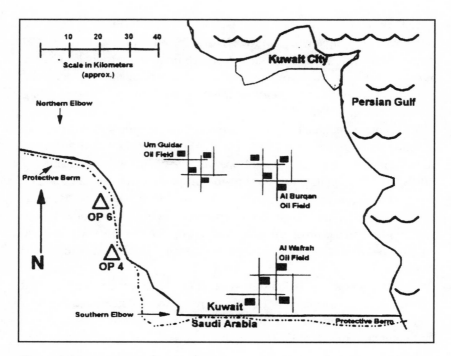

Figure 3. Movement north.

places along the border where traffic could pass. To me it seemed that the Saudis had constructed the berm and the police posts as a means of controlling immigration in this vast expanse of desert.

We continued north without incident until we reached a site defined as checkpoint thirteen. This was the northernmost police post before the border turned from north to west. Checkpoint thirteen also went by the name of OP 6. Reconnaissance marines had established an observation post at that location to watch the zone between Kuwait and Saudi Arabia. At OP 6, 1st Platoon turned west to establish a company assembly area. We pulled into the predetermined spot and started to set up. Just as we were dismounting from the vehicles, a loud boom echoed across the desert. To a man, everyone recognized the noise as an explosion, and we all flinched and ducked our heads. We quickly mounted onto our vehicles and started the engines in preparation to move.

What had happened was that 2d Platoon, the company tail, had come under attack from Iraqi artillery while moving from checkpoint thirteen to the assembly area. Fortunately the barrage was not accurate, and no one was hurt. But now we knew we were being watched: the Iraqis were well aware of our presence. We found that their artillery was generally ineffective, however—a fortunate thing because we could always count on the Iraqis to throw something our way when we moved.

We spent most of that first day near the border either in a company coil or moving to another location to establish a coil. At each location we stopped, it seemed as though a unit had been there before us and had abandoned the position in haste. Propaganda leaflets littered the desert for as far as the eye could see. We picked up the leaflets and read them. There were a number of versions, in color and in black and white, but they all had a common theme: a dead and/or dismembered Iraqi soldier lying on the battlefield who had been killed because he hadn't surrendered. There were captions under the pictures that we could not read, but I assume they told the currently fighting Iraqi soldier that he would be treated fairly if he surrendered. The effort that had been expended in producing and scattering the leaflets paid off: hundreds of Iraqi soldiers walked across the border to surrender to Allied forces.

We went to sleep that first night in a company coil well away from the berm. We dug holes in the ground so that we would be afforded at least some protection against an artillery attack during the night. The crew of Blue 5 was still very motivated about digging, and in fact, from that point on we dug holes each and every night—elaborate two- and three-man sleeping holes complete with taut peeked roofs, made of ponchos, to deflect the on-and-off rain.

Our next trip to the berm took place the following day. We traveled along the mound from north to south to show our constant presence to the Iraqi forces that were watching. As we passed OP 6, someone reported an armored vehicle adjacent to the police post building on the Kuwait side. When we were in a position to see it, we were able to identify it as a ZSU 23-4 (an antiaircraft vehicle). I used the handheld laser range finder and was able to determine that the vehicle was 1,150 meters away.

I reported the sighting and requested permission to fire but was told to stand by. This would be the first direct-fire engagement of the war, and probably half the company could see the target. I don't think Captain Shupp could see it, though—he wanted us to hold off on shooting until he was sure of our sighting. In retrospect this was probably the best call for the situation: we certainly didn't need half the company shooting from all directions at a single target across the berm. As the company moved south in formation, the chances of someone's shooting someone else were quite high, and target orientation changed as we moved. If I had ended up shooting, I would have done so along the long axis of the company formation, a situation that may not have been good.

The target slowly slipped from my view, and I think the captain called in aircraft to deal with it. So went the company's first opportunity to engage the enemy. Frustration reared its ugly head as we continued our show of force along the berm to the south.

The ZSU had been parked next to a building, and someone higher up the chain of command figured that the enemy was probably using the building as a place to watch us from. Consequently we received orders on 19 January to conduct a raid by fire on the building. Excited about the prospects of a raid, we stepped off from our company coil to move back up to the berm.

We drove in company formation up to OP 6 and linked up with the reconnaissance team located there. The building had no activity around it, and Captain Shupp decided to move the antitank variants up to a position where they could use their thermal sights to look at it. (Until 4 February the only vehicles with thermal sights were the LAV-ATs.)

The building showed up cold on the thermals, and the raid was called off. We spent the next day and a half in the same manner as before: we moved to the berm and from the berm, anticipating enemy contact, and found nothing. It was very tiring and very frustrating.

During that first week on the berm, we had our first electrifying incident, however. Nothing spectacularly overt happened, but the tension created by radio traffic was enough to get the blood pumping hard throughout everyone's body. It was late at night, and we were standing off on some high ground about three kilometers from the berm. The company was spread out on line with all the turrets of all the vehicles facing east, toward Kuwait. We hadn't been in the position long when somewhere along the hundreds of miles of border someone called in a gas attack. We neither heard nor saw anything that led us to believe chemical warfare had been directed toward our positions, but we had heard enough about the immediate effects of nerve gas to know that if someone said it was there, it was there, period.

We put on our gas masks immediately and struggled to find our chemical suits. The masks went on fairly easily, but the suits were another story. All the time that we imagined sarin nerve gas moving undetected across the desert toward our positions, we tried to get our chemical suits on to protect our skin from the volatile chemical.

This was the first time we had to use the suits, and we hadn't even taken them out of the packaging yet. And we had traded our American suits, which were packed in an easy-to-open opaque foil, for the higher-quality British suits, which came in vacuum packages. So tightly were the suits compressed into the five-mil-thick packaging that it was nearly impossible for us to free them. As we struggled, we looked around for the telltale cloud of gas that would penetrate our thin clothes and contaminate our skin. The darkness and the reduced visibility caused by the gas masks compounded the problem.

It took us about half an hour to finally get our suits on, and I remember listening to my increased breathing pushing through the tiny diaphragms of the mask as I struggled to get purified air into my system. It turned out that the whole ordeal had been a false alarm, however. We were all relieved, but I couldn't help wondering how we would have fared had the gas attack been bona fide. It was a no-win situation. As soon as the suits came out of the plastic packs, the charcoal inside them started to break down. As the charcoal broke down, the suits became less effective. So you couldn't take your suit out of the package until you needed it. If you left it in, it took you forever to get it out and onto your body.

On 21 January the frustrations of constant, uneventful trips to the berm ended, and the chemical-attack issue was revisited. The weather was particularly nasty and overcast that day. We were established in a company coil until late in the afternoon. Shortly after lunch we received word through the chain that an Iraqi commander had walked to OP 6 and given himself up to the reconnaissance marines manning the OP. Further, he wanted to surrender his entire unit. And so he was allowed to go back to get his unit of approximately a hundred Iraqis and march them back to the OP for that very purpose.

Higher headquarters had arranged for five-ton trucks to move up to OP 6 in order to provide transportation to take the prisoners to the rear. Alpha Company had been assigned the specific task of providing security for the trucks as they moved south with the prisoners. Captain Shupp had ordered 1st Platoon to provide four vehicles—mine, my wingman's, the platoon commander's, and the platoon sergeant's—to escort the trucks and to provide the security required of the prisoners on the trucks. The rest of the company was assigned as reserve in case anything happened.

Additionally air was stacked (staged at various elevations in the sky) on station to provide any support we required. We were ordered to stand-to at 1830 and were scheduled to pick up the trucks at OP 6 at 2100.

We received the order to move and transitioned the company coil into the march formation we used. Just as we began to move, Sergeant Long came over the company tactical net in a very rushed and excited voice: "Gas! Gas! Gas! I've got gas rolling in on my pos!"

Without stopping our movement, we held our breath and donned the gas masks that were constantly at our side. I half-expected the captain to stop the march column, but he kept moving, and since we guided our movement on his movement, we kept moving as well. But because we were in motion, we couldn't get to our chemical suits and put them on. We did put on our rubber gloves to protect our hands, and we did cover all exposed skin with our clothing and rubber gas-mask hoods. Having no idea what was going on at that time, I waited impatiently for traffic on the company net.

"Red 5, this is Black 6. Report, over." Captain Shupp came over the net and very calmly asked Sergeant Long what was going on. It was unreal how calm Shupp was when he faced the uncertainty of this situation.

"Black 6, this is Red 5. Just as we moved, a huge white cloud came rushing out of the desert and engulfed us. I started feeling weird in the throat, and I masked up the crew, over." Long was very excited right then. I could tell he was terrified: it was easy to detect the nervousness in his gas-mask attenuated voice.

"Roger, Red 5, stand by." I assume that the captain was getting on the net with higher headquarters to see if they had any intelligence about this gas. While he was off the company net, sporadic radio traffic dominated both the company and the platoon nets. First someone came over one of the nets and said that his crew were starting to feel burning sensations in moist areas of their bodies. This type of radio traffic continued until one of my crewmen told me that he was feeling symptoms as well. I didn't know what to think, but it didn't matter. As I listened to my breathing through the gas mask, I believed my respiration was beginning to grow rapid and irregular. With the seed planted in my mind, I began to feel the symptoms of nerve-gas exposure: rapid breathing, involuntary muscle action, and loss of body control.

The imagination is a very powerful thing. One crew reported they were feeling symptoms, and pretty soon those symptoms were everywhere. The fact that it was a chemical agent we were dealing with compounded the issue. We were warriors—professional marines—and the world of chemicals was something we had only heard about. But we knew the symptoms, we knew what the effects were, and we were deathly afraid of this thing that we could not combat.

I don't know how long we waited for Captain Shupp to come back over the radio—it couldn't have been more than a few minutes—but it was long enough for the company to imagine the worst of the situation, fabricating the symptoms of something that we were ill-equipped to combat. Finally Shupp did come over the net to bring his traditional calm and rational thought to bear on the situation: "Listen up, Alpha. There has been no, I say again, no gas attack. Gentlemen, take off your gas masks and stand by for FRAGO."

I couldn't believe it. Just like that, Captain Shupp reached into each and every mind within Alpha Company and brought it back to reality. If someone today were to ask me what a leadership challenge was, I would say that it was executing unmasking procedures. I cannot think of anything more challenging than turning to a young marine and telling him to go ahead and break the seal of his gas mask.

Captain Shupp approached the situation not only with confidence but with wisdom. Within one minute we were unmasked and copying a FRAGO—the thought of a gas attack completely gone from our minds. That was the type of leader that Captain Shupp was; that was the type of presence with Alpha that he had.

The FRAGO itself was not exactly pleasant news, though. The hundred Iraqis who came to surrender had jumped the reconnaissance team, blown up their HMMWV, and kicked them out of OP 6. The mission had changed: we were no longer going to escort prisoners; now we were going to reinforce recon.

Our journey to OP 6 to reinforce recon was not without adventure. With all the confusion regarding the suspected gas attack, we had managed to lose our attachment of mortars somewhere in the desert. At that time the battalion had a weapons company; as part of it, all LAV-ATs and LAV-Ms were detached to the other companies as needed.

What made this a good situation for the battalion was the fact that the marines in Weapons Company received uniform instruction on the use and employment of their respective weapons systems. All mortar and anti-tank personnel received the exact same training on mortars and TOWs. A lot of things made this a bad situation, though. First, the companies operated on SOPs. Every company operated differently, and each time Weapons

Company detached an element to another company, the marines joined the unit with absolutely no idea how to operate within it.

Second, we didn't always receive the same crews from Weapons Company, so when they were attached, they usually had to be brought up to speed with the way our company operated. Unfortunately there was not always enough time to do this.

Finally, not all weapons variants were equipped with SINCGARS radios, and therefore when the company was frequency hopping on the radios, the weapons variants were left out of the loop. What usually happened was that one of the vehicles dropped down to a single-channel frequency with one radio in an attempt to keep the marines informed.

What all this meant on 21 January was that the mortars got lost. I don't know if it was a matter of a communications breakdown, ignorance of company SOP, or just sheer confusion after the "gas attack," but we had traveled almost forty-five minutes when the captain tried to call mortars and got no response.

I didn't understand how it happened. We always traveled in formation, so it was difficult to get separated, but the mortars had missed a portion, if not all, of the movement to OP 6. Shupp was irritated. Here he was moving up to support the reconnaissance element, and his only indirect-fire asset was not with him. He told the trains to go and find them and to guide them to the OP while the company continued. He didn't tell them how to find them, and no one asked: Captain Shupp expected them to be found —no *if*s, *and*s, or *but*s.

When we approached the OP, Shupp came over the net to tell us that the recon element was occupying a position in a road culvert west of checkpoint thirteen. Whoever found that point was to let him know so he could move to affect a linkup. No sooner did the captain pass that word than my gunner saw the culvert in question through his night site. I peered diligently through the night-vision goggles that were fixed to my face and was finally able to see the culvert about eight hundred meters to my direct front.

I called the captain, and he told me to stand by so I could guide him up to the spot. Within minutes Shupp's vehicle was behind mine, and we closed on the culvert. The culvert went under an elevated road surface that ran east to the actual OP and west out into the desert. I pulled up and parked behind the elevated road adjacent to the culvert and scanned the horizon near the OP.

My first indication that something was going to happen was this: my back hatches opened, and two reconnaissance marines jumped in with my scouts. Before I could decipher what was going on, Captain Shupp came over the net, "Alpha, this is Black 6. Stand by for FRAGO, over."

"This is Black 6. The situation has changed, break. . . . The Iraqis jumped the OP and forced them out under fire, destroying their HMMWV and disabling their five-ton in the process, break." Captain Shupp spoke in short transmissions with periodic breaks in order to keep his electronic "footprint" low so that the enemy could not use direction-finding techniques to locate the company. His FRAGOs were always issued in that manner.

"The OP was abandoned in haste, and there are still some sensitive items of gear at the OP. We have to go get that gear, break." At that time we knew someone was going to have to physically drive to the OP and pick up the gear. The reconnaissance marines did not have an operative vehicle, and we had arrived—it wasn't too hard to figure out who had to drive to town.

"We don't know if the enemy is still at the OP, so we will move in with one platoon and mortars providing fire support, break . . . and one platoon maneuvering with the recon marines to pick up the gear."

This was not good. I don't think that anyone wanted to move into a built-up area that was recently occupied by a hundred angry Iraqis, let alone move in the area with the huge, vulnerable LAVs. Secretly we all crossed our fingers. The captain took a few seconds before he gave his next transmission, and in that few seconds we all hoped that our platoon would be the base of fire, or supporting element—not the maneuvering or going-into-town element.

Then, before the captain spoke, the fact that the marines had already jumped into the back of my vehicle hit me. I knew our platoon was going into the town. "The base of fire will set west of checkpoint thirteen, and orient to the north end of the actual OP, break. . . . That element will be" —we all crossed our fingers tighter— "2d Platoon."

"First Platoon, you will move in transporting the reconnaissance marines, drop them off, provide security, get the gear, and get out, break."

It was a done deal. This was not the way any of us would have preferred to conduct business. The LAV was a terrible choice of vehicle to move into built-up areas. The armor protection barely stopped small-arms fire, and the LAV's hallmark, mobility, was nil in city streets. We would be sitting ducks without the ability to stand off from the enemy.

The captain continued: "Mortars, I want you to set south of checkpoint thirteen and begin a continuous volley of fire into the OP while 1st Platoon maneuvers up." The captain continued for a few more minutes until everyone was up to speed. When he was done, each unit acknowledged understanding of the order—each unit but mortars, that is.

The mortars still hadn't arrived. The captain was very frustrated. "Mortars, mortars, where are you?" he queried over the open company net. When they finally did arrive, the captain had to issue portions of the FRAGO again. This gave us all a little time to think about what we would do. On Blue 5, we checked all the weapons again, sorted out the areas of responsibility for scanning in the OP, and reflected.

I remember exactly what I was feeling at the time. This was by far the most serious moment that the company had encountered. The ground war had not even started, and I was really angry that I might actually die before that happened. I was scared of dying, and further I did not want to die in the air war. I know this sounds stupid, but for some reason it was very important to me. Yet even with the fear I was angry more than anything: distressed that I might be remembered as dying in the air war.

After about two minutes of silent frustration, I said consciously to myself, "Oh, well. Nothing you can do about it, Greg. Just do your job right, and if you die, you die." That short statement to myself cleared everything up for me. After that night I never had those feelings again. It was very surreal: I went through danger again, but it did not matter—I was never afraid of death again. After that, I always assumed that each and every warrior had to come to terms with the fear of death at some point in time. I remember how scared I was, and I feel sorry for any warrior who has not yet resolved this internal issue. I can't imagine having to deal with fear of death every moment of the day. It would be like living in hell.

The time came for us to move—2d Platoon called in that they were set in overwatch, and the mortars started firing rounds into the OP. I think they were firing a mix of high explosives and white phosphorus. When the rounds began to impact, 1st Platoon moved rapidly from behind the elevated road to the OP.

Lance Corporal Uke was scanning back and forth with the turret as we approached. I was standing in my hatch swinging the pintle-mounted machine gun in the opposite direction the turret faced as the gunner scanned, and the scouts in back were watching the area to our rear. We entered the town, and two things happened. First, I noticed that we were entering adjacent to a service-station island and that there was gas all over the ground. I could smell the oily liquid and see its shiny surface around the gas pumps through my night-vision goggles. Then an 81-mm round landed right in front of our vehicle. It's funny that I don't remember its being especially loud, but it washed out my vision momentarily. Another round landed near the first one, and I was concerned not only about the gas on the deck but about the fact that I was in the impact area.

I called my platoon commander. "Blue 1, this is Blue 5. I think someone forgot to turn off the mortars." When you move under indirect fire, the fire is shifted or ceased before you enter the impact area. This was not happening now.

"Roger, Blue 5. I've got them here too, break. . . . Black 6, this is Blue 1, shift fire on the mortars over." Lieutenant Tice was remaining calm, which was good.

"Roger, Blue 1." Captain Shupp would take care of it for us, and sure enough, the mortar fire immediately stopped. I was just glad that I wasn't fifty feet farther forward.

Second, I noticed that the buildings were extremely large and close to us. These tight quarters caused the gunner to have to increase the length of each sweep though the area—and caused me to get out of my hatch. The pintle-mounted machine gun on the LAV-25 is positioned to allow the vehicle commander to engage targets out to a range of 1,100 meters. You could engage these targets while standing comfortably in your hatch: your body was protected by the armor of the turret. With close targets the spade of the gun had to be elevated to a point that forced the vehicle commander to fully extend his arms over his head in order to aim at the ground and ground targets near the vehicle.

The situation was disadvantageous. I could not aim the machine gun at anything from inside my hatch, and I doubted my ability to bring fire to bear on a potential target with any rapidity. I experimented for a few moments and soon found that I actually had to sit on top of the turret to man the weapon. I was very uncomfortable with my entire body in an exposed position eight feet in the air, but the only other option was not to man the weapon at all—unthinkable with the narrow field of view that Uke had in the gunner's sight. There was no way he could pick anything up unless he was pointed right at it, so I sat on the turret. I didn't like it, but I sat there looking where the gunner was not looking, and I maintained positive weapons orientation with the pintle mount.

When we moved to the center of the OP where the recon post had been set up in a large, multistory structure, we passed a long single-floor building with doors on either end and windows every three feet along the sides.

"I've got movement! There, right there, the door!" Lance Corporal Uke was scanning the side of the building and had picked up a door opening and closing.

I looked to where the barrel was pointing, but didn't see any movement. "What was it, Uke?"

"I don't know. The door opened, then closed. . . . I swear, I saw. . . ."

"Got ya, Uke. Let me take a look." He had seen something for sure. It could have been that someone had decided this wasn't the best time to come outside. It was really hard to use the electronic night-vision devices to stare intently at anything. Pretty soon you started interpreting the green images for exactly what you wanted them to be. I was concerned about that possibility and constantly changed the angle that I looked at the building. I finally figured that if there was someone in there, he was hiding.

I wanted to fire up the building—put a round in every window. That would have been the safest thing to do. The Iraqi inside could pop out at any time and fire an RPG (rocket-propelled grenade) the twenty-five meters to my vehicle before I could react. I definitely couldn't move in time to avoid the explosive projectile. Unfortunately, though, I couldn't fire into the building. Somewhere on the other side of it was Lieutenant Tice's section. Any ammunition I fired into the wooden structure would travel right through. It was another no-win situation.

I directed the driver to move forward to the left and repositioned the vehicle to offer a smaller target to anyone inside the building. I told Uke to watch the building with the night site and 25-mm chain gun. I reported to Lieutenant Tice and continued on the mission. Within minutes we had passed through the puddles of gasoline and established a perimeter around the former OP. All was going well, and I reassigned each marine in the vehicle a sector of observation while we waited for the recon marines to get their gear out of the building.

The gear was swiftly recovered. We mounted up onto the vehicles and took a head count, and Lieutenant Tice gave us the word to leave. We left the OP a lot quicker than we had entered. Within minutes we were south of OP 6, crossing the hard-surface road. Then someone came over the net and asked where the TOWs were. I had no idea what they were talking about. *What TOWs?* Apparently we had dragged our TOW attachments into the OP with us so that they could observe to the north from the confines of the OP. I questioned that call, but the facts remained the same: we went into the OP with an attachment of LAV-ATs, and we left the OP without them.

I looked back and then radioed Lieutenant Tice: "This is Blue 5, I'll go get them." I immediately turned my section around, and we went back to the OP. We didn't have to travel far—just on the south side of the OP, next to the berm, the attachment of TOWs sat looking north. I drove by, got their attention, and signaled for them to follow. We left without incident.

That evening lasted a long time. It was 2100 when we were supposed to leave to conduct the original mission of EPW escort, and it probably took us four hours between the "gas attack," lost mortars, and FRAGO before we were even able to move into the OP proper. When we had finished the mission of getting the gear out of the OP, we dropped off the reconnaissance marines who had been riding along and got into company march formation to head back to our company assembly area.

About half an hour into our trip back to the assembly area, my night-vision goggles fluttered blank. I figured it was the battery because I had been wearing them all night long. Without taking the goggles off my eyes, I reached into my flak jacket and drew out a spare battery. I replaced the battery by feel, without taking the goggles off, and flipped the power switch back on. To my surprise the goggles flickered momentarily and shut down again. I didn't think I had two bad batteries, and I took the goggles off to look at them more closely. I was greeted with the morning sun already above the horizon to my left.

It was morning! The light of the sun had overtasked the light-intensifying goggles and shut them down. We had been up for twenty-four hours, and right then, I realized just how tired I was. Not just physically but mentally.

This was my first experience with adrenaline deprivation. This is something you can never duplicate in training. No matter how late you stay up training, no matter how taxing on the body the deployment is, you can never duplicate the reaction of the human body after an adrenaline rush.

With the threat of danger, the adrenaline pours through your body, heightening the senses. With the danger gone, the adrenaline is gone, and the mental fatigue sets in. Without that adrenaline reserve to keep you awake, your body shuts down. As we traveled back to the company assembly area, there was absolutely nothing I could do to keep awake. I kept nodding off in the turret. I banged my head against the sight in front of me; my knees buckled; I got lost in the middle of conversations with my driver while trying to keep him alert.

After that, I knew for the first time what it was like to be completely exhausted mentally. And after that, I paid particular attention to sleep plans for the marines on Blue 5. I couldn't combat this phenomenon, but I could make sure that we knew about it—that we could anticipate when it was going to happen and that we were prepared to deal with it.

When you can, put your marines to sleep, rotate your drivers, and shorten watches. The one thing a leader can do is to ensure that when marines are working on adrenaline deprivation, they have the benefit of a smart sleep plan to help them cope. I cannot overstate the fact that this physical shutdown of the body is a totally natural occurrence and there is nothing you can do to combat it—it simply happens. Mental toughness and strength are not enough to fight the body's desire to shut down when depleted of adrenaline.

That evening I learned a lot. Aside from the effects of adrenaline, I learned that in the future we would be required to do a number of tasks that we normally wouldn't do just because we were available. The job we had been tasked was much better suited to a mechanized infantry asset, but we had superior mobility and position, and thus we had to be flexible as the needs arose. This fact would ring true throughout the remainder of the war. Whereas the LAI battalion was suited to the reconnaissance and security role, the very capabilities that allowed us so much success in this arena—mobility, firepower, and flexibility—put us into a position that forced commanders to use us to accomplish missions outside our doctrinal realm: we were always in the right place at the right time.

During the week after our incident at OP 6, Bravo Company experienced the first tragedy of the war for Task Force Shepherd. On the morning of 25 January three marines died after a successful artillery raid on Iraqi positions near OP 6 on the enemy side of the Kuwait border.

The mission started out straightforwardly enough: Allied forces had begun artillery raids on select points in Kuwait on 21 January. This raid was just one of the many artillery raids designed to disrupt and confuse the enemy in Kuwait. The target of the raid that was assigned to Bravo Company was a police post on the Kuwait side of the border near OP 6. I assume this target was chosen not only because Alpha had experienced difficulties with this particular post but also because it provided excellent cover for the Iraqis as they watched our actions.

The order for the raid was actually issued on the twenty-second or twenty-third and scheduled for the early morning hours of the twenty-fifth. Taking advantage of the time they had, Captain Hammond ran the company through rehearsal after rehearsal. Bravo cleaned and checked their weapons, made checks on the vehicles, and then conducted rehearsals again on the twenty-fourth.

Captain Hammond worked Bravo hard to prepare for the raid. In fact Corporal Buntin recalls that they didn't get much sleep at all in the last twenty-four hours prior to the raid—a situation not too uncommon for a mission of this sort. The raid was scheduled for just after midnight on the twenty-fourth (the morning of the twenty-fifth), and if a night rehearsal was conducted and weapons and vehicles were checked before moving off to conduct the mission, it would be pretty easy to use every bit of the available time prior to the actual mission.

On the evening of the twenty-fourth, the marines of Bravo Company were ready. They looked forward to the mission, which they expected to execute in a credible fashion. They left their company assembly area after dark and moved off into the desert to link up with the artillery battery that would actually fire the rounds on the raid. This was common practice. Any artillery raid that Alpha conducted always started with linking up well to the rear with the artillery unit. Then the unit would be escorted forward to a position from which it could fire on the intended targets. Things were no different with Bravo.

Once linkup was made with the self-propelled artillery pieces, they were escorted forward toward the berm by Bravo Company. The company initially assumed a tactical column formation with Captain Hammond's (Corporal Buntin as gunner) vehicle in the lead on point. This meant that the company would be traveling one vehicle behind the other in two long, snakelike columns. Such a formation is called a staggered column because the vehicles are staggered, or offset, from one another to maintain dispersion. This type of formation is used to maximize speed and march control.

Once the company got to the point where the artillery battery would fire from, which was a few kilometers back from the berm, the self-propelled pieces dropped out of the formation, and Bravo Company transitioned into a wedgelike formation without stopping. More security was required as the company drew closer to the berm, so Captain Hammond spread his company out laterally with maximum eyes and firepower forward. From this formation Bravo could screen forward to the berm and drive right into positions from which to provide not only observation of the target area but security for the artillery unit as they fired.

All had gone well up to this point, and when the company reached the berm the FAC (forward air controller) and FOs (forward observers) moved out of the vehicles to a position where the target area could be observed. The FAC was toting a MULE (modular universal laser equipment), a laser targeting device for terminally guided munitions, and was forced to get on the forward side of the berm in order to set the MULE up for targeting. With him he took a team of marines who provided security and served as forward observers. That group included a staff sergeant, a lance corporal, and a PFC.

The FAC set up the MULE and started to guide in munitions from aircraft before the artillery rounds began to pour in on the target area. When the aircraft's bombs were striking the earth, a number of enemy actions were presented to Bravo Company.

Sergeant Ramirez remembers eavesdropping on the company radio net from the battalion CP when the first enemy action was reported. Vehicle 1-4, manned by Corporal Sparks, reported that two jeeps were trying to leave the area of the police post. They were almost two kilometers away, and Captain Hammond simply told Sparks to go ahead and light them up. Buntin recalls that there was not much more involved in the engagement with the jeeps. The captain spoke and Sparks executed, destroying the targets quickly with 25-mm cannon fire.

Artillery rounds started to impact hellishly in the target area. Almost simultaneously an Iraqi element—Sergeant Ramirez thought it was squad-sized—got caught up in the action and started to move around. Whether they were simply moving away from the police post or exercising futile maneuver, they let off some small-arms fire toward Bravo Company. The FAC and his small detachment of marines were on the forward slope of the berm, a terribly exposed position. The marines escorting the FAC returned fire, and they got the FAC and the MULE up and over the berm to safety without incident.

Corporal Buntin saw the targets over the berm and fired a long burst of fire at them with the coaxially mounted machine gun. Because the vehicle was in almost complete defilade—only a portion of the turret was exposed—the machine gun simply fired into the berm in front of the vehicle and the rounds glanced off into the air. The sights were high enough that the targets could be seen, but the machine gun was masked by the elevated berm in front of the turret.

The whole evolution went by very quickly for Bravo Company: the raid lasted for less than half an hour. After almost twenty-four hours of continuous operation, Bravo had successfully executed the artillery raid assigned to it. The company left the target area, keeping an eye out for the enemy, and displaced back to the protection of friendly ground.

When the fear of danger was no longer a factor, the strain of the continuous training and the mentally tiring raid started to set in. Bravo was nearly back to the location of the battalion CP when tragedy struck.

At 0515 on 25 January the sun was just starting to creep over the horizon. A thick, cool fog, typical of desert mornings at that time of year, was rolling in over the sand. Bravo Company was traveling in a staggered column en route to a company assembly area. The driver of the 2d Platoon commander's vehicle had dozed off during the slow and methodical movement. When he woke up, he saw the vehicle to his side moving, and he picked up his vehicle speed to catch up.

When he realized there was a vehicle in front of him it was too late to do anything to avoid the collision. The vehicle rammed into the back of vehicle 1-5 and split a gaping hole in the three-eighths-inch cold steel rear doors. The collision occurred with such force that three of the marines in the back of vehicle 1-5 were killed and four other marines were injured— including a PFC who was medevaced to have his spleen removed.

Sergeant Ramirez remembers being in the battalion CP when the light started to illuminate the horizon. He recalls that very suddenly there was a lot of activity in the battalion CP. Through word of mouth he heard that three or four marines from Bravo Company had been killed, and he didn't understand. He knew only that the artillery raid had gone well. Through the dim light of morning Ramirez could see Bravo Company on the horizon. Having joined the corpsmen who rushed to that position to offer help, he saw immediately that the marines had been killed in a vehicle accident.

Corporal Buntin was assigned a serialized gear inventory while other marines tried desperately to provide first aid and CPR (cardiopulmonary resuscitation) to the casualties. Captain Hammond, deeply concerned about the fate of his marines, moved back and forth between the dead and injured men and the vehicle radio, trying to get a medevac chopper in. A CH-46 helicopter arrived rather quickly and took the casualties away. It was a tragic day for Bravo Company, Task Force Shepherd, the Marine Corps, and the families and friends of the marines who were killed.

Captain Hammond and the rest of Bravo were pretty upset about the whole ordeal. The mission had gone so well; it wasn't right to lose marines the way they did. Corporal Buntin remembers that the captain got the company together and talked to them about the mission, the unfortunate tragedy, and why it had happened. Hammond had been so broken up that he wept; after that, he was quiet for a while. Buntin says that the marines of Bravo did things a little differently from that day on—they watched their drivers religiously and frequently rotated them with the scouts in the back of the vehicles. It became almost standard procedure.

The whole situation reaffirmed my beliefs about mental fatigue. Marine Corps training always focused on the enemy. We knew what we were supposed to do, we knew how to operate our equipment, and we were ready to face the enemy. But we didn't know about mental fatigue—not the kind caused by adrenaline deprivation. After that incident I think we doubled our efforts with special precautions to prepare the marines for the situations where they might face such fatigue. We were very fortunate that we didn't have more incidents like this.

Sergeant Ramirez watched the whole ordeal from the battalion perspective. What really got to him was the fact that the marines who died were the very ones who had initiated the raid and had ensured the safety of the FAC when the Iraqi squad showed up. It just didn't make much sense: if there is justice in fate, this just didn't make sense.

Appropriate to the tragedy, the weather for the next few days was miserable and nasty: cold, biting wind; overcast skies; piercing rain. Alpha Company spent those days moving up the berm, showing our presence, and backing off from both OP 4 and OP 6.

News of the ill-fated artillery raid reached Alpha Company when we passed through Bravo Company's coil on the afternoon of the twenty-fifth after having spent an evening near OP 2 observing the southern east-west leg of the sandy berm. We saw the vehicle that had been destroyed by the collision, and the magnitude of the damage reminded us that tragedy had indeed struck. It was all too easy to make a mistake in armored warfare that could cost young men their lives. We went about our business solemnly after that, continuing to rotate among the OPs along the Saudi frontier.

OP 4 was a police post like OP 6 but much smaller in scale. Whereas OP 6 was a miniature city—complete with gas pumps, barracks, and overhead shelter for parking—OP 4 was an afterthought that consisted of two small structures and a water tower. OP 6 was located at the northern elbow, where the border turns west from north; OP 4 was nearer to the southern elbow, where the border turns north from west.

At OP 4 there was a hundred-meter break in the high sand berm that protected the Saudi frontier. The buildings of the OP were located at that break. The length of the break was reduced by the addition of a short length of three- or four-foot-high chain-link fence. That fence allowed a twenty-five to thirty-meter gap for traffic to pass through into Saudi Arabia from Kuwait. The fence had become a warped and wavy line, affected by time and the shifting sands of the desert. Normal vehicle traffic was restricted by the fence, but heavy armor formations could easily breach the flimsy structure.

On or about 23 January, Sergeant Negron led his section to the break in the fence and installed a hasty minefield with the few mines that the platoon had. Tactically this was a very sound decision. While armor could easily breach the chain-link fence, the natural tendency of the enemy's armor formations would be to break through the border at the natural gap: armor, like electricity, tends to follow the path of least resistance. With a minefield in place, the armor formation would meet resistance, probably unexpected, and be forced to back off and make a decision as to how to breach the slight obstacle. This action would buy the time we needed to coordinate combined arms assets against the formation.

So no matter how ineffectual the minefield may seem from our perspective—scattered with just a few mines—the Iraqis would certainly be placed off balance at the discovery during the attack. Unfortunately the minefield remained in place only while Alpha stood back well off the berm and observed. When the company moved on the next day, the minefield was recovered and the opening in the sand left free of obstacles.

On the twenty-seventh we established a position back from the berm in the cold desert to support the rest of the battalion. Movement to and from the berm was frequent, and each company in the battalion spent time both in the reserve and on the front line watching the dead space beyond the berm. This is the way things were until 29 January.

9

ON 29 JANUARY, Task Force Shepherd faced an Iraqi attack for the first time—and tragedy for the second time. Not only did the battalion come face to face with enemy armor, but we lost eleven more marines. The worst part was that they all died as a result of friendly fire.

There have been numerous accounts written about what took place on the evening of 29 January at OP 4. In doing my own research I scoured not only official Marine Corps reports but eyewitness accounts from within Delta Company, Task Force Shepherd, and the reconnaissance platoon involved in the incident. I conducted interviews to gain an even broader perspective, and I also have the benefit of my personal recollections of those events.

As my research revealed, there are significantly different versions of what actually took place that evening, depending on the nature of the source and the whereabouts of that source while the battle was going on. I do not intend to attempt to clarify for posterity exactly how the events of the battle for OP 4 played out: such an effort would only add to the confusion and do certain injustice to those who fought in the battle and those who died in it.

I accept that in war there will be an opinion from each and every warrior present, and that these opinions may differ markedly from one another. This is natural: each person sees and feels different things from dif-

133

ferent points on the battlefield. I recount this narrative as objectively as I can from my own perspective. Where actions of other units are concerned, I give their recollections the benefit of the doubt and use these memories to tell the story.

The Saudi police post, al-Zabr, was known to the marines in theater as OP 4. Across the desert from OP 4 was the Kuwait police post, al-Sur. About three and a half kilometers separated the posts, and somewhere within that distance the actual border between the two countries lay in the rolling sand.

A platoon from 1st Reconnaissance Battalion occupied OP 4 and the area around the OP in order to provide early warning of Iraqi attack and "eyes-on" of Iraqi forces inside Kuwait. That platoon had established four distinct sites at the two-building police post. Three hundred meters north of the post proper, an eight-man observation bunker was established. About the same distance south, another bunker, similar in construction, was established. Within the police post itself the headquarters element of the platoon had established a command post. The final site was a horse-shoe-shaped berm located about four hundred meters west of the OP. This protective berm was to be the initial rally point (IRP) for the platoon in case they had to withdraw from the OP. When given the signal, the platoon would abandon their bunkers, mount their vehicles (three HMMWVs and a five-ton), and assemble behind the sandy berm of the horseshoe.

In late January, Task Force Shepherd was participating in a large deception operation designed to keep the enemy confused as to our actual intentions in the area. At 1200 the companies of Shepherd received orders to configure forces in a fashion that would continue the deception operation. Company C, who just the night before had been screening north of the coastal town of al-Kafji, was ordered to screen at OP 6. Captain Sellers deployed the entire company on the northern side of the OP and oriented his platoons to the east.

Company D was ordered to occupy a four-kilometer frontage behind OP 4. Company A was sent to an assembly area about ten kilometers behind and between OP 6 and OP 4. Company B was positioned about twenty-five kilometers south and west of OP 4. Alpha and Bravo were positioned outside of enemy artillery range but within range to support either Delta or Charlie if something were to happen.

A leader's reconnaissance was conducted at OP 4, and at 1500 on the twenty-ninth Delta Company occupied the required frontage slightly northwest of the OP. Attached to Delta were seven LAV-ATs from weapons company. The company was positioned about three and a half kilometers from the berm with the right flank of the company about two and a half kilometers from OP 4.

Alpha and Bravo Companies established their assembly areas at the required locations to support Charlie and Delta. All was quiet when the marines of Shepherd settled down for the evening.

At 2000 the monotony of the cool, dark night was broken when the marines of the reconnaissance platoon at OP 4 sighted a column of armored vehicles rolling in from the north heading toward the al-Sur police post. The team radioed to report contact with approximately thirty armored vehicles. Almost simultaneously the AT section leader attached to Delta Company reported that he had sighted approximately thirty-five armored vehicles moving in from the north.

Things happened quickly from that point on. By 2015 the reconnaissance team reported that two BMPs rolled up to the small Kuwaiti police post, quickly followed by five tanks (T-62/T-55), and two more BMPs. Those vehicles formed an assault formation—the tanks on line leading the BMPs—and turned west, moving directly across the desert toward OP 4.

The recon team struggled to get support with their radios. They contacted a FACA (forward air controller airborne) in an OV-10, and he responded that he had air support inbound.[1]

Meanwhile, Captain Paster, Delta Company's commanding officer, had already started moving his marines to the south in order to support the OP. He moved his log trains well to the west to get them out of the potential fight and maneuvered his company to a position directly west of the OP. The AT section leader followed up his initial report by telling Captain Paster that he now had a sighting of at least fifty armored vehicles across the desert in Kuwait.

Many kilometers to the west Sergeant Ramirez was on watch in the battalion CP. He was sitting with the colonel, carrying on a casual conversation. Then the reports started coming in from Delta Company. Ramirez recalls they were getting reports from Delta that armored vehicles were moving across the border, but it took the CP about thirty minutes to confirm that there was actually a threat to OP 4. About fifteen minutes before the attack started, radio checks had been made with all of the companies; now, however, with the Iraqi attack imminent, the battalion CP could not get Delta Company on the net with any regularity. The Iraqis had precipitated the attack by jamming VHF (very high frequency) radio traffic. Delta Company was operating in the single-channel covered mode—that is, they were not frequency hopping like the rest of the battalion. In fact only the company commander's vehicle was equipped with SINCGARS to "hop" with. With the Iraqi jamming, it was very difficult at the battalion CP to figure out exactly what was going on.

It took the battalion CP about thirty minutes to get accurate reports on the situation. Ramirez recalls that they received reports of enemy vehicles in strengths between ten and eighty BMPs and tanks. Taking no chances, Colonel Myers dispatched Alpha and Bravo to OP 4 in hopes of reinforcing the situation. The worst-case scenario was that there were eighty tanks attacking into Saudi Arabia, and Task Force Shepherd was the only unit capable of slowing down their movement long enough to get help from other units. Without Shepherd, the Iraqis would be able to move unimpeded into the Saudi desert and threaten Allied logistics points to the southwest.

We in Alpha had just dug our sleeping holes and erected shelter from the rain when the call came from Captain Shupp that we were moving. It took us about two minutes to get underway. Looking back I cannot believe how fast we moved to support Delta. PFC Dudley, who had been sleeping in the driver's compartment, dressed in his combat vehicle crewman's uniform and put on his boots while driving as we moved southeast across the desert. We left all the gear that was not already on the vehicles where it lay in the sand. Bravo Company, Corporal Buntin recalls, left their camouflage nets standing where their vehicles had once been. The rapid response allowed Colonel Myers the flexibility he needed to deal with the situation at hand.

While the battalion CP was trying to sort out the issue and Alpha and Bravo were en route to reinforce, the reconnaissance platoon lived through a nightmare. They had already called to Delta Company for support and had made contact with the FACA orbiting high above them in an OV-10 when the formation of tanks and BMPs crossed the border fourteen hundred meters away. Two A-6 attack aircraft responded to the FACA's call for help and started bombing runs on the armored formation. They dropped CBUs (cluster bomb units) that scattered hundreds of explosive bomblets across the path of the advancing armor. There was no effect: the Iraqis continued to advance. Drawing even closer to al-Zabr police post, they began to fire their 115-mm main guns at the building occupied by the reconnaissance CP.

Fortunately for the reconnaissance marines, the tanks fired nonexplosive sabot rounds that whistled through the masonry of the building without causing any casualties. The reconnaissance team quickly called to Delta Company, again requesting assistance. Delta Company answered and requested permission to engage the lead tanks that were now within range, and battalion approved the request.

When the tanks drew within small-arms range of the police post, one of the reconnaissance marines fired an M203 grenade launcher loaded with an illumination round at the lead tank. Luckily the round landed on the front deck of the tank and burned brightly, serving as a beacon as the tank advanced. AT-4s (handheld antitank rocket launchers) were fired in quick succession at the tanks with no effect.

The tanks raked the police post with machine gun and main gun fire. The reconnaissance marines responded with more M203 rounds and AT-4s. But they were having a big problem with some of the AT-4s: not all of them were firing. The AT-4 has a number of safety devices—a transport safety pin, a cocking lever, a safety catch—all of which must be activated for the weapon to fire. The reconnaissance team members were so flustered by the quick advance of the Iraqi tanks that they were forgetting to activate one or more of these devices. Under the circumstances, with plenty of AT-4s available and the Iraqis still advancing, the marines were simply throwing misfired AT-4s to the side and grabbing other ones from the pile.

Around this time the first TOW missiles were fired by the ATs attached to Delta Company. The result reported was two tanks destroyed, but the advance continued. The reconnaissance platoon commander fired a red star-cluster into the air—the prearranged signal to withdraw—and under fire the platoon moved to rally at the horseshoe.

Under interrogation some of the EPWs captured from the battle confirmed that they had been very much surprised to find anybody manning OP 4. Their attack was part of a multipronged advance that included the famous events at al-Kafji to the south. An enemy RPV (remotely piloted vehicle) flyover early in the day had spotted no American forces at the al-Zabr police post. The presence of the reconnaissance marines and Delta Company surprised the Iraqis and caused them confusion: they expected to move quickly through the gap in the berm and head deep into our rear to disrupt our logistical base to the southwest.

Captain Paster had decided that in order to aid the beleaguered reconnaissance platoon gathered at the horseshoe, he would have to draw even closer to the OP to effect their withdrawal. He personally moved forward with 2d Platoon and an AT section to extract the reconnaissance unit. Captain Paster left his remaining platoon and the rest of the ATs in a line about fifteen hundred meters back in overwatch. The captain wanted to move up on line, but because of the dark evening, enemy action, and communication problems, he and 2d Platoon had formed more of a wedge.

When the LAVs moved forward to relieve the reconnaissance platoon, the first three tanks and two BMPs occupied the actual police post that the reconnaissance platoon had just evacuated. The FACA brought in another section of A6s to attack the Iraqi vehicles at OP 4. The CBUs still had little effect on the armored vehicles. The horseshoe was only four hundred meters away from the tanks being bombarded by the A6s. In order to avoid being killed by an errant CBU, the reconnaissance platoon marked its position with an IR (infrared) strobe that the pilots could see.

Unfortunately the Iraqi tanks used IR for sighting their huge main guns at night, and they quickly picked up the reconnaissance platoon's beacon in their gun sights. The IR must have glowed like a candle in the passive sights of the Iraqi tanks, and almost immediately 115-mm sabot rounds were impacting on the berm of the horseshoe and deflecting skyward. The reconnaissance platoon quickly realized its folly and extinguished the strobe. Fortunately for the platoon the tanks did not fire high-explosive rounds. Had HE been fired, the platoon would have certainly perished: the rounds would not have deflected skyward but would have exploded into balls of hot fire and steel that would have shredded the marines and their equipment.

At 2045 while Captain Paster advanced with 2d Platoon, he saw the AT on his left fire a TOW missile and watched four tanks near the police post return fire. When he looked to the left again, the AT beside him disappeared from the battlefield in a ball of fire. At the time, Captain Paster thought the tanks had fired and destroyed the AT. What actually happened, however, was an LAV-AT from the second line, 1500 meters behind them, acquired the LAV-AT next to Captain Paster and misidentified the vehicle as enemy. The missile he fired downrange impacted into the back hatches of the forward vehicle and exploded. Over a dozen TOW missiles were stored where the missile impacted, and the resulting explosion literally disintegrated the vehicle. Four marines died.

It is possible that Captain Paster observed the tanks firing at the reconnaissance platoon in the horseshoe and thought the tank rounds were directed at the AT beside him. Regardless, the captain had no time on the spot to sort out the situation. Lighting up the dark night, 25-mm tracers were on their way to bounce ineffectually off the tanks at the police post.

Out of the confusion Captain Paster saw an AT-3 "Sagger" coming toward his vehicle.[2] Just as he backed up, the missile flew past the right side of his vehicle and exploded behind him. Two other vehicles reported avoiding Sagger missiles. After the battle, five Sagger impacts were found, the missiles having been fired from the Iraqi armor.

Shortly after the AT was destroyed, Captain Paster linked up with the reconnaissance element and withdrew them from the horseshoe. The firefight was still going on, but with the reconnaissance platoon in hand, Delta was able to withdraw to the west. Delta did withdraw and stopped its movement to form a screen line three kilometers west of OP 4. The reconnaissance team was hastily protected by the LAVs, and the XO of Delta tried to get air support from the FACA in the sky.

About this time Alpha Company rolled up behind Delta. We were still moving in the company march formation, about to link up, when the following incident happened. I remember watching the tracers of the 25-mm fired from several locations converging on a distinct point and knowing we were getting close. We watched the aircraft munitions explode on the deck, and we cheered each drop as we moved. Suddenly there was a bright explosion on the deck—much closer than the previous ones, it seemed to be right in front of us.

At the Delta Company screen line, the XO was trying to guide in an A-10 attack aircraft on the enemy armor at OP 4. In Alpha we watched as 25-mm HE fire was used in that effort. But the XO, having a particularly difficult time achieving the objective, had decided to give the plane only one more attack run before going to another aircraft.

At the same time that Delta's XO was trying to work the air, the reconnaissance team was talking on the radio to the FACA. The team was trying to get the air support but was informed that the control of air had already been turned over to Delta Company. While this conversation was taking place between recon and the FACA, a flare from the OV-10 was launched, and it dropped in front of one of Delta's LAV-25s. The confused reconnaissance team saw a crewman get out of the vehicle and kick sand over the flare in an attempt to extinguish it. The team thought the flare marked the position of the attack for the A-10s.

Delta Company was confused, too: marines were asking why the flare had landed on top of them. As the crewman attempted to extinguish the flare, the XO explained that it had been intended to mark the company's position. With the flare burning on the ground, clearly visible to the aircraft orbiting high above, the XO could transmit a magnetic azimuth and the distance from the flare to the enemy tanks. The flare was a common reference point between the pilot and the company. After explaining this to the company, the XO radioed the nearest unit to the flare. He wanted that unit to provide the azimuth and distance from their position adjacent to the flare to the enemy tanks. Just as that requested information was submitted, a maverick missile left the launch rails of the A-10.

A marine in the reconnaissance team saw the exhaust flash of the heat-seeking missile just before it pierced the left flank of the LAV-25 adjacent to the flare. The reconnaissance marines scrambled for cover, hoping that the A-10 wouldn't attack their positions as well. One of the reconnaissance marines stayed on the radio and talked directly to the A-10 pilot, telling him that he had destroyed a friendly vehicle. The A-10 pilot acknowledged, very shaken. Seven more marines died.

At 2100 Captain Paster watched these seven marines die. The missile impacted behind the emergency escape hatch (which is just behind the driver on the left side of the vehicle), blew the turret of the LAV-25 through the air, and set the vehicle on fire. Unlike the LAV-AT loaded with high-explosive missiles, the LAV-25 did not disintegrate. The vehicle burned throughout the night, its rubber tires feeding the flames for hours as a solemn reminder of what had happened.

Captain Paster, who didn't see the missile's exhaust flash, thought that Iraqi tanks had flanked his position, and thus he quickly ordered the ATs to scan the area. They found no evidence that the tanks were in the area.

Sergeant Ramirez remembers the call to battalion from Captain Paster: a vehicle had been hit, it looked like one of his, and it looked bad. Not ten seconds after that call, Captain Shupp came over the battalion tach net confirming that a vehicle had been hit. He went on to inform battalion that it looked as though it had been friendly fire, possibly air, and that the hit was catastrophic.

Soon after, Captain Shupp came over Alpha's company tach net and informed us that Delta had lost two vehicles to catastrophic kills, possibly friendly fire. The explosion we had seen suddenly took on a deep significance. I now knew why it had been so close: it wasn't because the Iraqi tanks were near us; it was because Delta was. We were very quiet on the intercom of Blue 5, and both the platoon and company tach nets were deadly silent. There was so much to say but no way to say it, so we did not say anything.

Captain Paster recalls linking up with Alpha at 0055 on 30 January. The official history has that time as just slightly before midnight on the twenty-ninth. I don't recall the actual time, but it seemed to be just after the LAV-25 was destroyed by the A-10. At any rate, we moved forward and relieved Delta in place, the burning LAV-25 about a kilometer ahead of us. I didn't see Delta pass through us; I was on the left flank of the company, almost directly behind the burning LAV-25. As we advanced, Lieutenant Tice came over the radio: "Blue 5, this is Blue 1, over."

This may seem funny, but it was good to hear his voice. I could tell from his tone that he had business for me, and as far as I was concerned, this was exactly what we needed—business. "Go, Blue 1."

"Blue 5, we're screening to the east, break. . . . I want your section to refuse our left flank, over."

I was expecting his order. We were the leftmost section of the company, and we had no idea what was out there. At this point, there were still thoughts that Iraqi tanks and BMPs were rolling around on our side of the border. Captain Paster's initial assessment of our being flanked by tanks was taken seriously even though the friendly air strike was confirmed. I turned my section to a forty-five-degree oblique and watched the company's left flank.

To the south Bravo Company pulled up to provide support for Delta as ordered. Bravo most likely got to the scene just after 2100. Corporal Buntin recalls that the initial position of his vehicle did not allow him to see very far to the front: the terrain was masking his line of sight. While Captain Hammond maneuvered the company to support Delta, Buntin was breaking into the intercom system between the captain's radio transmissions, telling the driver to creep up. (You cannot use both the radio and the intercom at the same time; they are tied together, and the crewman of an LAV must wait for a break in radio transmissions to talk on the intercom.) Buntin could see the tracers now, and Captain Hammond kept stopping the vehicle every time Buntin crept forward. Buntin clearly wanted to get into the mix, but the captain had other things on his mind.

The AT section attached to Bravo reported they had four vehicles sighted twelve hundred meters out, and they wanted to fire at them. Captain Hammond had the gunners get out of their vehicles and shoot magnetic headings to the contacts. It turns out that the turrets of the ATs were facing due south, pointing at the company headquarters element. The captain averted a friendly fire incident within his own company through sound judgment. This is just an example of how disoriented armored-vehicle crewmen can become when they are moving around the desert at night. The enemy was probably at least five kilometers to the northeast, and the ATs were pointing at targets twelve hundred meters to the south.

Captain Hammond put a freeze on the ATs for the rest of the evening.

We had just relieved Delta Company when Sergeant Worth's voice crackled reverently over the radio, "Blue 2, this is Blue 3, over."

Sergeant Negron, Worth's section leader, responded very calmly, "Go ahead."

"Simmons is dead." I couldn't believe what I heard. How did Worth know something like that already? Corporal Simmons was an LAV-AT vehicle commander. In fact throughout Desert Shield and Storm almost every time we had ATs attached to our platoon, Simmons was one of the vehicle commanders. He had become part of the platoon—as much a part as any of us.

I pictured Simmons's smiling face as Negron answered, "Roger." And that was it. Everyone with a CVC helmet in Blue 5 heard the transmission over the helmets' built-in speakers. Those not on helmets were quickly informed by those who were. I don't recall there being much conversation about that subject. We knew that marines died, but learning that a friend had been killed was like having a stake shoved through the heart. I remember I swallowed hard and tried to remain calm. My stomach felt a little light with butterflies as I tried to put the vision of Corporal Simmons out of my head. I didn't want to think about it then, and I didn't: I concentrated on the situation. Only now, as I write these words, am I recalling my thoughts and feelings during the situation.

Almost immediately after that incident, Lieutenant Tice radioed me again. "Blue 5, this Blue 1, over."

"Go, Blue 1."

"Blue 5, I need you to move your section forward, link up with the reconnaissance team, and bring them back to Delta's position, over."

"Roger." This was the first I had heard about a recon team. "Where are they? Over."

"They have a five-ton and some HMMWVs and should be due east of your position. I don't know how far."

I don't know if those were the exact words, but if they weren't, they are pretty close. I called Matlain, who acknowledged that he had heard the order. We moved out in section wedge and drove due east. My senses were superhyped. My gunner was scanning back and forth for a purpose: we did not want to be surprised by a tank. I don't know how far we drove— maybe it was a kilometer or more—but I felt like I was traveling into the valley of death. The ground was starting to slope downward, and I noticed multiple tracked-vehicle marks on the ground. I radioed back about sighting the tracks and continued. Eventually I found the five-ton and the HMMWVs (I don't remember how many) and circled around them. I got their attention and led them back through the lines.

Driving back I could see that Delta Company was only about eight hundred meters behind us in an assembly area. The reconnaissance team saw this also and drove off to rejoin Delta. I let out a huge sigh of relief and assumed my position on the left flank.

The Delta Company commander recalls taking the reconnaissance team with him when he withdrew through our lines. I distinctly remember going forward and finding the five-ton and bringing it back—it was an incredibly huge target that night, and I felt sorry for the guys driving it. When I researched this battle, I had a hard time reconciling some things, especially those events that I was personally involved in. I think the only explanation for this particular event is that one or more of the vehicles were inadvertently left behind when the recon platoon withdrew. That fact would account for Delta's taking some of the marines and my section's leading the rest of them back.

We spent a great deal of time just sitting there that night. We surveyed for any signs of enemy movement, and we watched as the Marine Corps Cobra helicopters lofted flares into the air in an attempt to find the targets.[3] It had gotten incredibly dark, and we were not having any success finding the enemy. We crept forward and scanned; we crept forward and waited.

At some point we drew very close to the burning LAV-25 that was the grave of seven marines. Sergeant Sweeny—the same Sweeny who found the map on the highway—was peering through a starlight scope (passive night-rifle and/or machine-gun scope) held in his hands and noticed movement in front of the burning LAV. He thought it was a marine.

We were some four to five hundred meters away, and when Lieutenant Tice informed me of Sweeny's sighting, I found it hard to believe—even knowing the scope he was using. Lieutenant Tice wanted to move forward under overwatch and investigate. He took Corporal Matlain with him and instructed me to overwatch. As he moved out toward the burning vehicle, I crept forward until my gunner could see down into the desert beyond the vehicle. Within minutes they had found a survivor from the destroyed vehicle. He was crawling in the sand in front of the vehicle in a dazed state of mind. They quickly picked him up and transported him back to the company trains, where the corpsman took over.

The corpsman wanted to medevac him by helicopter, and initially Captain Shupp was going to approve. Soon, though, it became apparent that aside from flash burns and a possible concussion, the marine was in fair condition. The captain delayed the helicopter for the time being and opted to transport the wounded man by ground. I don't think the corpsman liked it, but it was a sound decision. The marine was injured, but he was going to survive. Eating up precious air assets or bringing a medevac chopper into the hostile area might not have been wise.

The marine turned out to be the driver of the burning LAV, and he didn't remember anything but trying to get back to save his buddies after the explosion. We had no idea how he had survived. When we looked at the vehicle in the daylight, it was hard to believe this marine had been blown out of the driver's hatch. The missile impacted no farther than one meter from where the driver would have been sitting, and it had exploded with a force great enough to blow a two-thousand-pound turret thirty feet through the air, buckle every weld on the vehicle, and blow off every hatch, including the driver's.

If this marine had been in the vehicle, he most certainly would have been killed instantly. Initially the predominant thought was that the seventh man killed on the vehicle (the crewman placed behind the driver to load AP ammunition) had shielded the driver from the blast and had thus allowed him to be blown out with the escaping gases of the explosion. After seeing the vehicle, however, I found this hard to swallow.

While we were recovering the wounded marine, Captain Shupp had directed the company also to search for any survivors from the crew of the destroyed AT. Warily the company moved about in an effort to find the wreckage, but the AT had exploded so completely that it didn't burn like the LAV-25. We looked and looked but never found anything. Eventually, when it was light out, 2d Platoon succeeded in locating the charred area of sand that marked the AT's final position.

There were no whole bodies to be found; in fact there was no vehicle to be found. Chunks of it were scattered about, but if you didn't know that you were looking for an LAV, you would never know that you found one. I remember much later seeing the remains after they had been moved to the rear. It was shocking to find that the entire vehicle fit onto two wooden pallets—a fourteen-ton vehicle was reduced to two small piles of twisted and unidentifiable metal.

The battalion commander had decided sometime earlier that Alpha was going to sweep through the area and that Bravo would remain just south of Alpha and block enemy action. The sun was fully up on the horizon, and visibility was perfect when the final phase of the battle for OP 4 started.

Alpha was reinforced by air force A-10s and marine Cobra helicopters, and the company XO and FAC started to guide the aircraft in on the Iraqi tanks that were still hanging around in the area. From my position approximately twelve hundred meters directly west of OP 4 I could see that the multitude of tanks reported the prior evening were gone. There were still half a dozen tanks that we could see, but it was clear that they were the last ones left. Marking the slight break in the chain-link fence at OP 4 were two T-55 tanks that had been destroyed by TOW missiles. From their hulks, which did not burn, a thin trail of ugly black smoke escaped into the sky.

On the friendly side of the OP was a white civilian vehicle that had apparently been abandoned some time earlier by the Saudi police manning this checkpoint in the sand. When I looked left and right, I saw that the entire company was on line, perched in an advantageous position twelve to fifteen hundred meters from the sand berm. In front I watched the A-10s make their steep dives, attacking with devastating accuracy the tanks that were on the other side of the berm. With every attack I saw a belch of gray smoke emanate from the nose of the ugly aircraft and heard seconds later the deep roar of the 30-mm cannon in that nose. I watched as the depleted uranium rounds struck the steel of the hidden tanks, sending sparks and tiny flames skyward. This went on for at least half an hour.

The Cobras were up next. They were about to commence their run when Captain Shupp called "Wildman" (our FAC) and told him, "They don't go hot until they count our vehicles." I listened as the vehicle count was reported from the helicopters. Initially they were one vehicle short. Having none of that, Wildman and Captain Shupp aborted the mission. But eventually the Cobras counted all of our vehicles, and above me in a high hover the first Cobra let loose with a TOW missile.

The missile immediately dove to the deck and exploded about four hundred meters in front of us.[4] I remember thinking *Oh, this is great!* Ultimately the missiles flew straight and found more tanks to destroy. The Cobras then flew in close, toward the OP, to use their 20-mm cannons. It was really an impressive show of air power. In due time, though, something was bound to happen to muck it up.

About twenty minutes into the Cobras' gun runs, one of the pilots reported he was receiving small-arms fire from the top of the building at the OP. He had to pull back and wanted us to take care of the problem before he continued. Instantly Lieutenant Tice was calling me on the radio. "Blue 5, this is Blue 1, over."

"Go."

"Blue 5, the Cobras are taking fire from the top of the OP. I want you to go in and suppress the shit out of that building."

I had absolutely no problem with this mission. I acknowledged the lieutenant and gave a section fire command. "Blue 6, move out, section on line, suppress building with mix of HE, AP, and coax, over."

Matlain copied my transmission, and we moved out over the desert toward the OP at about twenty miles per hour. I laid the gunner on target, and he started firing HE at the building in a wide pattern. I watched the tiny explosions creating a cloud of mortar and dust, and I ordered him to switch to AP. He did and quickly engaged the abandoned vehicle and then the building, again in a wide spread. I wanted to ensure that I put fire inside the building itself. I wasn't sure how thick the mortar of the walls were, so I used both ammunitions, hoping one of them would do the damage I wanted.

As we drew closer, I ordered the gunner to fire a burst of HE on the roof top, followed by a burst of coax. Again I wanted to ensure effective coverage of the target area. I looked over and saw that Matlain was firing into the area as well. It was really a beautiful sight: the walls and roof of the structure were literally peppered with 25-mm and 7.62-mm fire. Everything was going well until my gunner yelled out, "Jam! I've got a jam!"

I picked up the spades to my pintle mount and began to fire at the target area. I keyed my helmet to intercom and said, "Fix it, Uke. I've got you covered!"

I fired in short, controlled bursts to conserve my ammunition until Uke yelled again, "Hey, Sergeant Michaels, look at this!" I told him to get up and reach over to the pintle mount as best as he could, and I dropped into the turret.

The main gun was stopping just before sear (the ready-to-fire position). I was able to turn it manually to sear with the hand crank, but with HE selected it would fire only one round before it jammed again—stopping again just before sear. *This is great. Come on, Michaels, what do you do?* I felt the vehicle pick up speed, and I heard the short burst of the pintle as Lance Corporal Uke tried to lean over my hatch to fire the weapon. I finally got it to sear again, switched to AP, sighted in, and fired the weapon. It fired fine. The M242 is dual fed—AP on the top side and HE on the bottom side—and for the most part the feeds are independent of each other. Fortunately only the HE side of the feeder was jamming now; the AP side was firing fine.

I popped back up in the hatch and told Uke to stick to AP. We were only about four hundred meters away from the police post at this time, and I made the decision to wheel slightly right, to the gap in the berm adjacent to the two smoking tanks. We fired and wheeled through the gap. The scouts in the back of the vehicle trained on the building as we passed it, and I brought the section to a halt at the old chain-link fence on the Kuwait side of the OP.

I immediately radioed Matlain to send his scouts to link up with mine: I wanted them to check the building, which was not twenty feet behind us. Within a heartbeat Lieutenant Tice was on the radio, denying that order —he didn't want anyone in the building.

I felt very uncomfortable sitting where I was without dismounting my scouts. I had in fact made the conscious decision to move quickly to the right, around the post, so that I could drop the scouts right in the post's back door. To stop on the other side of the building would put my section in a terribly awkward position. I would have no observation and would be restricted to reacting to the enemy action in the building. Our maneuver to the back side allowed me the freedom to move away from the building if need be. It also offered ample observation to al-Sur and beyond, and it put us in a good position to surprise the Iraqis who had fired at the Cobras: I don't think they would have expected us coming in from the rear.

I requested to dismount the scouts and pleaded my case to Lieutenant Tice, but he turned down my request. I was angry. I didn't always agree with the decisions Lieutenant Tice made, but for the most part they had no adverse effect on the situation. But I felt, and still feel, that he was clearly wrong in his decision to not check the building for the enemy. Looking back, however, I realize why he made the decision. It was a part of his leadership style—a part I had not yet figured out. I had always respected the way he developed his subordinates, and I admired his devotion to the marines of the platoon. This decision was just an extension of his concern for the marines, albeit an extension that went a little too far in my opinion.

Lieutenant Tice was the type of leader who would never put his marines in a situation that he himself would not have gone into. The lives of his marines were first and foremost on his mind. In this situation he saw great risk in checking the OP. Even though the building was small in comparison to OP 6, it was still large enough to hide a number of nonfriendlies from our scout teams. I think he felt the building was too large to check properly and that the chances of casualties did not outweigh the benefits of checking it. But I believe he let his concerns for the safety of his marines cause him to make a decision that actually put them at even greater risk. I don't think he realized this fact at the time, though.

I knew there had been active and aggressive enemy forces sighted by the Cobras, and I knew that without completing the maneuver I executed by dismounting scouts rapidly, we were at risk of taking an RPG from about twenty feet. I felt the sound tactical decision was the one I had made. Lieutenant Tice now has history on his side of the issue, however, because there was no incident. I posted a watch from the back of the vehicles, weapons trained on the building and, after arguing my case, bit my tongue in frustration.

Soon after I occupied the gap in the berm with my section, the OP was bustling with activity. Bravo came up and joined us at the berm from the south, and 2d Platoon from Alpha occupied the area north of the OP, capturing a number of Iraqi prisoners. I remember looking at the two destroyed Iraqi tanks that were within twenty meters of my position. By this time they were barely smoking. The holes where the TOW missiles entered just below the turret rings were so neat in appearance that the tanks' destruction seemed surgical. Besides the holes and the blackened appearance of the hulls, the only evidence that there had been a fierce explosion was the debris that was strewn for hundreds of meters in every direction. I didn't dismount my vehicle and check the tank for survivors.

The end of the whole engagement was anticlimactic. The few scattered and destroyed tank hulks in the immediate vicinity belied the reports of multiple formations of enemy armor. It was clear that the enemy had tried to penetrate the slight gap in the berm where I sat, but it was also clear that the actions of Delta Company and the reconnaissance team had disrupted the smooth flow of combat power into Saudi Arabia that the Iraqi commander may have desired. They had been surprised by our presence and beaten soundly. Then—before the light, Alpha Company, and aircraft had arrived that morning—they had withdrawn most of their combat power to the protection of the smoking oil fields in Kuwait.

We were relieved after a very short period of time and moved back to positions away from the berm. Lieutenant Tice came over the platoon net and directed Sergeant Worth to move to the destroyed LAV-25 to assist Graves Registration with recovering the bodies of the seven crewmen killed in the LAV-25. About a half an hour later Worth's voice, clearly shaken and disoriented, crackled over the platoon tach: "Sir, there were bodies, and they were . . . burned . . . and. . . ."

Worth was starting to lose control. I could hear a distinct sadness and frustration in his voice as he tried to explain his feelings to the lieutenant. It was obvious that the sight of the burned and disfigured bodies of the marines had been etched painfully into his mind. In a firm voice, tempered with extreme compassion, Lieutenant Tice comforted Worth as best he could. I listened to the radio conversation, I cataloged the event, and I understood the anguish.

Sergeant Worth had been the one who had initially told Sergeant Negron and the rest of the platoon that Corporal Simmons had been killed. I could hear the deep concern in his voice then, and I have always wondered why Lieutenant Tice assigned him to the body detail for the seven marines on the LAV-25. Perhaps the lieutenant had sensed Worth's emotion the night before and wanted to put him in a position where he would see the harsh reality of death firsthand—to delay no longer his coming to terms with the nature of war. Or it might have been a decision made solely to strengthen Sergeant Worth's resolve. To this day I am not exactly sure. Personally I'm glad I didn't have to do the job. Accepting the fact that marines die, accepting the fact that friends die, and accepting what it looks like to see those people die are three distinctly different things.

For a marine, and especially a marine of the combat arms, death is a very real part of business. As real as death is, however, you cannot prepare for the sight, smell, and feelings of death. You must face the reality head-on and battle the demons that run through your head. Maybe Lieutenant Tice recognized the demons materializing in Sergeant Worth; maybe he wanted to make him stronger by affording him the opportunity to chase the demons away.

When Bravo had relieved us, we pulled back off the line. I was tired, and I knew my crew was tired. We had peaked on adrenaline a number of times throughout the past twelve hours and our bodies' natural reaction would be to shut down. I didn't allow that to happen right then, though. I wanted to assure the crew that nothing had changed: the incident of the previous evening did not mean that solid SOP went out the window, only that the boundaries of our experiences within the SOP had broadened. Certainly it had been an exciting and stressful evening, but such was the nature of our business, and we had to accept that.

Therefore I ordered all the weapons that had been fired to be cleaned. The crew didn't like having to do it, but after about an hour of intense weapons cleaning and operational checks, I felt good about executing a sleep plan. On Blue 5 nothing indeed had changed.

The lull in action while we cleaned weapons allowed me to reflect on what had happened the prior evening. The destruction of the LAV-AT marked the first Americans killed by friendly fire during Desert Storm. In the blink of an eye four marines had lost their lives because of a mistake. Shortly thereafter seven more marines lost their lives to friendly fire. To this day I do not understand why there isn't more emphasis placed on distinguishing friend from foe on the ground battlefield. The onus is placed on the individual gunners and vehicle commanders.

Aircraft have IFF (identification, friend or foe) systems that help prevent them from shooting down friendly aircraft, but armored vehicles have no similar system. After the war there was a lot of talk in the Marine Corps about acquiring a system of identification for armored vehicles. The end result was a money issue, I believe. Imagine the costs associated with equipping each and every ground-combat vehicle and support-role vehicle with interrogator-translator devices that are reliable enough to accomplish the role assigned: eliminating friendly fire incidents.

But from a ground-combatant perspective, the money issue is an inadequate reason for not implementing a ground version of IFF. I remember that I was given a roll of IR tape and a green star-cluster to protect us from friendly fire. The tape was supposed to reflect upwards to the sky so that friendly aircraft would know that I was friendly too. The green star-cluster, when fired, would notify the attacker that I was a friendly target—that is, if he had missed me on his first attack. I considered these measures totally inadequate. The IR tape may have helped aircraft to identify me, but it also reflected nicely when a T-62 was hunting for me with his IR searchlight. I cannot imagine how happy an Iraqi gunner would be to find my glittering vehicle in his gun sights.

Many times during the war I remember grabbing the green star-cluster and preparing to fire it. What a feeling: white-knuckling the silver canister, hoping that the aircraft above me would exercise good judgment. With all the money spent on advanced weapons systems, smarter weapons, and sights that allow you to see beyond direct-fire range, it is a shame that money hasn't been invested to save the lives of the personnel operating the weapons. We can see farther than we can shoot, and we can shoot farther than we can see to identify targets. The situation is a recipe for disaster, and disaster struck too often during Desert Storm.

By midafternoon we had been called back even farther to conduct a resupply. I was surprised to find that the resupply was located right next to the destroyed LAV-25. When we got there and drove past, the rubber tires were no longer burning. The vehicle simply stood as the lone visible landmark on the horizon for the battle of OP 4. The bodies of our fallen comrades had been removed, and all that was left was the twisted and warped steel hulk that had once been an LAV-25.

Later the company armorer delivered to my vehicle a gun part that would correct my gun jam problem. When I asked him where he had gotten the part so quickly, he told me that it had been recovered from the destroyed LAV-25. I looked at him wide-eyed and didn't know whether to handle the part with extreme reverence or to give it back to him and say, "No thanks." I took it, however, and the jam problem for the HE side of the gun disappeared. I think that as a crew we handled the part solemnly in remembrance. It wasn't a curse. As far as we were concerned, the spirit of the warrior crew lived on, appropriately, in our chain gun.

Bravo Company occupied the OP when we left that morning. Corporal Buntin dismounted his vehicle and took up a position on the berm adjacent to OP 4. He brought a map, compass, radio, and laser range finder with him. Lying on the berm, he carefully ranged the al-Sur police post with the range finder; he deliberately determined the azimuth to the Kuwaiti police post with the compass, and he plotted his own position with his map.

Using all of these data he was able to determine a ten-digit grid coordinate for the enemy police post. He called in an artillery strike on the building that had served as a checkpoint for the advancing Iraqi armor—and was surprised at the results. After twenty or thirty rounds the artillery was unable to get onto the target. They hit deep, short, left, right. Finally, when Corporal Buntin figured he had bracketed them as close as they were going to get, he told the battery to fire for effect. The volley of rounds covered a huge area but missed the target completely. Frustrated, he ended the mission. He couldn't believe that with all the accurate data he had given them, they hadn't been able to hit the target.

Some time later Bravo had two electronic warfare variants of the LAV attached to their company near one of the OPs. These vehicles were able to determine that someone across the berm was attempting to jam Bravo Company's radios—a very difficult task with SINCGARS, which Bravo was operating on. The company was unaffected, but Captain Hammond wanted to eliminate the threat nonetheless. The vehicles determined that the jamming was coming from a small building across the border, a kilometer or two away.

Captain Hammond directed the attached mortar section to fire onto the building, and after a while it became apparent that they were not going to be able to hit it. Buntin did not understand. The mortarmen could see the building, so they could directly lay onto target, but they could not hit it.

Eventually frustrated with the mortars, Captain Hammond ordered a TOW vehicle to back off the line, get a clear shot, and fire a missile at the building. The AT backed away about four hundred meters from the berm and fired. The missile traversed the distance to the building quickly and exploded fiercely into the thin mortar structure. The jamming stopped.

When Shepherd set up on the evening of the twenty-ninth, all eyes were to the north on OP 6. The response to the deception operations was never received at OP 6, though. When Delta Company and the reconnaissance platoon became engaged with the enemy at OP 4, all was quiet at OP 6.

At 2200 Sergeant Hernandez was woken from sleep, and Captain Sellers ordered the entire company to mount the vehicles and move in support of Delta Company. Captain Sellers wheeled the company from facing east to facing south. The company moved out, left flank on the berm, and headed on line toward OP 4.

They hadn't traveled very far when Captain Sellers received a report of an enemy convoy of vehicles in Kuwait near OP 6. He immediately turned the company around and moved back toward OP 6. Visibility was poor, the desert fog had moved in, and Captain Sellers stopped Charlie Company about a kilometer south of OP 6. For the rest of the evening, the company oriented north, in positions perpendicular to the berm, expecting to make contact with an enemy armored convoy. The enemy never showed up.

When the sun rose in the morning, visibility returned, and Sergeant Hernandez could clearly see the OP from his position to the south. Captain Sellers wanted to move back to the north of the OP and assume his screening positions of the day prior, but he was concerned about the OP. With visibility as poor as it had been during the evening, Captain Sellers was concerned that the enemy may have been able to move in undetected to occupy the buildings within the small city.

Captain Sellers maneuvered the company within eight hundred meters of the OP and ordered that a platoon of dismounted scouts clear the buildings. Under overwatch from a company of LAV-25s the scouts swept through OP 6 and found nothing.

When the captain was satisfied that the OP was clear, he maneuvered the company back up to their screen line on the north side of the town. It wasn't long after the company reassumed their positions that an Iraqi tank was spotted by one of the TOW vehicles. Two kilometers east, a lone tank defiantly sat adjacent to a small building on the Kuwaiti side of the border. It would have been easy to launch a TOW missile at the tank and destroy it, but Captain Sellers was concerned about gathering information: he wanted the crew of the tank captured so they could be interrogated.

In order to capture the crew, the captain decided to send a section of LAVs out to the tank under overwatch by the rest of the company. He planned to fire a TOW missile toward the tank to initiate the movement. He called 1st Platoon's commander and gave him his orders. The platoon commander ordered Sergeant Hernandez to ready his section to accomplish the mission.

Hernandez acknowledged the order, but as he briefed his section, he expressed his reservations about the whole event. If the tank were not destroyed by the TOW missile, it could easily dispatch his entire section with its large gun. Additionally Hernandez was concerned about what might be hiding in the terrain beyond the tank's position. Since the tank was already two kilometers away, he knew that if a platoon of BMPs appeared from beyond, the company would be too far away to effectively support his section, who would be hanging out alone on the tip of the spear.

Having maneuvered to a position where he could move toward the tank, the sergeant waited for the TOW missile to fire. Then he moved out rapidly and watched the flight of the missile as it closed on the tank. Hernandez was surprised when he realized that the crew of the tank had seen the missile too. The crew quickly evacuated the vehicle and, toting their weapons, rushed for cover behind the small building.

Sergeant Hernandez closed on the tank with the section on line. The marines fired AP at the tank as they advanced so the Iraqis would know they meant business. But Hernandez had directed his section not to shoot at the Iraqis unless the enemy shot or aimed weapons at the marines first. The sergeant planned on stopping five hundred meters short to dismount the scouts, but when he was actually at that distance, he felt it was too far for the scouts to move if he wanted to maintain the initiative. He moved the section to within two hundred meters of the abandoned tank and dismounted the scouts to round up the Iraqis.

While the scouts moved to capture the tank crew, Hernandez searched for potential deep targets. He continuously moved his vehicle to reduce the ability of the unseen enemy to effectively track him.

One, two, and finally all three of the tank's crew appeared from behind the building with their hands in the air. The scouts bound their hands and blindfolded them. Then suddenly a fourth Iraqi appeared from behind the building. Covered in bandages and wearing a pressure dressing over an ugly shoulder wound, he was dragging a limp leg. The busy scouts quickly rounded him up.

When the prisoners were gathered and Sergeant Hernandez moved in to pick them up, he noticed that the wounded Iraqi was in really bad shape. In addition to the obvious injuries, he was covered in black soot from burns, and his boots and hair were smoking. When he was loaded onto the vehicle, Hernandez could smell his burned flesh and clothing; the sergeant quickly called in a report and asked that a corpsman be ready for the wounded prisoner.

When the section returned, mission completed, the prisoners were interrogated. What Sergeant Hernandez found out was that the tank had been involved in the incident with Delta Company at OP 4. Apparently the crew had fled and ended up adjacent to OP 6, waiting to surrender.

The night of 29 January had been Task Force Shepherd's first face-to-face standoff with the Iraqis. The task force emerged victorious—but at a cost of eleven marines killed by friendly fire. Throughout history, warriors have been killed by their own comrades. It is part of the chaos of war. But clearly the events of the twenty-ninth could have been avoided. Where the key to that fact lies, though, is unclear.

Is any one person to blame for the events that unfolded that night? Personally I don't think so. Marines were facing an imminent threat and reacted to that threat the only way they knew how, head-on. Confusion resulted in a TOW gunner's misidentifying a friendly vehicle as an enemy vehicle. Only that gunner knows exactly what he saw that dark evening. When radio calls are made up the chain of command to engage a target identified on the battlefield, the commander bases all decisions on the present situation. Unable to see what the gunner of each vehicle sees, the commander knows only that the enemy is being engaged.

Captain Hammond's deliberate actions with his ATs saved his company trains from destruction because he had the time to send the marines out to shoot an azimuth. Even then, those targets had been reported to higher headquarters and had been considered for a potential artillery strike. Things happened so fast for Captain Paster that it would have been impossible for him to do anything more than he did from his position on the battlefield.

Captain Paster now speculates that maybe he should have stayed back behind the first line of vehicles, in a position where he could see more of the battlefield. He may be right in this assessment: he might have been able to gain a position that would have enabled him to see the situation as it was developing and thus perhaps to take some action to prevent the deaths of the four marines on the LAV-AT. But then again, maybe it wouldn't have made a difference at all.

Captain Paster, like any good leader, placed himself at what he thought was the critical point on the battlefield. He was where he thought his company needed him at the time: where the action was, where the enemy was, and where the decision to withdraw would have to be made from. You cannot second guess that decision. Even Captain Paster should remember why he decided to move forward with the 1st Platoon and the two ATs.

The friendly fire from aircraft scared me. In fact, to this day I am deathly afraid of friendly air. It seems so glamorous to envision the returning pilots jumping out of their cockpits after a successful mission, the air crews painting the silhouettes of the destroyed vehicles on the sides of the aircraft—the motivation, the stories, the celebration. Then a mistake is made: out of eagerness, out of weariness, or out of confusion. A mistake is made, and friendlies are killed. What then? And why? There is nothing you can do as an armored-vehicle crewman to evade an aircraft, friendly or enemy, that is intending to kill you.

The air wing and the ground element are two islands within the Marine Corps. No matter how often we work together, and no matter how hard we try to combine arms, there is an ocean of differences separating our islands. Aircraft move at such great speeds, attack from such great heights, and use weapons that are so smart that it is inevitable that the human aspect of the equation will be the deciding factor.

The man at the controls of the aircraft will ultimately decide whether the slight speck on the ground below him is friend or foe. To me that seems like a huge burden of responsibility. The shifting lines on the maps that represent boundaries for friendly units are not good enough to ensure the survival of ground combatants. What is needed, and what is needed in the here-and-now, is a technological advance in IFF to aid the pilot in making the decision about the speck on the ground below him.

For the rest of Desert Storm, I didn't worry so much about the enemy: I worried about the friendlies. I worried about buzzing aircraft intending to drop their bombs, and I worried about itchy fingers on triggers, combatants eager to be involved in the shoot-out.

The enemy I could deal with. I had the training and the experience required to move tactically, to scan properly, and to maneuver for cover when required. My gunner had the skill to pick up the targets in the sights before they picked us up, and he had the skill to destroy those targets. I had to let the enemy situation rest in my training. The friendly situation, though, was different. I had no control over what I looked like in the gun sights of another armored vehicle or aircraft.

With the literally thousands of vehicles on the battlefield in Kuwait it was inevitable that American personnel would be where they weren't supposed to be and that some other American personnel would misidentify them and shoot them. I felt very comfortable that no one in our company would be involved in these situations—we had met the enemy and realized the cost of human error firsthand. But I wasn't confident about others in theater.

After the battle for OP 4 the mood in the company was a bit more somber. We were professionals as before, but now we had experienced the harsh realities of armored combat, and we knew the penalties enforced by confused execution.

The EPWs interrogated after the fight let us know a number of useful things. Besides the fact that our presence had surprised them and caused some initial confusion, we found that the 25-mm HE fire was very scary for the Iraqis. Although the HE did not penetrate the thick armor of the tanks, the hundreds of tiny explosions on the tanks' hulls did blind the Iraqis in a sense: their IR sighting was overwhelmed by the sudden and furious insurgence of light created by the explosions, and the tank commanders—forced to remain buttoned up inside the vehicles—were further blinded. This was welcome news because we had always thought we were ill-equipped to fight these monstrous tracked vehicles with our tiny cannons.

After the battle Bravo Company established a hasty minefield in the break in the berm at OP 4, and I couldn't help but wonder if the permanent existence of a minefield prior to the attack would have helped us. The berm's construction along the border made it almost impossible for the Iraqis to cross at any point other than at the OPs where the breaks were. The Iraqis could have breached the berm, but it would have required a coordinated and concentrated effort including engineer, artillery, air, and heavy tank support. With the distance between the Iraqi positions and the berm it would have been impossible for them to amass the appropriate combat forces undetected, and if they were detected, our commanders could shift the necessary forces required to the appropriate place on the battlefield to counter the enemy thrust.

Using this logic, I think that we probably should have focused a bit of energy on the construction of hasty minefields at the critical points along the sandy berm. These minefields would have bought us the time and space required to shift combat resources in the event of another surprise push by the Iraqi armor. As history shows, however, this was never an issue. The Iraqi thrust of 29–30 January was countered, and after that, the Iraqis lost the resolve required to mass the necessary forces again.

10

AFTER OP 4, Alpha Company moved back up to familiar ground around OP 6. During the day we stood back off the berm approximately two kilometers. We were spread out over about four kilometers, fifteen hundred meters north and south of the OP proper. The visibility allowed us to see five to six kilometers across the berm and into Kuwait, preventing any chance for the enemy to move undetected across the open desert between the two countries.

At dusk we fired up our vehicles as a unit and moved to the berm. Three to four hundred meters short of the berm, we dismounted our scouts ahead of us to check our night positions. Under overwatch of the 25-mm main guns the scouts hurried to the berm, checked the near side of the berm, and then quickly scurried to the far side to check for signs of enemy presence. When all was clear, the vehicles were called up, and we assumed turret-down positions—which allowed only the sights of the vehicle to peer over the berm into the desert beyond—and set up armored observation posts.

On the evening of 1 February my night position was at the elbow created by the intersection of the north-south berm and the sandy east-west wall of OP 6. The crew spent hours digging in the corner of that intersection, creating both a turret-down position and a higher firing position that allowed the weapons system to crest the berm. On the Kuwait side of the berm the scouts dug a hollowed-out cave into the slope of the berm itself that allowed the team to observe the open desert from a position of limited cover and concealment.

To my immediate left, the sandy road that led into the OP from Kuwait and beyond twisted through two high walls, a line of wrecked cars, and a sharp L-shaped turn to the right before entering the small city of OP 6. To my right, the rest of the platoon was nestled behind the berm, with scouts out to observe the desert. Our line continued for about fifteen hundred meters. With an observation post established in the multistory structure five hundred meters to my left, 2d Platoon had their vehicles positioned farther north along the continuous berm.

It was very late, and I was on watch in the turret. I had scouts forward of the berm in an observation post. I alternated my watch by scanning with the vehicle optics and with my NVGs (night-vision goggles). First I traversed the turret manually from the extreme right (roughly southeast) to the extreme left (roughly northeast) of my assigned sector of observation. As I traversed, I peered through the M36 passive night-sight elbow.

The green glow of magnified and amplified light allowed me to see only the very obvious on the horizon. When I got to the left end of my sector, the sights completely washed out due to the fires burning in the al-Burqan oil fields ten to fifteen kilometers away. So intense was the light that the light-amplifying sights were completely overloaded. I scanned back to the right, and after detecting nothing obvious I stood in the turret to listen and scan with the NVGs. I continued alternating between the sights and the NVGs in this fashion for about two hours.

I remember standing in the turret scanning with the NVGs when I heard voices to my left. There were people not thirty feet away from me, carrying on a conversation. I peered to my left but could see nothing closer than fifty or sixty feet, due to the height of the berm and the bright light of the fires burning in the distance.

The voices continued, and I quickly woke up the crew and pointed to the left. I radioed the OP on the field phone, and within minutes the marines on watch had captured a number of Iraqi soldiers, with weapons, who had strolled along almost the entire company frontage from left to right. I do not know exactly what the enemy soldiers' intentions were. They may have been simply surrendering, or they may have been plotting an attack. Fortunately, we had heard their muted conversation, the quick actions of my scout team had surprised them, and the Iraqis were captured without incident.

After I reported the capture and coordinated the turnover to the company gunny, I was livid on the platoon tach net to the lieutenant. I explained to him that enemy soldiers had walked right in front of the 2d Platoon screen, had continued to walk right in front of the 2d Platoon OP in the multistory structure, and had been stopped only when I heard their voices. I explained that I was blind to the northeast because of the fire and that I was counting, personally, on the abilities of 2d Platoon to cover these types of things. He said he understood, and that was that. From then on, I repositioned my OP so that it had a better view to the northeast. Regardless of the enemy's direction—and of 2d Platoon's actions—I wasn't going to be surprised again.

We spent the next couple of days at OP 6 conducting screen operations. The platoon always left the berm just before sunrise and backed off about two kilometers. Just before dusk the platoon moved forward again, using the scouts to clear the positions, and occupied the night positions. The only exception was the position my section had in the crook of the elbow, which was so ideal for cover and concealment that I was allowed to stay on the berm twenty-four hours a day in complete defilade and undetected.

On 3 February, Bravo Company was preparing to conduct another artillery raid with one of the artillery batteries. Captain Hammond needed to conduct a face-to-face liaison with 5th Battalion, 11th Marine Regiment— the battery supporting the raid—and left his company position with the XO in tow in the C2. The two vehicles headed off into the desert on an azimuth that would lead to the artillery battery. By sheer coincidence the path that was chosen to drive inland to the artillery battery position intersected with the wreckage of a marine Cobra helicopter.

Captain Hammond stopped the two vehicles, and the FAC came out of the LAV-C2 to take a look. There, in the middle of the Saudi desert, a Cobra was crudely scattered around the desert after having run into the ground at a high rate of speed. Both pilots were dead; there was nothing the marines could do for them. The FAC, a CH-53 pilot, looked at the wreckage and surmised that the Cobra either had flown too low and run aground or had abruptly run out of gas.

The marines hadn't heard that there was any problem with a lost helicopter, and Corporal Buntin was very surprised to find one the way they did. Almost as soon as the LAV section stopped and began to look around, a CH-53 rescue helicopter came in to retrieve both the pilots and the wreckage.

From 4 to 6 February, Alpha Company was pulled back off the line for maintenance. I never understood why we periodically pulled back for that purpose: for the past five months we had performed maintenance on a continuous basis. Our failure to do it would have resulted in a vehicle that didn't operate. If your vehicle was nonoperational, you walked. Walking is something that a lot of marines do; however, it is not something that any LAV crewman relished or looked forward to. There was talk from some individuals about wanting to be on the ground during the war, away from the RPG magnet that the vehicle represented. But truth be told, I think that however much the LAV attracted rockets, it was still better than walking.

Looking back I realize how extremely lucky we were to be in LAVs and to be placed at the tip of the spear. One reason is that mistakes such as friendly mortars coming at you were less of a problem when you were wrapped in fourteen tons of steel. Small-arms fire was insignificant unless the firer was able to hit the portion of your body exposed from the vehicle. Additionally we moved so fast in the LAVs that by the time the enemy figured out what was going on and determined that someone hostile was in the area, we were gone. Unfortunately those marines who moved behind us were invariably harassed by the small pockets of resistance that we had stirred with our rapid passing.

This maintenance trip was different from previous ones: the LAV-25s were now equipped with an add-on modification, a thermal sight. Before this change the only night-vision instrument in the LAV-25 was an ancient, eight-power, passive night sight. If a target were more than five meters in size, the sight could barely make out the outline of that target at eight hundred meters. If there were no moon providing an ambient light source, the targets could not be acquired at all. The LAV community had been complaining for years about the situation. What it boiled down to was this: at night we were blind.

From somewhere in the supply system the same thermal sights that were currently in the LAV-AT vehicles had been procured in numbers large enough to outfit a number of the LAV-25s. The modification was only temporary, though. The sight was fixed outside the turret adjacent to the vehicle commander's sight block. It pointed straight ahead and could not be moved. In order to use the sight, you were required to traverse the turret in the direction you wanted to see. Only the vehicle commander could use the sight; the gunner still had to use the M36 passive night sight to engage targets. Hence the sight could be used for scanning only—and only from the vehicle commander's position.

Even though the addition of the sight offered limited help in the engagement of targets at night, we heartily welcomed it. Looking through the sight at either four or thirteen power, you could pick up any object in your field of view that had a temperature differential of less than one degree from the surrounding terrain. Targets as small as field mice showed up as bright red dots scurrying across the desert floor. Armored vehicles and troops were impossible to miss when you scanned across your front-age. The warmth of the human body and metal, even after cooling all night in the desert, translated into sharp red images within the eyepiece of the sight.

Aside from the fixed position to which the sight was mounted, there were a couple of other drawbacks to the system. In order for the sight to operate properly, the scanning elements within the sight had to be super-cooled. But the cooler was incredibly noisy—so noisy that when walking, you could find the vehicle's position in the dark from more than five hundred meters away, just by using your ears to guide you. I did not find this a very pleasing advantage, especially since Iraqi troops had walked up on my flank a few nights earlier. I wondered at the time if I would even have been able to hear the enemy soldiers' conversational tones had the sight been attached and cooling.

An additional problem was the oil fires. Their bright lights overloaded the passive, light-intensifying M36. And their heat produced such a differential in the temperature of their surroundings that the sights washed out in a smeared red glow when pointed near the fires. However inconvenient the positioning or operation of the sight may have been, though, it was a far cry better than nothing. We dealt with it.

When we were in maintenance, we had a chance to catch up on the mail and current events. Finally we were able to read about the OP 4 battle in the newspapers. I had postponed telling my wife about the incident for fear of worrying her. Once we read about the event in the papers, however, I felt safe to write to her about it. Additionally we read a news story about seventy-five thousand protesters who supported the troops but didn't support the war. After reading that particular article, I got mad all over again.

We knew there was wide variation in the degree of support President Bush was receiving, and I still believed in the precious rights that every American citizen was accorded—free speech included. But even so, the protesters still bothered me. To them the war was about oil. They were concerned about the welfare of the American forces deployed, but in their opinion America had no interest other than oil in the desert. I just didn't buy it. Politically oil may have been an issue, but we had already established in our own hearts what the war was about. It was about the people of Kuwait; it was about freedom.

American citizens were not allowing us to do the job required without distraction. To me the demonstrations were a huge distraction. I had already seen how the attitudes of the protesters affected other military personnel. I wanted no part of that. And finally, if freedom was not a viable American interest, then to hell with it all.

I know this may sound as though I was brainwashed or wearing blinders, but nothing could be further from the truth. I understood that political concerns stood in purview over all of our military actions—war is in essence just an extension of politics. To me, however, this was not the issue. I had enlisted in the Marine Corps to serve my country. I needed something in my life, and I found it under the scarlet and gold flag that flew to the left of the red, white, and blue. As romantic as this may sound, it is true and heartfelt. In Kuwait I found out why we were there. I saw the faces of the Kuwaiti citizens who had regained their country. I saw the children standing in the streets waving the small American flags, staring up with jubilant smiles as our convoys drove past. It was never a mystery to me, and if people in America could not understand that we had all freely chosen to join the service and had fully known the consequences of that choice, then I feel sorry for them.

Whenever I read negative things about what we were doing in the Persian Gulf, I became melancholy. But that depression just fueled my already deep desire to make the situation right. These feelings were very common among those that I talked to. Sure, we wanted to be home with our families, but it was very important to set things right in the theater before we left.

When Alpha was relieved from duties at OP 6 to pull back and conduct maintenance, Charlie Company pulled in to assume responsibility for the desert outpost. Captain Sellers handled the problem of watching for an enemy attack differently than we in Alpha Company had done.

During the day Sellers put both of his platoons up on the berm to observe—if you remember, in Alpha we kept the platoons back during the day. Behind the protective walls of the berm his marines diligently watched into Kuwait. The ability to see a vast distance across the empty desert between the two countries allowed Sellers to position vehicles right on the sandy berm. At night—with visibility and, accordingly, reaction time limited—he pulled his two platoons back from the berm to observe from a distance with the thermal sights mounted on top of the TOW vehicles.

Because there was always dismounted Iraqi activity in the form of surrendering soldiers, Sellers wanted to be able to keep an eye on the berm and the immediate area beyond it at night. In order to accomplish this he sent out one section of LAV-25s with an attached LAV-AT to patrol the berm north and south of the police post every night. That section conducted a two-hour patrol, stopping periodically adjacent to the berm to observe; the marines were then relieved by another section of similar composition.

Sergeant Hernandez led his section and one of the attached LAV-ATs on one of these patrols when the horrific incident that had happened between the A-10 and the LAV-25 at OP 4 was almost repeated. On patrol Hernandez noticed a distinct pattern in the skies above Kuwait to the east. He recalls that the night was especially active with Allied air strikes on the fortified Iraqi positions.

He saw the blinking lights of aircraft from Saudi Arabia turn off as soon as they crossed over his position on the berm. Shortly afterward he saw parachute flares dropping from another aircraft and illuminating a target area far to his east. Immediately following each flare Hernandez saw either the flash of a missile fired from an attacking aircraft or a destructive explosion taking place on the illuminated ground. It was a regular pattern: lights off, parachute flare, ordnance dropped on target. As he conducted his patrol, he saw this again and again.

About an hour into his two-hour patrol Sergeant Hernandez stopped about two hundred meters south of OP 6 to check the area. He was leading the section with the TOW following him and his wingman following the TOW. The section stopped within a hundred-meter radius of the berm, and the scouts from the two LAV-25s scurried out of the vehicles to take up positions of observation on the berm. The LAV-AT erected its hammerhead turret and began to scan the terrain beyond the berm for hot spots. Hernandez planned to spend a few minutes doing this and then move on to another spot to repeat the action.

Suddenly a parachute flare erupted in the dark sky above the halted section. Their entire position was illuminated, and in the sergeant's head something clicked. *Shit! This is the pattern! They're going to drop on us!* Hernandez went into immediate action. He yelled at the dispersed marines, "Take cover!" He then jumped down into the protective hull of the LAV.

The armor wasn't as thick as a tank, but it was thicker than his skin.

He looked straight up through his hatch at the sky, and an aircraft flashed quickly through the narrow field of view offered by the tiny hatch opening. He distinctly remembers seeing the belly of the aircraft as it flew over and thinking it must be Iraqi because it was coming from the Kuwait side of the berm.

An intense explosion rocked through the protective ear pieces of Hernandez's CVC helmet, violating his eardrums. The vehicle started to rock violently back and forth. The sergeant looked out of his periscopes on the side of the turret and watched as the cluster-bomb munition began to activate. From north to south, the thousands of tiny bomblets of the munition exploded. It looked as though they were setting the desert on fire in a methodical fashion. Fully expecting his armor hull to be pierced by the fiery shells, Hernandez awaited the pain of burning flesh. But that never happened. The explosions ceased, and the fierce jerking motion of the vehicle gradually subsided.

Sergeant Hernandez's thoughts were first on the safety of his section and then on detecting an enemy attack that was sure to follow this intense bombardment. He stood in his turret, checked the vehicle intercom to see if the crewmen in the vehicle were all right, and turned to check the scouts. The crew was unharmed. The scouts were already running back to the vehicle, and he counted them as all four returned safely.

Someone was already on the platoon radio net: "We've got to move! We've got to move!" Clearly upset, he continued to dominate the net: "We've got to leave the berm and go back to the company. Let's go!"

Sergeant Hernandez was trying to get the marine off the net so that he could make an assessment of the situation, but he just kept sputtering on about leaving, and Hernandez couldn't get a word in. Finally Hernandez had to yell over the radio, "Shut up! Shut up and listen!" The radio traffic died down, and Hernandez continued. "First, is everybody OK?" After a few moments of checking, he found that no one had been injured. Hernandez now was able to take care of his second concern, the Iraqis.

He radioed a quick report to his platoon commander and then radioed back to the rattled marine. "Look, I know you want to get out of this spot, but this is the most critical time." He struggled to formulate the most concise words in his head. "If the Iraqis are going to attack, it will be now. We need to have eyes out up here. We are the only ones in the company who can see. We have to stay." Although the marine didn't like that too much, he had no choice but to accept it. Hernandez did move the section farther south a few hundred meters, but they stayed on the berm until they were relieved by the next section.

Sergeant Hernandez remained very cool under the fire that he thought was delivered from Iraqi aircraft. Always his first concern was to be there for his section. He was committed to providing them the direction and leadership required for them to stay alive in combat. On top of that, he was always logical in his thought process. It wasn't until later that he realized he had been fired on by an American pilot. He was angry, but still his predominant thought in action had been to be prepared for the enemy.

In the morning they went out and found where the bomb had struck the earth. Not all bomblets in the cluster bomb had exploded on impact; some of them had fallen harmlessly into the sand. What they found was that the rattled marine's vehicle was within fifty meters of the trailing edge of the impact area. Lucky for Sergeant Hernandez and his section, the pilot had missed—if you could call fifty meters off a miss.

As soon as we completed our maintenance, Alpha headed to OP 6 to relieve Charlie. When I pulled back into the position south of the OP that I always occupied, the first thing I noticed was a field of unexploded bomblets on the ground behind the berm. Having no idea where they had come from, I steered clear of them when I moved into position.

Our screening duties at OP 6 started all over. In addition to the constant flow of Iraqi soldiers walking over the border day and night, the higher-ups had escalated the psychological warfare in our region. The pamphlets we had seen our first day at the berm amounted to the solicitation of defectors to this point. Now, at night, we were frequently joined by a U.S. Army PSYOPS (psychological operations) team. They had come to us at OP 6 with nothing more than a pair of HMMWVs.

I didn't think that these two vehicles would be very imposing, but as soon as it got dark, I found I was completely mistaken. These HMMWVs had a sound system that would be the envy of nearly every hard rock-loving teen in America. Sitting no more than fifty meters behind our positions, the vehicles turned on their music system and blasted American heavy-metal music across the open desert toward Kuwait. Song after song played at a sound level that quickly produced an ache in my CVC helmet-protected head. I had been to a number of concerts when I was young, and I must candidly say that this music was at least as loud as any concert I've been to—and all out of a pair of HMMWVs. My head was hurting so badly I was almost ready to surrender myself.

I distinctly remember AC/DC's "Back in Black" being played over and over. After every couple of songs the PSYOPS team paused to play a prerecorded message in Arabic. I assume the message was urging the Iraqis to surrender immediately or face the wrath of the heavy metal-loving American soldiers having a bad-hair month.

Apparently the music and recordings did the job because after that, even more Iraqis surrendered to us day and night. That last week at the berm was characterized by long nights of peering into the darkness followed by days of making trip after trip to the rear, thirty kilometers away, to drop off prisoners at the EPW collection points. Every morning, it seemed, I moved my section to the company gunny's position to pick up a group of EPWs that had joined us during the evening. Whenever I got there, I always had to wait while our interpreter interrogated them.

The interpreter was a Kuwaiti Air Force pilot who had been in school in the United States when the war broke out. My first impression of the officer was that he was effeminate. He spoke softly and was very well-groomed. He was tall and slender, and I felt that if I were to come up and slap him on the shoulder, he would break, fragmenting into bone shards. I watched time and time again as he calmly talked to one of the prisoners being kept in a shallow sleeping hole. He would be on one side of the hole, legs crossed and dangling to the sandy bottom of the hole while he took notes in a small notebook. The prisoner would be on the other side of the hole, meekly answering his questions. I was not very impressed by the stature of this officer. As it turned out, though, I was dead wrong in that assessment.

During one interrogation, he began as usual, speaking very soberly to the prisoner while writing on the notepad. The prisoner, sitting across from him, shook his head and mumbled a few indiscernible words. Suddenly the interpreter's eyes turned to fire; he reached out his hand and slapped the prisoner and then chastised him with a sharp verbal rebuke. The prisoner immediately turned to jelly and began speaking rapidly, apparently giving the officer what he wanted. The interpreter then returned to his normal demeanor. I stood back and said "Damn!" not believing what I had seen. After that, I knew there was something I had missed in my assessment of this individual. I laughed and walked away.

One of those evenings I was on watch in the turret when the lieutenant called me on the radio: "Blue 5, this is Blue 1, over."

"Go ahead, Blue 1."

"Blue 5, 2d Platoon has reported contact with troops crossing over the border to their flank, break." Thus far it sounded like the most exciting thing to happen in a long time. "You and I are going to move over to the company's rear and try to find them before they get to the CP, over."

"Roger, Blue 1, I'm moving." I alerted the crew and quickly looked at my map to try to visualize the area he was talking about. Mentally I divided the area behind 2d Platoon into four squares—bisected by the hard-surface road that ran roughly northeast and a dry wadi that ran perpendicular to it. If Lieutenant Tice approved it, we would check the sections one at a time using the thermal sights, with the scouts starting at the northeast square and moving clockwise from there. I called him with the plan while the crew was mounting up, and he approved it.

As soon as the driver fired up the vehicle and backed away from the berm, I saw a series of bright flashes on the horizon to the east. We had seen these flashes before—they were an Iraqi rocket battery firing at some target. As standard procedure I reported the firing and the azimuth to the firing and didn't give the rockets another thought. They were usually aimed at something far away from us to the south.

When I rounded the south end of OP 6, a quick series of explosions rumbled about a kilometer to my left. I glanced quickly in that direction and saw the sparks of the rockets' impact subsiding. This was the first time since 17 January that they had fired the rockets at us. I was glad they were poor gunners. Apparently they had heard the engine noises of our two LAVs starting up and had fired the rockets toward that sound. Later, when I'd had time to think about it, I found it hard to believe they had missed us. Our positions were no secret—we were adjacent to OP 6, and OP 6 was on the map.

We continued with the search after that but never found the Iraqi soldiers. It surprised me that we never found them. We were using the same technique that Negron and I had used with the reconnaissance team at Manifa Bay the previous fall. In fact this time we had the luxury of not only the thermal sight but the time to use dismounted reconnaissance with our scout teams.

We searched the open areas, the wadis, the culverts, the bushes, and the steep road shoulders but never found the Iraqis. We searched for hours, and in the end, I was very disappointed. I don't know what else we could have done. I thought we had responded very quickly and had attacked the problem with a solid plan. Such is the way things go at times. We went back to our positions and resumed screening—we watched our six o'clock the entire evening, but we kept screening.

On 13 February we started getting visitors. On one of my trips to take

EPWs to the rear I passed a formation consisting of hundreds of tanks and armored personnel carriers (APCs) belonging to the U.S. Army's Tiger Brigade. I was astonished at the magnitude of combat power being moved into our area. To date I had never seen so many tanks, Bradley Fighting Vehicles, and other specialized APCs in one place at one time. So congested was the *open desert* on my trip to the rear that I literally had to pull over and stop, breathing road dust for half an hour, until I could find a wide-enough break in the armored convoy to cross their path to my destination.

On my return trip after dropping off the EPWs—carefully watching to see that they were treated properly—I moved quickly on the east side of the convoy, passing as many vehicles as possible. The LAV really moves fast over the flat desert, and I was able to pass almost two-thirds of the slow-moving convoy before I returned. When I got back, the desert behind our positions was littered as far as the eye could see with massive armor assembly areas. There was not a single visible area of empty desert, and I said to myself that as poor as the Iraqis were at gunnery, they could now launch rockets anywhere and hit something.

As the forces moved into our area, one thought dominated my mind: I hoped that they didn't ruin it for everybody. I remembered how anxious we had been for contact when we first moved up to the berm. Alpha Company had adjusted well, but I was unsure how Tiger Brigade would do.

We had been up and operating near the berm for almost a month. We had been in contact and had taken prisoners, and we were very single-minded about how the prisoners were to be treated. We knew that in LAVs, our success and survivability depended on the disposition of the Iraqis that we met. Every Iraqi who surrendered was one less Iraqi who could pop out of an unseen hole to fire an RPG into the rear of our vehicle.

I was very concerned that the soldiers new to the area or new to contact with the Iraqis would be overzealous—aggressive to the point that they shot first and asked questions later, white flag or no white flag. I had already seen how our own company matured in its handling of the enemy, and I didn't want to be around when this huge armored formation adjusted and matured.

As it turned out, we didn't stick around long. That night we were joined on the berm by the leaders of Company C, 2d LAI Battalion. They were not from Task Force Shepherd but the 2d Marine Division, and they were assuming control of the area around OP 6. Their platoon commanders and company commander spent the night with us on the thirteenth in order to prepare for a relief in place the following day.

I was sleeping next to my vehicle when, midway through the night, a huge rumbling explosion rocked the entire frontage of the company. I woke quickly and sat up in my sleeping bag. Looking at my vehicle I saw that the scout who had been in the turret was now eight feet in the air, executing a beautiful swan dive to the deck. I listened to the echoes of the explosion and recognized it as a cluster bomb, but I didn't know why it was so loud or so close.

I jumped to the radio in the turret, and Wildman, our FAC, was already on the company tach explaining the situation. Apparently a friendly air-craft had come back from a run in Kuwait with an extra bomb that he needed to get rid of before he landed. He decided to drop it about eight hundred meters in front of us near the border.

I shrugged off the explanation, posted the watch, and went back to my bag. Too tired to catalog yet another experience with friendly air, I quickly drifted off to sleep. In and of itself this incident was not very remarkable. However, years later, while serving in Company C, 2d LAI, I met a marine officer who had joined us that evening. We were talking about it, and he told me how his crew had been so startled by that explosion on their first night on the berm that none of them was able go back to sleep. I got a real kick out of the story. One of his crewmen was now in my platoon, and I gave him a serious ribbing about the matter that same day—and at every opportunity thereafter. He didn't know that the only reason I had no prob-lem sleeping was that I was dead tired. He didn't need to know, as far as I was concerned; we were two NCOs, and I had him right where I wanted him.

That evening was the last one we spent at OP 6. We were relieved by Charlie Company, 2d LAI, and moved down to "Q-town" to rest, refit, and receive orders for the ground war. It had been an incredible month on the berm. Sadly the battalion had lost fourteen marines. Each and every one had been killed by other Americans: this reality weighed heavily on all our minds.

There was never any blame cast from our corners, however. In war good men die. It is unfortunate that they die by our own hands at times, but we have to learn from that. My hopes are that we have learned; my hopes are that the mistakes we made that cost men their lives will even-tually ensure that others live. Unfortunately I don't see concrete evidence of this today. The onus of the responsibility to avoid these instances is still on each individual. I am not saying that each individual should not be responsible for stopping this fratricide, but I am saying that you cannot make it go away simply by saying to each marine, "Make it go away." With the massive increase in technology there has to be more involved.

I have seen much written about how we are going to stop the problem, but I have not seen much done. To date I still haven't seen a marked increase in the quality of armored vehicle identification programs. I still haven't seen technology, aside from IR light sources, that will help identify friendlies on the battlefield. I still haven't seen the solution to managing the situation on future "joint" battlefields, where you have multiple nationalities and multiple vehicle types involved.

Military technology has advanced so rapidly that it has outpaced our ability to manage it. Helicopter pilots can now shoot missiles from a distance of more than four miles to a target illuminated by a spotter over a mile away. Gunners in armored vehicles can shoot munitions that travel to targets more than eight miles away. They can see the targets with advanced technology, yet they can barely recognize them as friend or foe. Mobility on the battlefield has increased so greatly that units can displace over vast distances into other units' zones before the radio traffic catches up and notifies the adjacent forces.

Situational awareness is highly touted along with individual responsibility. The ability to manage information and create a mental picture of the battlefield is essential for leaders in today's armed conflicts. As a nation we must do everything possible to give the commanders of our forces the available technology that will allow them to create and disseminate this mental picture. We should never send men to fight wars where they are required to pause and wonder *Is that really a bad guy, or is it a friendly who is where he or she shouldn't be?* Position reporting systems, IFF for all elements, and solid communications are essential if we are to capture the beast called fratricide. It is an arduous task ahead, but it is a task we can handle if we focus on it. When we ask Americans to die for their country, we should be able to reasonably guarantee that their deaths will not be at the hands of other Americans.

Yet in our endeavor to protect fighting Americans we must try to avoid creating for them a sterile, overly safe environment. Like the AT 4, which has too many safety devices to make it fully successful as a combat weapon, such an environment creates a tendency in a fighter to falter when a decision must be made. The initiative is lost, not gained, and the enemy will be able to exploit the situation. We must not create a clearing barrel of sorts with a list of procedures so long that it hampers the warriors at the triggers. In short we must allow commanders to use the available technology to dictate the tempo of the battlefield, but we must be able to do that without killing each other.

These thoughts were forming in my mind as we moved to Q-town, which was nothing more than an open area of the desert that the marines had turned into a large encampment area where we could rest and take showers. Alpha Company spent the entire week there. Gone were the daily turret watches and the chasing of EPWs. It turned out to be our first real break since the air conditioning of Stalag 3.

At Q-town my professional differences with one of the staff sergeants finally received the attention they deserved. Lieutenant Tice pulled me aside one day—much as he had pulled me aside months ago at Stalag 3——and we took a walk. During the course of our conversation he admitted that I had been correct in my assessment of the staff sergeant, that he wasn't qualified. The lieutenant even went so far as to say that the staff sergeant probably had no business at all in a leadership role in the LAV community.

I was relieved, to say the least. I had always been concerned that the staff sergeant might be put into a situation he could not handle, a situation where the lives of other marines may be involved. Throughout the course of the deployment I had had my differences with the staff sergeant over little things, but his role in the platoon was so minor that big problems never arose. And now I understood why he played such a minor role in the tactical functions of the platoon. For the most part he had been relegated to accomplishing a myriad of mundane, administrative tasks. I knew why I wouldn't give him a major role, but until now I was unsure of what the platoon commander's rationale was.

As we walked, it became apparent to me that Lieutenant Tice had been true to his word. He had asked me to give him time to observe so that he could fully appraise the situation. I had given him the time, and he had figured out the staff sergeant. I think the biggest reason that he pulled me aside that day was to justify his actions. I think he realized I was on the mark, and he wanted to make sure I understood why he had made the decisions he did. At that moment I probably wasn't very sympathetic to his words, however: things were too real to be playing games, as far as I was concerned.

Captain Shupp talked to me about the situation shortly after Lieutenant Tice did. His words weren't as concise as the lieutenant's had been; he was more vague, more aloof about the whole situation. I am not sure why he approached me, and I probably will never know. I don't even remember being aware that Captain Shupp knew what was going on in 1st Platoon. I listened intently as he formed his words into what I gathered was something between an apology and a pep talk. When he finished speaking, that was it—he had said what he had to say and was gone. I was unsettled. I knew now that he had been aware of the situation the whole time, but I was unsure what he was going to do about it, if anything.

When I interviewed Sergeant Ramirez in writing this book, things became a little clearer for me. The whole time that Ramirez had been trying to get into Alpha Company, he was aware that Captain Shupp was trying to replace one of his SNCOs. No name was ever spoken in Ramirez's presence, but based on what he had seen of the company, he had deduced that this SNCO was the same guy I'd had problems with. Ramirez recalls that it wasn't difficult for him to figure it out. But, ironically, the company waited too long to replace him. Had it been done earlier, the process would have gone smoothly. Now it was too late to replace a cog in the wheel without creating the possibility of even greater problems in the ground war.

As we waited for the ground war to happen, the days of rest and relaxation quickly turned into a period of heightened anxiety. We were pretty sure that the ground offensive was about to kick off: they told us that outgoing mail had been suspended indefinitely.

One afternoon I walked over to Gunny Chevice's vehicle and asked him if he had any ammunition he would like to give away. The word was out that we were short on 25-mm ammunition in-country, and that Gunny Chevice had been tasked with distributing what he had to the platoons. When I asked him the question, I half-expected a prolonged period of bargaining as I attempted to squeeze the ammo from him. So I was surprised when he told me I could take whatever I could carry.

Our vehicles were already full of ammunition. We had an entire upload (210 rounds) in the ready boxes of the vehicle and at least two more uploads stored inside the vehicles. Although I would have loved to take every bit of ammunition off Chevice's hands, I had the room for only one more upload. When I returned to the vehicle, I spent the rest of the day trying to find places to secure the ammunition we had received. Finding a place for the ammunition was difficult. In the end we secured a hundred rounds of ammunition to the outside of the vehicle, in wooden crates underneath the muffler. The remaining ammunition was broken down into twenty-round belts and laced over the troop seats in the back. The vehicle was not designed to carry more than two uploads of ammunition in reserve, so in adding a third, we had to be innovative.

Just a few days before we received our orders to go into Kuwait, the company participated in a battalion awards ceremony. We had to get in battalion formation and stand at attention while the marines being honored were recognized. On the surface this job didn't sound too threatening to any of us. We hadn't stood formation in a while, but how bad could it be? If I knew then what I know today about this formation, however, I think I would have looked for some bad food to eat so I could have gotten dysentery and missed the whole thing—the trots would certainly have been more pleasant than what was in store for us.

Once the battalion was formed and at attention, the sergeant major announced, "Personnel to be recognized, center, march!" A column of forty marines marched in front of the battalion and came to a halt, centered on the battalion commander. As we stood at attention, a speaker started reading out the citations for each marine. When each citation was read, the battalion commander went to the marine, pinned on the appropriate decoration, and shook the individual's hand. Then the next citation was read.

When the battalion commander got about three-quarters of the way through the marines, my mind went into a daze and I couldn't wait for him to finish. My legs were beginning to get numb, and the balls of my feet were beginning to burn. When the colonel shook the hand of the last marine—whose award had something to do with running the supply-issue point in a credible manner—I snapped back to the present and was thankful that it was finally over.

The column of forty marines marched off, and I waited to hear *Company commanders, take charge of your marines and carry out the plan of the day.* Instead the sergeant major commanded, "Personnel to be recognized, center, march!" It must have been a bad dream. Forty more marines marched in front of the battalion. Before it was all over, more than 120 marines were recognized in that ceremony. Ironically, as good as I thought we were, I don't remember any of those marines coming from Alpha Company.

11

ON 20 FEBRUARY, Alpha Company received something we had waited six months for: the orders to move into Kuwait. It is hard to describe the feelings I had when we assembled to receive the order to complete the mission of Desert Storm. Surprisingly I do know that fear of death was not one of the feelings I had. We were told to expect up to 80 percent casualties within units participating in the breach of the Iraqi minefields. I heard this, but never for one moment did I believe it. We were told that we had combat replacement platoons to draw from when we took casualties. I heard this, but somehow I knew that we wouldn't need them.

I don't know exactly why I didn't put too much stock in those things. Maybe it was because I had seen how the enemy was reacting up until this point and I expected more of the same: surrendering en masse. Perhaps it was because I truly believed in our cause and had been raised to believe that things always work out for the best in the long haul. I don't know. What I did know was that Alpha Company was ready. We had trained hard, and we were ready for any task. And Captain Shupp is the one who can take the credit for that.

Participating in the ground war allowed us to see clearly the light at the end of the tunnel—the light that marked the freedom of Kuwait and, eventually, the trip home. Of course I expected some casualties. I was not so naive as to think that we were bulletproof, but I knew that we knew our

177

business. I hoped I personally was a hundred percent ready for the operation, but I was certain we would prevail in our endeavor.

For this mission we were given a full-blown five-paragraph order. I was so accustomed to working off of FRAGOs that I found it difficult to sit through the lengthy, drawn-out order. Looking back I realize this is one tangible mark that Captain Shupp has left on me forever: he led us so well, with so few words, that anytime I have to sit down and go through a well-choreographed order, I become frustrated and impatient. There are so many ways to waste both language and time.

I see certain things about a unit when words are wasted. I see a lack of training that requires marines to memorize long lists of coordinating instructions—how many of those details should be rehearsed drill? I see the lack of leadership when marines are required to draw out endless control measures on maps—where is confidence in the subordinates' ability to maneuver and make decisions? Most of all I see the lack of cohesion when marines look at fellow platoon members with blank stares, confused and wondering what they are supposed to be doing.

It is unfortunate—albeit unavoidable in the garrison Marine Corps—that all marine units cannot be in sync the way we were in Alpha Company at that time. So little time is available for marines to grow accustomed to their commanders and for commanders to gain trust in their subordinates. Development of leadership at the small-unit level is not where it needs to be—not if we want the leaders of these units to make decisions based on intent alone. The most combat-ready unit will always be the one where the marines know and understand the commander, the commander trusts the marines, and the marine mind is actively operating with coordinated initiative tempered by a common intent.

Lieutenant Tice gave the vehicle commanders the order. He started out by giving us a rough time line for the ground war. Our "G day" was 24 February. In the time remaining before that day arrived, friendly forces were going to infiltrate Iraqi minefields in preparation for a breach. In the early morning hours of the twenty-fourth Task Forces Ripper and Papa Bear would breach the minefields created by the Iraqis. At 1500 Task Force Shepherd would move through the U.S. breach lanes. The time line was not very specific beyond these general events.

When the lieutenant completed this orientation, we knew it was going to take two full days for marine forces to position themselves for the assault on the Iraqi minefields. We knew that on the twenty-second there would be an amphibious deception raid on an island in the Gulf, and we knew that on the twenty-third, artillery preparation of Iraqi positions would begin. Beyond that, we didn't know much.

Lieutenant Tice described the enemy situation. In our sector we would be facing three enemy armor divisions—the 29th, the 7th, and the 8th. All three were comprised of Iraqi regulars, but they were reported to have poor morale. Additionally these units had lost so many personnel during the air campaign that they were operating as skeleton crews at best. Two additional units, the 80th and the 5th, were expected to be farther to the north. Their exact locations were unknown. The lieutenant told us how the enemy was expected to react to our attack: they would use the oil fields as obstacles to our mobility and would counterattack by using the hard-surface road networks to heighten their own mobility. The terrain in our sector of Kuwait was low, rolling, sand hills that resulted in poor off-road maneuverability. The enemy was expected to use the roads because traveling on the rolling terrain was slow and cumbersome and because they were accustomed to using them as their primary avenues of movement. That was fine with me; I didn't want to use the roads anyway.

The initial threat to our forces was enemy artillery batteries firing standard munitions, chemical munitions, and scatterable mines. There was a slight possibility that we might encounter enemy helicopters. As Lieutenant Tice closed out his description of the enemy situation, he reminded us not to touch anything we found on the battlefield. He did not want us picking up things that might be booby-trapped by the Iraqis. This made perfect sense to me at the time, so perfect that I hadn't even considered the caution worthy of mention: we were professionals, and picking up things left on the battlefield was not one of the practices of our trade. Unfortunately Allied forces were to suffer casualties in this area.

Before the lieutenant outlined our mission, he relayed the division commander's intent: for us to move through the breach quickly. Additionally the commander wanted us to fight dirty: if chemical warfare were initiated by the Iraqis, we would don protective gear and fight in that contaminated environment. Our priority was to uncover the enemy artillery and destroy it. The division commander's basic plan of attack revolved around two basic points. One, the Iraqis were probably going to use chemicals. And two, this being the case, our first objective was to seize the al-Jaber airfield so that we could conduct chemical decontamination if it were required. The airfield had a water source that would make such an operation possible.

Task Force Shepherd was told to move well forward and screen for an enemy counterattack while the division moved combat forces through the breach and conducted decontamination operations at al-Jaber. This involved the battalion's moving forward quickly, once we were through the breach lanes.

The first phase of the plan required Task Force Shepherd to give up companies to reinforce the breach operation. Initially Alpha had been attached to Task Force Troy (this lasted until 22 February, although word of our attachment never got to me). Charlie Company was attached to Task Force Taro to screen while the task force moved to protect the division's left flank during the breach (Charlie Company returned when Taro completed its movement). Delta was parceled out to Task Force Ripper.

The second phase of the plan started with Shepherd's moving through the breach. Once we were clear of the breach, we were to seek out Iraqi artillery while we moved north into Kuwait to screen for enemy counterattacks. Our orders were to engage counterattacking forces before delaying them: because of the time and space involved in the operation, we did not have a lot of room to play with. We would not have the luxury of delaying an attacking enemy force by withdrawing and maintaining contact. Behind us was the center of gravity: the movement of forces through the Iraqi obstacle belts. There was no place for us to fall back.

Our company mission was issued to us as follows. One, move in a march column to Assembly Area Pacific. Two, move through the breach and destroy all enemy uncovered en route to the screen line. And three, screen from grid 8926 to grid 8198. We were tasked to provide early warning of an enemy counterattack and eliminate enemy forces encountered. We were given two fall-back positions to use if we had to withdraw. Both positions were within fifteen hundred meters of our initial screen, so that for us, falling back would be more like repositioning. We were directed by Lieutenant Tice to break contact when the enemy advanced to within two thousand meters. Given the fall-back positions, I didn't know if this distance would leave us enough space to maneuver, but with the activity going on behind us it didn't matter: maneuvering room was a luxury we did not have anyway.

Our platoon had been designated to lead the company march formation through the breach and on to the screen line. This was nothing new. Throughout the deployment 1st Platoon had been at the point of the company march formations. I don't think it had anything to do with ability so much as with the order in which the platoons were named—the point was 1st Platoon, the trail element was 2d Platoon.

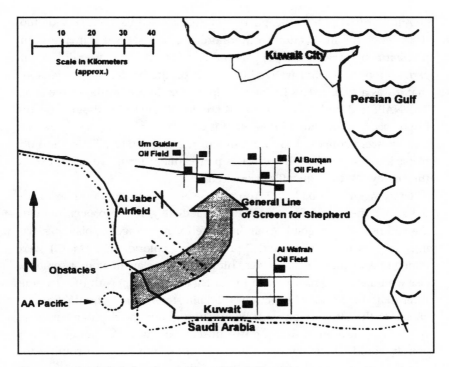

Figure 4. The initial plan for movement into Kuwait.

The order went on to direct that the uniform of the day for the war would be MOPP-2, which meant we would be wearing our chemical suits (tops and bottoms) and rubber boots. Our gas masks and rubber gloves would be at the ready, should the MOPP level increase. This particular part of the order was probably the most shocking element in it for me. I hated the prospect of having to fight a chemical war. I felt comfortable fighting against an enemy I could see, maneuver on, and fight back against. But I felt extremely uncomfortable fighting something I could neither see, nor avoid, nor combat. We did not have chemical alarms on our vehicles. Our only aid was chemical-detection paper—basically a roll of specially treated paper that was sticky on one side. We were ordered to put a strip of it around one wrist, the opposite bicep, and one ankle. Additionally we were to put a foot-long strip of the paper on each of the vehicle's four corners: if the paper came into contact with a chemical agent, it would change from brown to a scarlet color. I knew after the order that I, for one, would watch the tape.

Another part of the NBC plan—one that caused us some mixed emotions—was the medication we were ordered to take: NAPP (nerve-agent pretreatment, pyridostigmine) pills and an antibiotic. The latter didn't concern us too much after we read the labels on the bottles and understood that it was a standard antibiotic to help us if biological warfare were used. The NAPP did bother us because there wasn't anything about it on the bubblepack, so we didn't know what it was. The only thing we knew was that we were supposed to take three of the tiny white pills in the bubblepack every day and that it was a pretreatment for nerve-agent use by the enemy. We took the pills as ordered.

Nerve agents are bad stuff. You can die almost instantly from exposure to some of them, and if you don't die immediately, your prospects of living are still not all that good. As an antidote for nerve-agent poisoning, two injector sets of atropine and 2-pralidoxime chloride (2-PAM Cl) were issued to each marine. If you were hit with a nerve agent, you or someone else would stab the meaty part of your leg (or buttocks) with the atropine. After that, the 2-PAM Cl injector was administered to counter the harmful effects of the atropine on your body. Throughout the deployment, word was making it around that the two injector kits weren't enough to help you. It would take many times that amount of the drugs to counter the effects of nerve agents on your system. This was not good news.

Finally we were issued the signal plan for the war. The most important part of this plan was the green star-cluster flare, which was the abort-air signal. As ridiculous as it sounds, whenever I heard an aircraft, my hand wrapped around the slender tube of the pyrotechnic. I don't think that any of us had much confidence in the ability of friendly aircraft to distinguish friend from foe at the time.

The order culminated with a long list of checkpoints to be used in Kuwait, along with the challenge and the password for each day. When it was all over, we asked our questions and went back to our respective crews to reissue the order. By the end of the day each and every marine knew what was going to happen. We were ready to free Kuwait.

Far to the north, adjacent to OP 6, Charlie Company, 2d LAI, pulled back from the screening mission they had assumed from Alpha Company, 1st LAI, on 14 February. They were relieved by the U.S. Army's Tiger Brigade, and on 18 February they moved back to an assembly area deep inside Saudi Arabia. The order I received in Q-town did not mention what 2d LAI Battalion would be tasked with during those days before the ground war.

Captain Donnelley, the commanding officer, gave Charlie's leaders their orders: the company was to rest, relax, and get the vehicles ready to go; and on the morning of the twentieth, Alpha and Charlie Companies, 2d LAI, would move into Kuwait. Tiger Brigade was tasked with digging lanes in the berm that would allow 2d LAI Battalion to pour into the flat expanse of sand between Saudi Arabia and Kuwait.

The battalion would have the support of close-air and counter-battery artillery, which could quickly squelch any resistance the unit met.[1] Beyond the penetration into Kuwait, Sergeant Smith was unaware of the purpose behind the mission, but he looked forward to it with zeal. When I interviewed Smith, he recalled that it had been very important to him to apply his training and experience in this environment. I asked him if he had been uncomfortable with the mission—a light armored unit spearheading against reinforced hard points and Iraqi armor—and he replied that he had put full faith in the abilities of both Charlie and Alpha (2d LAI).

On the morning of the twentieth, before the sun rose over the desert, Charlie moved to the berm and prepared to move through Tiger Brigade. As the tension built within the crews of Charlie, Captain Donnelley came over the company radio net and told the marines that the mission had been delayed. It was an overcast morning with a very low ceiling of clouds, and the aircraft could not support the company's movement in those conditions.

The result of the delay was an increase in tension. Each marine had mentally prepared to cross into Kuwait that morning. With the morning's passing, everyone was given an additional amount of time to ponder the future. One marine on Sergeant Smith's crew requested to see a chaplain —apparently his fears had overcome his ability to produce the rational thought that would probably have calmed him. Every marine deals with the fear of death in a different manner. Some use humor; some use silence; some use solitude. The only common element is that each marine must indeed deal with that fear.

Unfortunately for that particular marine, a chaplain was not available to assist him. In the hours before sunrise on the twenty-first, he struggled to find reassurance from the marines around him. Sergeant Smith wasn't worried about the marine, however. He understood what the individual was going through and knew that when he was required to perform, he would do so.

Finally 21 February arrived. In the early morning Charlie Company mounted up and moved back to OP 6 to link up with Tiger Brigade. The mission had not been called off this time. Captain Donnelley gave the company words of encouragement. Over the company radio net, he passed these words: "Good luck, God be with you, and happy hunting." With that, the company moved out. Over every helmet and radio speaker in the company Wagner's "Ride of the Valkyries" blared. Captain Donnelley had chosen to motivate the company by broadcasting the powerful music as they crossed through into Kuwait. Sergeant Smith recalls that it had motivated him, striking him as a replay of scenes from *Apocalypse Now*. The salty force of marines was boldly advancing to contact with the enemy, finding strength and confidence in music.

Shortly after 0700 each platoon of Charlie Company—it was organized into three four-vehicle platoons—moved through a different lane in the berm. Once clear of the sand walls Captain Donnelley moved the company into a wedge formation, with 1st Platoon on line in the center. Sergeant Smith and 2d Platoon were in a left echelon on 1st Platoon's left flank, with 3d Platoon in a right echelon on 1st Platoon's right flank. The weapons variants (TOWs and mortars), the company trains, and the LAAD (low-altitude air defense) stinger team fell into the center of the wedge, protected on three sides by the advancing platoons.

Almost immediately after the company crossed the berm, they received an extensive barrage of artillery and mortar fire from the Iraqis. Sergeant Smith had expected it, and he knew counter-battery fire from Saudi Arabia would diligently respond to destroy the Iraqi indirect-fire positions. That didn't happen, though—for some reason the counter-battery fire did not act to combat the threat facing Charlie Company. Instead of being destroyed, the Iraqis continued to fire at the advancing Charlie Company.

The enemy's first hit was a mortar round that sailed over 1st Platoon and landed directly on top of the HMMWV carrying the LAAD team. The HMMWV, equipped with dual stinger pods straddling its bed, was immediately disabled. The mortar round landed on a crossbar directly behind the vehicle's cab and between the dual stinger pods. The shrapnel pierced the soft skin of the vehicle and damaged all the stinger missiles. The two marines in the cab were spared because they had their sleeping bags behind their heads. Through an incredible stroke of luck the shrapnel missed the soft skin of the marines.

Sergeant Shelly, commanding the LAV-R in the company trains, watched the marines pour out of the damaged vehicle. Referring to the stinger team as the "sagger team" for some reason, he radioed the company commander, "Sagger team! Sagger team has been hit!"

Captain Donnelley directed that the HMMWV be completely destroyed. In the middle of an artillery barrage the company had neither the time nor the inclination to attempt a recovery of the damaged vehicle. Sergeant Shelly picked up the two bewildered marines and proceeded to fire the 7.62-mm pintle-mounted machine gun of the LAV-R at the HMMWV. Soon it was burning, a billowing cloud of black smoke rising over it in the desert.

The company continued to move east, and the Iraqis continued throwing shells, at a rate of fifteen rounds per minute, at the marine formation. Charlie still had not received any support from the close-air or the counter-battery fire.

Aside from the one mortar round, Iraqi artillery was generally inaccurate that morning. Nonetheless, Sergeant Smith lowered his seat in the turret until he was standing with only his head outside the vehicle commander's hatch.

All of this action took place in the span of fifteen minutes. Finally Captain Donnelley directed the company to turn and move back to the protection of friendly lines. Without the support promised, the company was just asking for casualties.

When the company moved back through Tiger Brigade's positions at OP 6, everyone in the company was angry. *What the hell is going on? Where is our support?* Captain Donnelley and the commanding officer for Alpha Company drove off to talk to the battalion commander about the situation. When they returned, the support problem had been ironed out. Sergeant Smith recalls that they were directed to move across again in an hour.

Shortly after 1030 Charlie Company retraced its steps and moved back through the berm. Again the Iraqis started shelling the advancing formation with artillery and mortar fire. This time, though, the fire-direction center came up on the company radio net. "We've got a position on that one battery. Do you want us to fire it?" Captain Donnelley told them to fire. Because of the support he was about to move Charlie Company about five kilometers, where they reached the first Iraqi minefield belt.

The company moved from the wedge to a line formation and halted. Fifty meters ahead Sergeant Smith could see a mélange of concertina wire and exposed land mines. At that time Charlie received the rest of its promised support: F-18s and Cobra gunships started to hit targets overlooking the minefield. The coordination of the air strikes was done at the center of the company line by the 1st Platoon commander.

While the aircraft searched for and destroyed targets, the company saw enemy troop activity in a complicated network of trenches about five hundred meters in front of them. Adjacent to the trenches was a small brick building. The Iraqi troops were moving back and forth between the building and the trenches.

Sergeant Smith recalls that before he could discern what the activity was, a TOW missile was let loose by one of the attached ATs. The missile rapidly traversed the distance between the company and the building and exploded on contact with the building. When the smoke cleared, there was a huge gaping hole in the center of the structure. Iraqi troop activity at the site ceased.

The Iraqis were still active in the trenches, however, and the company fired the coax machine guns and 25-mm HE at the enemy troops in an effort to suppress them. The fire was very effective; enemy were falling at a rapid rate.

Iraqi armor supported the minefield from dug-in positions behind the trench network. Sergeant Smith recalls that the tanks were difficult to detect: they were deeply entrenched and expertly camouflaged. As each tank was discovered, the LAV-25 crews marked the position of the target with 25-mm HE, and the TOW gunners quickly launched a missile at the marked target to expedite the destruction.

As this was going on, Sergeant Smith spotted what he believed to be a command and control bunker. At about fifteen hundred meters out, his gunner spotted a high concentration of antennae protruding out of a reinforced position. Smith issued the fire command, and his gunner started shooting at the target. A small secondary explosion occurred, and Smith saw what looked like plywood flying through the air. Simultaneously an F-18 picked up the target, rolled in, dropped a bomb, and destroyed the target in a volatile fireball.

Shortly thereafter an Iraqi BTR-60 (a wheeled armored personnel carrier) pulled up to the destroyed command bunker. Seeing the vehicle approach, Smith directed his gunner to fire 25-mm AP at the exposed vehicle. The AP rounds found the target, and the BTR immediately started to produce black smoke that was soon followed by fire.

The volume of enemy artillery fire had slacked off due to the efforts of the counter-battery artillery, but the company was still receiving sporadic—and generally inaccurate—fire from the Iraqi artillery.

Alpha Company was to Charlie's right flank and had been pinched into their area—they needed more room. Sergeant Smith, in the far left vehicle of the Charlie Company formation, was directed to shift about a kilometer north. When Smith moved, he saw a large finger of sand extending perpendicular to his northward movement. The finger blocked his view of the terrain on the opposite side, and as he maneuvered around the terrain, his wingman covered him. Soon it became apparent that the only way Smith could safely get to the other side of the terrain was to blast around it. Moving slowly would only give the enemy an easy-to-hit flank shot at his LAV.

When he blasted behind and cleared the terrain, Smith immediately acquired Iraqi troops five hundred meters to his right flank, firing rifles and machine guns at him. His adrenaline was up, and instinctively he pulled in, offering the Iraqis a smaller frontal view of his vehicle, and started firing. Eliminating the troops as a threat, he received no more fire, scanned the area for potential danger, and called in that he was set.

The company maneuvered around behind him and fell in on Smith's left flank. He was now the extreme right flank of the long line of Charlie Company. And he stayed in that position until he was wounded.

When the company completed the movement, the 1st Platoon commander continued to call in air strikes on Iraqi targets. Captain Donnelley looked at the land mines in front of him and decided to fire at them to see if they would explode. His gunner fired 25-mm HE at the mines, and sure enough they exploded. Donnelley started to try to clear a lane in the minefield in case Charlie was later directed to pursue withdrawing enemy forces.

Just before dark the situation had begun to settle down. Enemy artillery was still sporadic and inaccurate. But the combination of Charlie's boldness and the application of supporting arms had created a relatively stable situation. Charlie Company sat awaiting darkness.

When the sun set, the only illumination provided to the marines of Charlie Company was the burning oil wells to the front. The light was only bright enough for the marines to be able to see the obstacle belt in front of them. Other than that, the marines were forced to use the thermal and passive sights in an attempt to detect any signs of an Iraqi assault.

The company gunnery sergeant took advantage of the impending darkness to resupply the company with ammunition. He drove his LAV-L behind the platoons and stopped at each position. "What do you need?" The marines had been shooting all day long at awkward intervals and needed to replenish their ammunition stocks. When the crews answered him, he simply kicked the requested ammunition out of the back of his vehicle and drove on to repeat the process at the next vehicle. Sergeant Smith's crew had fired almost four hundred rounds of 25-mm during the course of that afternoon.

That night Iraqi activity in front of Charlie heightened. Through the thermals Sergeant Smith could see large formations of Iraqi troops gathering in the desert. Vehicles were moving about, and it appeared as if the Iraqis were being resupplied. The 1st Platoon commander saw the formations as well and directed artillery strikes against the concentration of troops.

As a rule, at night the company refrained from using their direct-fire weapons. The resulting muzzle flashes would surely give their vehicle positions away. Using artillery was the safest way to engage targets at night, but it wasn't very quick. Critical targets still had to be destroyed by direct fire.

On the company's left flank two trucks had joined the troops and appeared to be off-loading supplies. Corporal Darnay picked up the targets—perfect flank shots—and relayed his findings to his vehicle commander. Using artillery was possible, unless the trucks started to move away. The vehicle commander told Darnay to keep an eye on them and stand by. If the trucks so much as looked as though they were going to move, Darnay was directed to destroy them.

As his vehicle commander was making his report over the radio, Darnay saw the wheels of one of the trucks start to turn. He pulled the trigger and poured an incredible amount of accurate 25-mm HE fire onto the trucks. Sergeant Smith recalls that all four of 1st Platoon's vehicles actually fired at the trucks, which exploded hellishly and started to burn within a few seconds. Those trucks, which burned for the entire evening, provided additional illumination for Charlie Company.

The situation calmed as the night dragged on. Sergeant Smith was standing in his turret hatch looking out to the front, occasionally with his eyes and occasionally with his thermal sight. He plugged his Walkman into the vehicle intercom system and listened to music through his CVC helmet—a very calming entertainment for Smith and the crew of 666.

At 2300 the sporadic and inaccurate Iraqi artillery suddenly became very accurate. An artillery round cracked through the air and landed directly in front of Smith's vehicle. As the LAV rocked back and forth on its heavy suspension, Smith could hear the metallic *tink* of shrapnel as it rained against the front of the vehicle.

Sergeant Smith thought *What the hell?* and keyed his helmet. "Back this damned thing up!" His driver responded, and 666 backed up between fifty and seventy-five meters. When the vehicle came to a stop—removed from the initial rounds' impact area—Smith heard an ominous crackle in the air. It was not a whistle or a rushing noise, just a faint crackle. Suddenly two or three rounds landed immediately to Smith's right flank. The crushing power of the explosion rocked the vehicle violently and jerked the sergeant to his left. Feeling his right shoulder dislocate, Smith grasped the arm with his left hand and applied pressure until the joint fell back into its socket.

Sergeant Smith remained standing in the turret, the pain from the dislocation gone. The artillery round had shredded two of the eight tires on the right side of the vehicle, destroyed the two field packs hanging on the right side, disintegrated the vehicle antennae above Sergeant Smith's head, pierced the thin skin of the vehicle muffler, punched holes through the POL cans positioned in the bustle rack, and embedded shrapnel in the back of Smith's open turret hatch.

The shrapnel had also penetrated the bodies of Sergeant Smith and one of the scouts in the back of the vehicle. After two or three minutes of standing in the turret holding his right arm, Smith felt a sudden warmness in the hand that cradled his right elbow. Because he was wearing leather gloves, he was unsure about what he was feeling. Sitting down in the turret next to his gunner, he turned on the dome light behind his head. He looked at his left hand and saw that the gloved hand was covered in blood. He looked at his arm and saw the crimson fluid spraying out and onto the vehicle interior. Turning to his gunner, Sergeant Smith said, "Vega, I've been hit."

Vega looked at his vehicle commander in disbelief: "Bullshit! You have not!" When Smith turned so that Vega could see the blood pouring from his upper arm, the gunner exclaimed, "Oh, God!"

The shrapnel, which had penetrated Smith's right arm just above the elbow and traveled completely through the bicep on the opposite side of the arm, had come to a rest just beneath the skin on the inside of the arm. Yet Smith felt no pain or burning sensation at the time. Telling his crew to unkey their helmets, he called in to the platoon commander: "Fat Chick, Fat Chick, this is Juggernaut. I've been hit, over." After he made that call, Smith's vision narrowed and then dimmed. Sitting in the vehicle commander's seat, he blacked out.

In the back of the vehicle, when the artillery rounds had hit, one of the scouts had been reaching up and out of the open troop hatches to grab his canteen. The shrapnel had flown past him, ripped the left ear of his CVC helmet, and planted a jagged piece of metal in the skin between his thumb and forefinger.

Sergeant Smith had a medical corpsman in the back of the vehicle who attempted to give both of the marines first aid while they awaited medevac. Smith was unconscious when 666 left the line to link up with the company trains. When they pulled him out of the turret to put him on a stretcher at the company gunny's location, he regained consciousness and attempted to assist them.

After the marines dropped off Sergeant Smith, the platoon commander restructured the crew in order to replace Smith and the wounded scout. Once the replacements had been made, the crew was directed to go back onto the line, but the men were told they wouldn't occupy the same position they had before—the enemy obviously had that position registered as a target. However, when the vehicle came to a stop, Vega—the new vehicle commander—noticed that they had, in fact, pulled directly back onto their previous position.

Sergeant Smith was transported in the back of the LAV-L to the battalion aid station located at the same culvert (behind OP 6) that the reconnaissance marines had occupied as their command post during the air war. The corpsman with Sergeant Smith kept asking him if he wanted any morphine for the pain. He refused the offer—he still wasn't feeling any pain.

It wasn't until he was on the operating table in the battalion aid station that Smith felt any pain. As the surgeon cut away his clothing and started to irrigate his wounds, the sergeant immediately felt a strong burning sensation and requested the morphine. After the drug had been administered, he relaxed. A medevac flight was called in to take Sergeant Smith away: they couldn't do any more for him at the battalion aid station. When he had been put aboard the helicopter and was being flown away from his company, the last thing Sergeant Smith saw was the burning oil fields to the east.

12

SERGEANT RAMIREZ had given up his attempt to move to a line company—he had finally realized that transfer was a thing that was not going to happen. He approached the colonel a final time and said, "Sir, if you won't let me go to Alpha, how about giving me a permanent vehicle?"

The colonel replied, "Well, I need a platoon commander for these eight 25s." And the deal was struck. Just before the ground war kicked off, Ramirez was assigned as platoon commander for the eight LAV-25s that made up Security Platoon. It wasn't a line company, but he was at least aboard an LAV-25 and in addition had responsibility for the security of the Alpha and Bravo Command Groups of Task Force Shepherd.[1]

While Sergeant Smith was being treated for his wounds, Alpha Company, 1st LAI, was preparing to drive into Kuwait. We had absolutely no idea that 2d LAI Battalion had started the ground war with their daring push from OP 6. We knew only that the clock was ticking down and soon we would be riding across the border separating Saudi Arabia from Kuwait. On the other side of that border was the brass ring: freedom for Kuwait.

On 23 February, Alpha Company was in Assembly Area Pacific just west of the southern elbow, waiting for the ground war to begin. In the darkness of night we donned our NBC suits—for only the second time—and placed the chemically treated tape on our bodies and vehicles. It was very hard to sleep that night. The commonsense thing to do would be to get some rest, but anticipation of what would happen in the morning overrode both common sense and the natural desire to sleep.

Early on the morning of the twenty-fourth we got the word to move out. It was still dark when the company formed a long column —1st Platoon leading, followed by the headquarters element and then 2d Platoon —and drove through the freshly dug gaps in the sandy berm. When the light shone over the desert that morning, Task Force Shepherd had already assumed a large coil in an attack position seven kilometers into Kuwait. After six months of waiting we were in the country of Kuwait. It is hard to describe the emotions of the time.

We waited in that attack position for more than six hours, so our arrival in Kuwait was anticlimactic in a sense. After all the waiting it would have been so much more fitting to drive hard across the open desert and not stop until we had reached Kuwait City. But we couldn't do that. Ahead of us, combat engineers worked at a feverish pace to create lanes that would allow marine combat power, including Task Force Shepherd, to pass through the deliberate belts of Iraqi obstacles.

The combat engineers encountered far less resistance as they worked than had been expected, but they had to deal with a totally unexpected logistical strain: by midday, when the lanes were finally open, the onslaught of surrendering Iraqis completely taxed the system designed to handle them. The marines had been prepared to conduct a deliberate breach against a belligerent enemy. But instead the opposition was slight, and the enemy was willingly walking toward our lines, waving the white flags of submission. Thousands of Iraqi soldiers surrendered, creating a steady, moving roadblock of traffic to the south.

Alpha left the attack position just before midday and made an uneventful trip through the obstacle belt. Any battle that had to be fought at the minefield had already been fought by someone else. I remember as we drove forward thinking how incredibly lucky we were. Astride the snakelike lanes created by the engineers with line charges and mine plows were Iraqi weapons of destruction. We passed scores of unmanned weapons systems—recoilless rifles, dug-in tanks, and bunkers—aimed menacingly toward our formations of men and equipment. Any one of the weapons alone could have turned our column into Swiss cheese. I felt very fortunate that these weapons were not manned when we passed through the obstacle belt.

Since there were only a limited number of lanes through the minefield (the engineers could make only a few of them without slowing the momentum of the attack), and the Iraqis were moving south as fast as we were moving north, our column of vehicles was moving about as fast as rush-hour traffic on Interstate 5 in southern California. As we inched forward, I watched the show to the front. Black, ominous clouds were on the horizon, and I could see Cobra gunships weaving back and forth as they fired their munitions on targets I could not see. These dancelike maneuvers continued as our column pursued its slow progress.

Suddenly to my left, a marine HMMWV appeared over a rise. I could tell the driver was pushing the vehicle to the limits because it was barely keeping its four wheels on the sand. As it approached I saw that both the driver and the passenger were in MOPP 4—that is, they had donned their gas masks and protective rubber gloves. The vehicle swung by our column with the occupants waving vigorously, giving the hand and arm signals for chemical danger.

I didn't reach for my gas mask. A couple of things were on my mind. First, I couldn't understand why our column was stalled in the engineers' lane while the HMMWV rode across the open desert next to us with impunity. Second, the weather was extremely clear where we were, and there were no indications that any chemicals had been used against us. I radioed in a report and was told not to worry.

Almost immediately after the HMMWV left, the traffic in our lane opened up. Somewhere up ahead the cause of the jam had been remedied. We moved out to catch up to the vehicles in front of us. Sergeant Negron's section was in front, leading the platoon, and Sergeant Worth was behind him. I was behind Worth when I saw a huge cloud of black smoke emanate from his muffler. He pulled to the side and stopped—his vehicle had broken down. As I passed, I saw him standing in the turret, giving us a dejected stare. I really felt sorry for him. All the waiting we had done, and he ended up breaking down when we were driving to complete the task.

Although 1st Platoon was scheduled to lead the company's advance, the loss of Worth's vehicle caused Captain Shupp to order 2d Platoon—still at full strength—to assume the lead. That hurt. There was a certain pride involved in leading the company's movement. If there was a little bit of a leader in all of us, and I think there was, we all wanted to be at the focus of the effort. Good leaders instinctively go to where the action is. From that point they can make the hard decisions required to win the battles. It was very difficult to relinquish our position at the tip of Alpha's spear to 2d Platoon, but reluctantly we did.

We finally cleared the minefield, and Captain Shupp ordered the company to continue movement to the northeast. We assumed a staggered column formation—1st Platoon on the left, 2d Platoon on the right—and moved out. There was about a hundred-meter dispersion between the vehicles and about a hundred-meter distance between the two platoon columns.

There still wasn't much going on. We passed intricate Iraqi trenchwork that had been abandoned during the surrender, but we had yet to face any hostile action. As we moved, one of my scouts yelled at me from his open troop hatch. When he finally got my attention, I turned in my hatch to answer him.

"Sergeant Michaels," he yelled over the noise of the engine, "They're shooting at us!"

I didn't understand what he was saying. "What?"

He pointed and looked nervously to the right. "They are shooting at us!"

I looked to the right and saw what he was talking about: a very large tracer round came directly down the center of the company, evenly bisecting the two platoon columns. The round's axis was exactly parallel to the company's axis of movement. The first tracer round was quickly followed by a second one that repeated the same flight path. The round seemed so incredibly slow. I followed its path easily and watched it until the tracer burned out, about two hundred meters behind me. I didn't know where it had come from, but I could tell it was a very big round. I assumed it had been fired from a vehicle main gun or cannon near the head of the column.

I looked to the front of the column and saw only black smoke on the horizon. The way we were configured, there was nothing I could do. We were in a column, so I couldn't shoot forward and I couldn't see the enemy that fired the rounds. I shrugged my shoulders and forgot about it; there was nothing I could do.

Just before we reached the black clouds, we intersected what was called Axis Stuart and turned directly north. This path would lead us directly in between the Umm Guidar and al-Burqan oil fields. Exactly as planned, we were moving north to screen for the forces behind us. We passed a significant number of friendly forces, and Captain Shupp guided us quickly past them and on to our mission.

As soon as we turned north, I saw red gaseous clouds venting out of the ground near an exposed pipeline to our right. We had been told about these clouds. H_2S is the name we were given—hydrogen sulfide. We had been told that if you breathed this gas, you died. That was all I needed to know. I reported the contact and made sure I kept well clear of that area.

It was at this point that Alpha first encountered in Kuwait surrendering Iraqis. As we moved in company column, we passed thousands of them marching south, carrying white flags. We had been directed to stop and assume control of all surrendering Iraqis who had not yet been gathered by friendly forces, but it was immediately apparent that this was an impossible task. The sheer numbers boggled the mind.

We passed formation after formation of these soldiers, and it was always the same: they looked at you, hands up, faces smiling, and you pointed to the south. I think they were disappointed that no one was taking charge of them, but they responded to our gestures and kept heading south. At the next vehicle they passed, the same thing would happen, and the prisoners continued their trek to freedom.

Once clear of the EPWs we dashed along Axis Stuart in order to reach our initial objective ten kilometers to the north. About halfway through the movement we entered what can only be described as hell. The Iraqis had set fire to each and every oil cap in the al-Burqan oil field. The ominous clouds I had seen to the front were the result of hundreds of exposed well caps burning out of control. We met those clouds and drove into them without hesitation.

Immediately the ceiling of clouds lowered to only ten or twenty feet above our heads. In traveling fifty meters we had gone from having four kilometers of visibility to having ten feet. Until that moment the most impressive display of nature I had ever seen in the sky was the devil-like clouds and ashfall created by the Mount St. Helens eruption. That memory was quickly replaced by this unnatural environment that the Iraqis had created in the al-Burqan oil field.

The darkness enveloped us like an ink-black shroud, covering every part of our being. Then it started to rain—not the usual wet drops of precipitation but thick, soupy drops of crude oil. Our equipment and bodies were exposed to a relentless onslaught of the hazardous substance as it dropped from the oil-saturated clouds above our heads.

Captain Shupp directed that we change from the column into a line formation. I donned my NVGs and found that I could barely see the ghostlike silhouettes of vehicles to my right. I couldn't see very far, but it was far enough for me to know that I was where I was supposed to be: my section was traveling as the leftmost unit of the company.

Captain Shupp didn't slow us down much when we entered the darkness. He simply moved and expected us to move with him. To him, changing our system because of the darkness would demonstrate a lack of intestinal fortitude—that would not happen in Alpha Company.

I think this was the first time in Kuwait that our navigation training paid off. It was pointless to try to track your position on a map in the darkness, but the confidence we had gained from hundreds of hours of night movement allowed us to remain cohesive as a unit. I knew the azimuth we were moving, and I knew to keep abreast of the section next to me. So while the darkness presented control problems, Captain Shupp and Lieutenant Tice had prepared us to handle such matters.

About ten minutes into the movement I picked up a bright red hot spot in my thermal viewer. Directly in front of my moving vehicle, at about eight hundred meters, I spotted what looked like a dug-in vehicle. I gave my gunner a fire command, but he was unable to pick up the target in his passive sight—a sight that with the dim light of stars was effective to almost eight hundred meters was now completely blinded by the light-sucking darkness.

I reported the contact and attempted to guide the gunner on target using the thermal sight. Uke blindly fired an HE round that landed within a hundred mils of the target. For a split second he was able to see the target outlined by the light emitted from the exploding round. The target disappeared from the reticle again, but Uke had the presence of mind to memorize where it had been within his eyepiece, and he made the proper adjustments with his hand control. Still unable to acquire the target, Uke fired blindly again, quickly applying a deadly three-round burst. Through the thermal sight I watched as the HE hit the target and sent hunks of metal flying through the air. Satisfied that he had destroyed the target, I told him to cease his fire.

When I reported the target destroyed, Lieutenant Tice wanted to know what it was. I was still about five hundred meters away from it and had to wait until we drew closer—the target stood directly in my path of advancement—to determine its exact nature. When I finally passed the target, I saw it was a pickup truck that had been half-buried in the sand. Protective earthworks had been piled around the target, and I immediately recognized it as an improvised bunker. We didn't stop to see if there was anyone inside it.

We moved for about fifteen minutes more under the clouds when the captain came over the radio asking 2d Platoon to find a gap in a pipeline to our front. I looked out through the thermal and saw what he was talking about: not five hundred meters to our direct front an exposed oil pipeline bisected our axis, halting our movement. There was no way the vehicles would be able to traverse the pipeline; it stood about four feet above the ground. Breaching the pipeline and creating a gap would surely result in an oil conflagration that would prevent us from passing through any hole that we made. We would have to go around.

It is ironic that this pipeline proved to be as effective an obstacle to our movement as any minefield. The Iraqis took great care in deliberately creating obstacles for us. But here, directly in front of us, was a completely natural aspect of the land—an oil-rich land, that is—with the potential to stop us cold.

While 2d Platoon went searching for a gap in the pipeline, I figured I would look, too. I hadn't been told to do it, but since we were waiting, I thought it best to search out a gap that would allow the company to keep moving. I moved slightly to my left, parallel to the pipeline. I didn't have to say anything to Matlain off to my left—he guided his movement off of my movement, just as I guided my movement off the vehicle to my right. I looked to the left and saw the shadow of his vehicle supporting my movement.

Amazingly I had traveled only about a hundred meters when I saw a spot where the pipeline dove underneath the ground for fifty meters before reemerging. I called in my findings, but Lieutenant Tice was not too interested in my report. I couldn't understand why, but he simply replied that 2d Platoon was looking for a gap to the right. I don't know why the lieutenant wasn't interested in moving the company through this gap; at this point I was still learning about the depth of his character. He had pushed us and trained us so well during Desert Shield, developing us into adept thinkers, but he still made decisions that I did not understand. Maybe the captain specifically wanted to move to the right around this pipeline. I didn't get that idea from his radio traffic, but it is possible that Lieutenant Tice did assume exactly that. At the time, though, I cataloged this decision with the one not to check the buildings at OP 4. We were vulnerable standing still, waiting to find a gap in the pipe. The gap that I had found out of luck would have enhanced our mobility: it was an easy call as far as I was concerned.

I radioed the lieutenant and told him I wanted to take my section through the gap to overwatch for the company as they searched for another gap. I was already moving toward the gap at the time, and he gave approval. In the end another gap was found to the right. About half of the company moved through the gap that I was overwatching from, and half moved through the gap that 2d Platoon had found. The company was advancing again.

When Charlie Company met Axis Stuart, the company was traveling in a staggered column, as Alpha had done. Captain Sellers had planned to move the company into a line formation from the base of Stuart north to the assigned screen line. The pipes of al-Burqan nixed that plan, though. Charlie Company was restricted to continuing in its company march column.

Sergeant Hernandez was the point vehicle for Charlie Company's column on the march into Kuwait. When he saw the black clouds of al-Burqan looming above the company, he felt that as the company moved, they were being sucked little by little into the hellish darkness before them.

The day turned to night, and Hernandez hadn't led Charlie Company very far into al-Burqan before he had his first encounter with Iraqi forces in Kuwait. In a classic meeting engagement, with the target-acquisition problem being compounded by the zero visibility of al-Burqan, Sergeant Hernandez saw two weapons carrying utility vehicles suddenly emerge 150 meters to his front on the black dirt trail. He was surprised, but fortunately the weapons carriers didn't see him until it was too late.

"Oh, shit!" Hernandez screamed through the vehicle intercom. "There's a truck. Right there," he slewed the turret on target, "Fire!"

The gunner rapidly brought the turret to bear on the advancing vehicles, switched to the coax machine gun on his hand control, and fired a long burst of bright tracers at the lead vehicle. Hernandez grabbed the spades of the pintle-mounted machine gun, aimed at the second truck, and fired a continuous laser of tracers at the moving vehicle.

He kept firing and firing, but the truck kept moving toward him. Hernandez couldn't believe the vehicle hadn't erupted into flames. He focused his attention on making a concentrated effort to hit the moving target and continued firing. The truck kept coming, and Hernandez kept firing. Finally the truck came to a slow halt right next to his vehicle.

When the truck stopped, Sergeant Hernandez noticed tracers lighting up the dark sky like dancing fireflies above his head. He turned in his hatch and discovered that the entire company, still in a column, was firing at the targets in front of him. Ducking down in his hatch, he keyed his helmet to the company radio net: "Cease fire! Cease fire! I'm up here! Cease fire!"

The next day when Hernandez was retrieving a meal from the MRE box behind his hatch, he found two small, blackened 7.62-mm bullet holes in the center of the box. During the company firefight his vehicle had been hit at least twice—in the cardboard box that was directly behind his turret hatch—by friendly machine guns.

After the encounter with the trucks Charlie Company continued into al-Burqan on the way to the screen line. It wasn't too long after the initial engagement with the trucks that Sergeant Hernandez acquired some hot spots to his front with the thermal sight. He stopped his vehicle and tried to determine the source of the target signatures. About five hundred meters away from him to the north, he saw a number of Iraqi troops moving back and forth along a deliberate series of trenchworks.

Hernandez reported the contact up the chain of command and recommended this course of action: one, bring the company up on line adjacent to his position; two, suppress the enemy position with the LAV-25s; and three, send out the scouts to sweep through the earthworks to clear the threat. His course of action was accepted in full by the company commander, and Charlie Company moved rapidly to a position to support the movement of the dismounted element.

Under the darkness of the oil-coated skies, the LAV-25s of Charlie Company reached out five hundred meters and raked the entire width of the Iraqi trenches with 7.62-mm and 25-mm fire. The scouts swiftly traversed the distance between the company and the trenches along the Iraqi flank. When they hopped into the enemy trenches, there were brief skirmishes and rifle fire between the Iraqis and the Charlie scouts, and then it was over: Charlie Company had moved too fast for the Iraqis to mount much of a defense against the two-pronged attack. The scouts captured three 30-mm antiaircraft weapons and over two hundred Iraqi prisoners from the trenches. The price in Charlie Company casualties was zero.

What worried Sergeant Hernandez about the engagement was the antiaircraft guns. Each and every one of the weapons captured was loaded and pointing parallel to the deck toward Charlie Company's positions. Hernandez was very thankful he had noticed the trench system with his thermal sight before the Iraqis were able to acquire him in the darkness with their naked eyes.

I don't know the exact time Alpha Company ceased movement that first day; I didn't have the sun for a reference. I believe it was just after sunset when we pulled into our screen positions. Alpha and Charlie were on line and screening to the north on the north end of the al-Burqan oil field. Bravo was trailing behind us in reserve.

Marine forces had moved a lot faster than anticipated and had enjoyed success not imagined by the planners of the ground war. Behind us, additional marine forces struggled to pour through the breach lanes to keep up with the rapid tempo of the war. There were numerous, sporadic firefights with the Iraqis behind us. As I look back, I see again how truly fortunate Task Force Shepherd was. We moved so quickly that we didn't give any of the belligerents the time to react to our movement. By the time any of the hostile Iraqis could react, we were gone and moving north. The end result was that the forces behind us were forced to ferret out the now-awakened pockets of resistance while we waited in screen positions to the north.

Sergeant Ramirez, who followed the line companies all day, recalls that the situation was, for the most part, uneventful for him. He had assigned four LAV-25s to guard the Bravo Command Group and the remaining four 25s, including his own vehicle, to guard the Alpha Command Group. Ramirez didn't move as fast as Alpha and Charlie had. Because of this fact he was more exposed to the onslaught of surrendering Iraqis than we were. However, the command group was not equipped to handle the EPWs. We in Alpha simply pointed to our rear and kept moving. We didn't give the EPWs a chance even to get close to us.

While setting security for the Alpha Command Group, Ramirez was stationary a good portion of the time and didn't have the luxury of pointing south and moving on. He knew that the Iraqi soldiers were not belligerent and intended to surrender, so he didn't even visit the idea of engaging the advancing hoards. Because of that, the soldiers were able to walk up to his position and hover around like vultures—a situation that was very distracting and made Sergeant Ramirez very uneasy. He had a job to do, and these soldiers presented the threat, albeit a small one, of disrupting the activities of the command group.

Finally Ramirez took action. He grabbed his pintle-mounted machine gun, pointed it at the gathering Iraqis seeking capture, and said, "Get the fuck away!" He accompanied this command with a hand gesture that would lead the Iraqis around their positions and to the south. The surrendering soldiers saw his hands on the spades of his pintle-mounted machine gun, heard his harsh tone, and understood completely what he wanted: they left. The sergeant wasn't sure if it was his machine gun or the harsh tone of his voice, but he didn't have any problems with the Iraqis after that.

When we settled in a screen that evening, Sergeant Ramirez recalls, Task Force Shepherd was basically separated from the friendly forces behind us. We had moved so fast that the pockets of resistance behind us had collapsed inward and put us in an awkward position. Any withdrawal we might have to make would be conducted through these Iraqi pockets, and any forced advance by friendlies behind us would send friendly munitions in our direction. There wasn't much we could do about the situation, so we were ordered to stay put and continue our screening mission.

Alpha was set into the screen line by the company commander. We had been directed to assume positions that overlooked a huge depression in the sand. When I pulled into position, I had two LAV-ATs fifty meters to my right and my wingman fifty meters to my left. Behind us, a hundred meters away, the company CP and trains had gathered in a makeshift coil. The mortars were positioned behind the lines near the CP, and we set up a continuous watch for an Iraqi counterattack.

In 1st Platoon one vehicle commander per section was required to be up and alert. This was Lieutenant Tice's call, and it made a whole lot of sense—it was extremely tiring, but it did make sense. If we encountered enemy action, there would have to be a vehicle commander awake to make the hard decisions required: when and what to report, when to call indirect fire, how to employ the attached ATs, and how to respond to the platoon commander's orders. While the gunners probably could have done this, Lieutenant Tice didn't want to make any stupid mistakes, so he ordered that a vehicle commander from each section be on the radio net at all times.

I decided to post myself in the turret for the duration of the evening. When I was not required to be awake, I would nestle down in my seat, attempting to doze off. But I kept my CVC helmet on so that I could hear any incoming radio traffic. Two other marines watched the terrain to the front while I was down in the turret. One of the things I noticed was that whenever I was up, Lieutenant Tice was up. And whenever I was down and heard the radio, he was up. I think he was determined to remain awake for the duration of the war.

In Desert Shield whenever I was out doing section training, I could always count on Lieutenant Tice's being up until we returned, and I admired this. He didn't micromanage my section, so I took it as a deep concern for the training. His people were up; therefore, he was up. This was one of his qualities I had respected. Now that we were in Kuwait, I had reservations about it, however. He still lived by the same rule, but I felt that we needed a platoon commander who was alert enough at all times to make hard decisions.

The next morning I walked to Lieutenant Tice's vehicle and asked him if he had been up all night. He stared down to me blankly from his turret hatch. He didn't respond; he simply shrugged his shoulders. I remember trying to talk to him about getting some rest—I could see in his eyes that he sorely needed it. The only response I received was a change in the subject. I cataloged the experience for future reference and moved on.

During my first watch on the evening of the twenty-fourth I saw something when I looked out from the rim of the depression in front of me. On the opposite rim I could clearly make out in the thermal sight Iraqi troops moving back and forth among their bunkers. I reported my initial contact and watched further to try to figure out what they were doing. Some Iraqis gathered in two- or three-man groups and sat around in the sand. Other Iraqis moved into bunkers and then shortly left, carrying something. As I watched, some of them talked while others were gathering objects from the bunkers.

The objects were large and square in nature. They didn't look like crates of supplies—the Iraqis were carrying them with one hand as if they had a handle. To me they appeared to be either suitcases or portable Sagger-missile kits. I think that if I had seen the soldiers putting things into the square objects, I would have opted for the suitcases. However, since the Iraqis were moving these objects to different points along their positions, I had to think they were positioning weapons—Sagger missiles.

I called Lieutenant Tice and wanted to engage the targets. We were only eight hundred meters away from them, and I felt it would be better to be safe than sorry. But the lieutenant didn't want to expose our positions by using direct fire—good call—and asked the captain to request indirect fire from our attached mortars.

Captain Shupp approved the mission but did something that I couldn't believe: he called the TOW section leader and asked him if he could see the Iraqis in question. After a few minutes the TOW section leader replied that he could in fact see them. The captain gave control of the mortars to the TOWs. I didn't understand why he had assigned the mission to them, but I believe it had something to do with the fact that they had been our eyes for so long that Captain Shupp figured they could see better with the thermals than we could.

The TOW section leader got on the radio to the mortars and gave a polar-fire mission.[2] The mortars knew his position, so the section leader simply gave the marines the direction and distance to the target. I listened intently on the company net until I heard the distance. The targets were only eight hundred meters out, and the distance given to the mortars was well over two kilometers.

I keyed my helmet on the platoon radio net. "Blue 1, Blue 5, that distance is way off. They are only about a click out, over."

Lieutenant Tice answered me immediately. "Roger, I know." And that was it. I expected him to call the captain or the mortars and correct the distance, but he didn't. I heard the mortar tubes expel their munitions behind me and watched in frustration for an impact. I didn't see anything, and neither did the forward observer. After about three rounds being fired like this and no one saw the impact, I finally saw the sparks from the explosion way out in the distance. The forward observer gave an adjustment, and the mortars fired for effect. The rounds were impacting more than two kilometers away, and as I watched the huddled Iraqis, they did not even flinch.

Then the forward observer called end of mission, target destroyed. I had no idea what he was talking about, but the threat to our front was still there, and the enemy were totally ignorant of the fact that we had fired at them. When I called Lieutenant Tice, he acknowledged the mission had been off, but he left it at that. Very frustrated, I spent the rest of the evening keeping a careful eye on the Iraqis to our front.

Midway through the evening, on the right flank, Captain Shupp ordered 2d Platoon to conduct a mounted security patrol to its front, which was open ground—the platoon was not sitting on the depression. The section responsible for the patrol, Sergeants Long and Davis (the latter the section leader), came up on the company net to report as they moved.

For thirty minutes I eavesdropped on the company net. I could tell that Sergeant Davis was very nervous. From the moment he stepped off, he was on the company net almost constantly. I could hear the reservation in his voice as he told the captain over and over again that he could not see anything. He had been tasked to go off by himself into Iraqi country and find out if there were any resistance in front of us. It was not a very rousing task for him, and you could tell he was worried as he kept transmitting on the company net. Finally the captain told him to come back. You could hear the huge weight lift off Davis's shoulders when he responded to the captain's transmission. He was very happy to come back to the comfort of friendly lines.

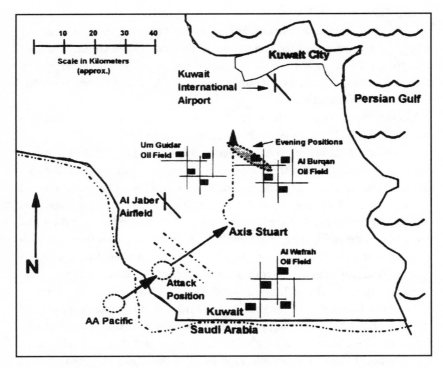

Figure 5. Task Force Shepherd's movement on 24 February.

When the morning of 25 February arrived, we were given a very welcome sight: the sun peeked through the gloomy overcast. We had exited the ominous darkness of al-Burqan and could again see out to the horizon. The ceiling of clouds was still very low, but the cloud cover was high enough that the light from the sun penetrated it down to where we were.

The first thing to happen was that the TOW vehicle next to me started to acquire dug-in tanks on the horizon. For the next hour I watched while the TOW vehicles fired missile after missile at exposed tank turrets more than three kilometers away. Each accurate missile was punctuated with a dramatic explosion and a showery display of fireworks. Each failure was apparent as the missiles simply flashed into the ground without any flare.

I was able to see the troops to my front very clearly that morning, and it was obvious they were not intent upon surrendering. In the first chapter of this book I describe the events that followed. Lieutenant Tice had given permission to eliminate the threat, and I had commanded Uke, the vehicle gunner, to set up on the target. The troops surrendered literally seconds before I had given Uke the command to fire, sparing their lives.

I am glad they surrendered. To this day I stand firm in my belief that every Iraqi who surrendered was one fewer Iraqi with the opportunity to kill us. Beyond this issue is a huge moral dilemma. Iraqis were surrendering in mass formations. When you approached a target area, you had to assume, for your own safety, that the targets were belligerent. You made this judgment with this question in mind: if given ten minutes to make a decision, how many of the Iraqis in front of you would surrender? When the enemy has weapons of destruction, you cannot afford to give them the ten minutes, and invariably passive soldiers who have not yet taken the step to surrender get killed.

Morally and ethically you are bound to accept the surrender of the enemy. In Kuwait we knew that the prevailing action of the Iraqi was to surrender. Even so, some Iraqis fought. The decisions made by individual marines to engage Iraqi troops were valid; however, in the back of your mind you knew there was a chance the troops would surrender. It was a no-win situation. Giving the troops an overt opportunity to surrender equated to giving belligerents an opportunity to engage you first. Giving no overt chance to surrender equated to the destruction of potentially surrendering troops.

The one clear-cut ethically and morally incorrect thing was to fire on troops who were carrying the white flag. The moral dilemma ended when the enemy gave up. I have no respect for anyone who would fire on a surrendering enemy. To do so is to have no honor or courage.

In this case, as I say, I was glad the troops surrendered. When I looked down to Uke, I could see a look of disbelief on his face. I could tell the situation had affected him: he had just realized in his own mind the moral dilemma imposed on us all. I think it shook him up that he had almost shot soldiers who had freely laid down their weapons. I nodded at him. Actually I was happy to see the confusion in his face. His expression told me he was concerned about doing the right thing—he had honor, and I couldn't ask for much more from a fellow marine.

13

CORPORAL BUNTIN and Bravo Company had been following up behind Alpha and Charlie in reserve on the movement north to establish the screen on the rim of the depression. On the evening of 24 February, when Alpha was busy setting in at the depression, Bravo was tasked with moving back to the division CP. The company was ordered to establish security for General Myatt's command post at the south end of the al-Burqan oil field. If the small pockets of resistance behind Task Force Shepherd turned into a counterattack, Bravo would be in a position to squelch the attack that could surely destroy the division commander's position.

Just south of the al-Burqan oil field, near the beginning of Axis Stuart, was a low area in the desert that had the underground water network required to support the existence of plant life. Copses of trees—growing in rows, apparently hand planted—created a miniforest in the desert. The lush green vegetation of the low ground stood out dramatically against the stark desert surroundings. The forest was spared the looming darkness of al-Burqan by mere kilometers. There was an overcast, as in all of Kuwait, but not the sucking and surreal overcast of the burning oil field to the direct north. It was at this oasis that the division CP was established.

On the morning of the twenty-fifth Bravo Company had established positions oriented northeast of the oasis in order to protect the division CP. The two platoons of Bravo Company were on line facing northeast, and

Corporal Buntin was behind that line in the company CP facing north. His vehicle—the company commander's vehicle—was nestled snugly among the long rows of trees. Next to his vehicle was the company LAV-C2. To his right front, the two platoons of Bravo protected the position; to his direct front and left, the company flank was open.

Early in the morning Corporal Buntin and the FAC, Captain Jack, walked around the area, checking out the abandoned enemy positions. They moved from bunker to bunker finding abandoned enemy munitions, weapons, and explosives. After gathering up the AK-47s they found, the two returned, and Buntin woke up his driver so they could make another trip to check for more enemy equipment.

When they returned from that second trip, a marine HMMWV mounting a .50-caliber machine gun appeared over a rise just north of them. From his position Buntin couldn't see very far in that direction. Less than a kilometer away the slight rise (that started in the low ground where the trees grew) peaked, and visibility of all terrain beyond disappeared. A distinct ridge of sand marked the limit of Buntin's visibility to the north.

The HMMWV appeared over this ridge as Buntin and his driver were walking back to the LAV. The driver of the HMMWV screamed at them, "There are vehicles coming this way!" When he saw Buntin's LAV in the trees, he pulled to a halt beside it. By the time Corporal Buntin and his driver mounted their own vehicle, small-arms fire and artillery had started to land around them.

Captain Hammond was informing the division CP that they were under attack when 2d Platoon, on the screen facing northeast, made contact with an advancing Iraqi armor formation. The platoon engaged the advancing armor at about two kilometers, firing upon enemy vehicles that quickly sought cover from the accurate 25-mm rounds.

The company's left flank, the same path that the HMMWV had taken, was exploited—probably by luck on the Iraqi's part. Hammond was directing the company activity from his vehicle when he saw a BMP appear over the ridge in front of him, less than a kilometer away. He slewed the turret toward the advancing vehicle and shouted to Buntin, "BMP over the hill! Right there in front of the building! Fire! Fire! Fire!"

Buntin selected armor-piercing ammunition, laid the BMP in the battlesight circle of his sight reticle, and started firing. His rounds went cleanly over the top of the vehicle. The battlesight reference in the sight reticle allows the gunner to fire quickly and without deliberately aiming at targets up to fourteen hundred meters away. The ballistic path of the round is supposed to hit any target within that fourteen hundred meters. Unfortunately the trajectory of the AP round goes higher than the height of BMP between about six hundred and eight hundred meters. This one was at six hundred meters and closing, its main gun oriented on Buntin's vehicle.

Buntin immediately adjusted his aim and fired again. This time he landed a burst of AP directly into the frontal armor of the BMP. Nothing dramatic happened when he hit the vehicle; it simply rolled to a stop (the driver and the vehicle commander most likely were killed), and Iraqi troops poured out of the back. Corporal Buntin flipped a switch on his hand control, selecting the coaxially mounted machine gun, and fired at the deploying troops. The coax promptly jammed, and the Iraqi troops continued to scurry behind the damaged vehicle.

Before Buntin could do anything to clear the coax, an RPG fired from the now-deployed Iraqis landed forty meters in front of his vehicle. Buntin didn't worry about the jammed machine gun; he selected 25-mm HE and fired into the attacking infantry with the explosive rounds. His aim was perfect, and the Iraqi troops started to fall dead in place. They didn't fly dramatically through the air as in the movies; they simply fell straight to the ground like bags of sand.

As soon as the first RPG was fired, Buntin's driver took the initiative, slammed the gear-range selector into reverse, and rapidly backed the vehicle farther into the trees, away from the RPG. Captain Hammond was in the vehicle commander's hatch, trying to organize the company to face the new threat to the company's flank. Bravo had contact in front of 2d Platoon, but more importantly the company was being flanked, and because of that, the division CP was in jeopardy. He directed the platoon commanders to wheel around to the left in an attempt to face the immediate threat.

When the first BMP came over the hill, the marines in the HMMWV tried to engage it with the .50-caliber machine gun mounted on top of their vehicle. Like Corporal Buntin's coax, the .50-cal promptly jammed. Lacking protective armor and means of self-defense, the marines abandoned the HMMWV and dove for cover in the trees.

While Captain Hammond was maneuvering the company, Corporal Buntin saw another BMP crest the rise in front of him, orient on them, and advance toward their position. Having figured out the range, Buntin immediately fired a burst of 25-mm armor-piercing rounds at the BMP six hundred meters away. The rounds stopped the combat vehicle in its tracks. Again the troops in the back dismounted, and again an RPG traveled through the air to Buntin's vehicle. That second RPG rocketed over the vehicle, barely missing the target, and exploded on a tree twenty meters behind them, rocking the vehicle violently.

When the second RPG was fired, the scout in the back of Corporal Buntin's vehicle was attempting to assist Buntin by engaging the Iraqi troops with his M60 machine gun. (Coincidentally the M60 was jamming just as the .50-cal and coaxial machine gun had jammed.) The blast and fragments of the RPG round forced the scout to seek shelter inside the hull of the armored LAV-C2.

Buntin engaged the troops with 25-mm HE and eliminated them from the battlefield. Captain Hammond was on the radio to the company, and Buntin had to stand in his hatch in order to maneuver the LAV-25 to a better position. Buntin was then forced to wait for breaks in the captain's radio conversations to be able to talk to the driver on the intercom.

The captain's LAV-25 was eventually repositioned, and Captain Hammond and Corporal Buntin again faced a BMP. The third BMP crested the hill in front of them, and Corporal Buntin again selected 25-mm AP on his hand control. The volley found its mark, and sparks cascaded on the BMP's hull. But still there were no secondary explosions—the BMP simply stopped. Buntin expected to see a number of escaping troops when the BMP stopped, so he was ready with HE selected when the Iraqis dismounted. He engaged the troops and killed them in place, without the customary RPG.

Throughout the whole engagement Captain Jack had been trying to get marine air support to fight off the attacking armor. When Buntin killed the third BMP, Cobra gunships appeared above the LAVs, and under Captain Jack's guidance the helicopters laid severe punishment on the attacking force. Four Cobras flew in a clockwise direction over Bravo Company. Every time one of the birds reached the enemy side of the loop, they let loose with a hellish volley of missiles, rockets, and 20-mm gun fire. The arrival of the helicopters marked the end of the enemy's initiative in their attack on the division CP.

Hours later, an aerial count revealed that more than sixty Iraqi vehicles had been destroyed by the Cobras and Bravo Company. Captain Hammond's quick thinking and sound deployment in the face of the enemy had allowed General Myatt's CP to go unscathed. The leadership of Bravo Company had remained cool under fire and reacted positively to meet the enemy threat.

Corporal Buntin had been in a terribly awkward position. Captain Hammond was forced to fight the entire company, and Buntin was left to fight the vehicle. It is very difficult to coordinate fighting actions from the gunner's hatch. When the commander is on the radio, you cannot talk to anyone in the vehicle. Buntin was forced to play gunner and vehicle commander while Hammond maneuvered the company and attempted to get the support they desperately needed through Captain Jack in the LAV-C2. Buntin was wearing these two hats without the benefit of being able to talk to anyone with any regularity on the vehicle intercom.

Corporal Buntin was highly impressed with the leadership of Bravo Company. While he was fighting the three BMPs, he was hearing all the traffic on the radio. Aside from Captain Hammond's orders and directions, Buntin now recalls only firm replies from the platoon commanders. No questions were asked; the company net remained functional.

Inadvertently, because of his actions to save his crew from the advancing armor, Buntin had also spared the marine HMMWV the fate of fighting the BMPs alone. When it was all over, Captain Hammond was awarded the navy's second highest decoration, the Navy Cross, and Corporal Buntin was awarded a Navy Commendation Medal with a V-device for *valor*.

Probably only fifteen kilometers separated Alpha from Bravo on the morning of the twenty-fifth, but we might well have been in different countries. I was totally unaware of what Bravo was going through. Somewhere in the desert that separated us, an Iraqi armor formation had materialized and attacked the company's position. We could have traversed the distance between us in as little as thirty minutes, but that could never happen. We had to watch for the counterattack where it was expected, and therefore we could not be allowed to leave the area to assist the members of Bravo in their fight against a concentrated enemy attack. They were on their own, and under Captain Hammond's leadership they performed gallantly.

It was past midday when Alpha Company left the screen to proceed north. The overcast skies were darkening as the winds above al-Burqan shifted as though they were attempting to envelop our formation in darkness. We headed north in company march formation, 2d Platoon leading in a wedge formation and 1st Platoon trailing in a close column. Soon we had outrun the wind and left al-Burqan behind us.

Within three kilometers of stepping off, 2d Platoon moved into the right flank of a battalion-sized armor position. The marines crested a slight rise in the terrain and saw, within five hundred meters of them, dug-in tanks and personnel carriers facing south. Alpha had inadvertently maneuvered into the enemy's flank. I listened to the company radio net for the next fifteen minutes as report after report came in. Having surprised the Iraqis in this position, 2d Platoon let loose with volley after volley of 25-mm fire and TOW missiles. By my recollection the platoon destroyed at least a dozen vehicles before the Iraqis started to surrender.

The enemy soldiers stopped running to man their tanks and BMPs and started running to find their white flags. Within thirty minutes of the encounter Alpha Company was in the middle of the armored formation, screening to the north while select personnel gathered Iraqi prisoners and other personnel destroyed the existing tanks by putting thermite grenades down their gun tubes.

We were nearing completion of the project when an OV-10 circling high above dove down and launched a marking rocket at our positions. The white phosphorous rocket landed next to the LAV-C2 and burned on the deck as a marker for the F-18s that were sure to follow. While crewmen scampered about trying to extinguish the flare by burying it, Wildman got on the net and chastised the OV-10 pilot. We avoided another encounter with friendly air, thanks to our dedicated forward air controller.

We spent the rest of that afternoon moving deliberately north to establish yet another screen. We had to move only five kilometers total distance, but moving in and among the Iraqi positions slowed us considerably. Every dug-in vehicle had the potential to come to life and fire at the company. There was no way we could have destroyed the hundreds of vehicles that we moved past; we did not have the ammunition required to shoot at them all. Fortunately for us the Iraqis were still surrendering. This meant that the crews of these vehicles didn't want to fight. I don't know if it was because their equipment didn't work or they were tired of fighting, but they did surrender. Had they elected to fight, we would have been hard-pressed to move through the formations of tanks and armored personnel carriers without catastrophic losses. I was glad they surrendered. Not all Iraqis surrendered, though, and I remained wary of unseen and belligerent enemy while we moved.

When we approached the location of our screen line, we shifted slightly to the east to position the company properly. We had just passed the last Iraqi dug-in positions and turned to travel on a slight rise behind them. Suddenly Uke came over the intercom. "Sergeant Michaels, I've got Iraqis out here!"

"Roger," I answered. "What are they doing?" We were pretty accustomed to seeing the troops. We saw them, they saw us, and then they surrendered—it was a nice little system. I wasn't too worried. Uke had them in his sights, and he would let me know where to direct the company trains to pick up the prisoners—or so I figured.

Uke continued calmly, "It looks like they're. . . ." He stopped midsentence as I waited patiently. "Wait! They're getting on BMPs!"

I peered down the gun barrel with my binoculars, trying to pick up the targets. I couldn't see them yet. It is common for the gunner to see targets the vehicle commander can't see. The gunner looks with a magnified and stabilized sight, while the vehicle commander uses his naked eye and an unstabilized set of binoculars. Trying to hold the binoculars steady while we moved, I asked Uke, "Are you sure? I don't see them yet."

He quickly replied, "Yes, they are getting on. . . . Hey! The BMP is moving out of its hole!"

The Iraqis had the chance to give up, but now that chance was gone. "Roger. Sabot [the command to fire armor-piercing ammunition], PC [personnel carrier], fire!"

Uke responded, "On the way!" Two sensing rounds left our cannon, and I watched them hit the deck about eighteen hundred meters to the front. I heard Uke say, "Shit!"

"What?" I was still trying to pick up the target. I finally saw a shadowy dot on the horizon.

Uke said, "That's short!"

"What's your range?" I was trying to determine exactly what kind of adjustment to give.

"I fired at two thousand," Uke responded.

"Aim at three thousand. Fire!"

"On the way!" A three-round burst left the gun, and I watched the rounds until the tracer burned out at seventeen meters.[1] I tried, but I couldn't pick up the impacts of the rounds on the ground with the shaking binoculars.

Uke was on the ball, though. "That's short! On the way!" For the next few seconds he fired and adjusted AP rounds onto the BMP that was backing out of its hole. I tried to help him, but the target was so far out that I couldn't accurately sense impacts for him.

Finally, after what seemed like hours but was probably only ten seconds, Uke said, "Target! Got him!"

"What happened?" I responded. I could no longer see the small dot.

"I hit him with that last burst. There was a puff of smoke, and he rolled back into his hole." He was still watching the target area, but he saw nothing else. After a few seconds, he said, "Shit! You know what, Sergeant Michaels?"

"What?" I said.

"That target was thirty-five hundred meters!" I was impressed. It had taken Uke about fifteen rounds to kill the target, but the range was incredible. At that distance the target would be barely distinguishable in his sight. I told him that I was impressed and then told him to keep looking —*impress me some more.*

When I went to report, I found that the rest of the platoon had seen targets in the same area and were engaging them. In the span of two minutes it was all over. I don't even know if Lieutenant Tice knew what was going on. It is hard to fight an immediate contact and report at the same time. I can't even remember what kind of traffic was going over the radio at the time. It all happened so quickly.

Just as darkness fell upon us, we reached our screen positions. We were about eight kilometers directly north of the northern end of the al-Burqan oil fields. Crossing in front of our positions was a major power line. A hundred feet above our heads I could hear the transformers crackle ominously when we moved underneath them to our positions.

Taking all of the EPWs caused us some problems. We couldn't just let them go south; there was too much deadly equipment that they could fall in on and attack us with. We had no transportation, so we couldn't truck them back to the rear. We had to guard them throughout the night. Gunny Chevice and the company trains were not equipped with the personnel to guard the prisoners, however.

As soon as I set into position on the screen line, Lieutenant Tice called me on the radio and told me to go back to the trains to assist the gunny with the EPWs. I moved south until I found him. The company was facing north, set in a huge arc. The attached TOWs were behind the line of LAV-25s oriented south, protecting our rear. Two hundred meters behind the TOWs, Gunny Chevice had stopped. I drove up to his position and parked perpendicular to the nose of his vehicle, facing to the west.

When I got there, he had already set up a ring of concertina wire to surround the EPWs. With approximately thirty prisoners huddled inside the circle, it was very cramped—the Iraqis, unable to lie down, were forced to sit upright. Off to the side was a dazed and wounded Iraqi; blood seeping out of his ears, he was being treated by a medical corpsman. I took stock of the whole situation and saw that it would take my entire four-man scout team to watch these EPWs properly. I told my scout-team leader to link up with the company gunny and establish a watch. When they left, only the gunner, the driver, and I remained.

I had to figure out where to put my vehicle that evening. The TOWs behind me were watching the company's rear, and I really couldn't move away from the gunny without being in their line of fire. I decided to remain with the company trains. Telling the driver to get some sleep, I informed Uke that he and I would share the watch. I knew I wasn't able to assume a battle position, but I still needed to have someone on the radio in case the platoon needed us. Additionally, if the prisoners got out of control, I had a good crowd-control weapon on the turret—the pintle-mounted machine gun. I reported my actions to Lieutenant Tice, told him we were here if he needed us, and settled in for the night.

During my first watch early that night, I listened to the radio while Sergeant Long of 2d Platoon tried to get support from Captain Shupp. One of the platoon's vehicles had moved into a sabkha and had gotten stuck. When Long's section went to recover the vehicle, they started receiving harassing small-arms and mortar fire from Iraqi positions to the east.

For about half an hour Captain Shupp tried to figure out what was going on, while Sergeant Long continually requested support. But Shupp did not reposition any vehicles to meet the harassing fire—such a measure could have compromised the security of the screen to the north. He consoled Long and told him to stick it out. Long, who ended up performing the recovery with Sergeant Walker under sporadic enemy fire, was upset about Shupp's decision. The captain had made a good call, however. What he hadn't known was that this action had not been designed to get us to reposition our forces. When the recovery was complete, the harassment stopped. That fact didn't stop Sergeant Long from having an adrenaline rush, but it did prove that Captain Shupp had again made the correct decision.

At about 0400 on the twenty-sixth I started another watch in the turret. Uke woke me from my vehicle commander's seat and told me it was my turn. I stood in my hatch and struggled to keep awake. To help me in that effort I turned on my passive night sight and scanned the area to the south and west. The burning fires of al-Burqan eight kilometers to the south totally washed out the light-gathering sight. Then I alternated between reaching across to the gunner's manual controls and traversing two hundred to three hundred mils and then standing in my hatch and looking out

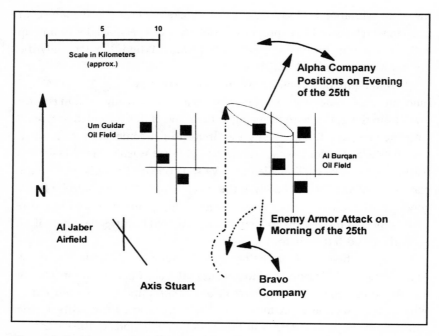

Figure 6. Positions on 25 February.

with my thermal sight. I did this for about an hour. The constant action of reaching across and turning followed by standing and looking kept me alert.

The only bad thing about the area was that to the west I could see fine with the thermal sight, but to the south the heat of the fire washed the thermal out just as it had done the passive sight. I looked south and saw the brilliant orange fire of the northernmost well cap and shrugged. I turned my turret to the west and then as far south as it would go before it washed out. I was pointed southwest. From that point on I looked southwest and west.

At about 0530 the sun was barely peeking over the horizon behind me, beginning a battle with the gloomy overcast to provide light to the desert. I was standing in the turret when I thought that I heard something. I took off my helmet and listened. Suddenly I could clearly hear the squeak of a tracked vehicle to the south. I couldn't see anything, but I knew something was there—and it was close. I reached down and powered up the turret. When I popped back up and traversed the turret under power, an MT-LB (a logistics variant of an armored personnel carrier) appeared five hundred meters to the south. Directly from the burning fire, the vehicle was moving toward our position. It was very strange.

Immediately the company net was active. *Where did this vehicle come from? Who was watching south?* When the MT-LB approached, I traversed my turret onto him. I saw a set of hands raised high above an open hatch, the signal of submission. I hollered at my scouts with the EPWs and told them to get someone over there. I let go of my joystick and grabbed the spades of my pintle mount as the MT-LB stopped twenty-five meters away. The scouts rushed to the vehicle and at gunpoint quickly took the surrendering Iraqis prisoners.

It seemed as if everyone in the company came down to look at the MT-LB. It was such a close call for the company. In the back of the vehicle at least twenty-five heavy-artillery rounds were stacked loosely on the deck. Additionally the vehicle was full of brand-new items, the type of things you might find at a Wal-Mart—shoes, pants, shirts, and a number of nice-to-have hygiene items still in the plastic wrap. It was obvious to us that the vehicle crew had looted a Kuwaiti store somewhere.

The TOWs hadn't seen the vehicle because it came directly out of the oil fire at the northern end of al-Burqan: their thermals had been washed out by the intense heat. For the Iraqis the situation had worked out perfectly. With the fire to their back, they probably could have seen the company as they advanced. But they were intent on surrendering, and I can only imagine the thoughts that were running through their heads as they drew closer to the company. It was at great personal risk that these soldiers drove an armored vehicle toward us. Had the oil fire not been where it was, the TOW vehicles certainly would have fired a missile into the enemy vehicle as soon as they saw it closing on the company. Fate had saved the Iraqis; they joined our cluster of EPWs within the ring of wire.

The company started moving again early on the morning of the twenty-sixth. Almost as soon as the curiosity over the MT-LB was over, I was sent back to my platoon, and we moved out again to the north. When I linked up with Corporal Matlain, he was exactly where I had left him. The platoon had a very uneventful evening.

We hadn't gone far—probably less than four or five kilometers—when I realized we had moved into another oil field. Not nearly as large as the al-Burqan field, it was nonetheless the same scene of pipelines and berms surrounding oil caps. Only about one-third of the oil caps in this new field were burning. To the west most of the field was ablaze, but where we traveled were scores of stagnate well caps. For that I was thankful.

Coming around one well cap, an armored vehicle appeared in Uke's sight at about fifty meters. I saw it and told him to fire. After about three rounds, we realized the vehicle was already abandoned, but the shock of its appearance caused our hearts to race. About five hundred meters on ahead, my section came around the west side of a gathering center. We were in a field where all the oil pipelines intersected within a square area, approximately two-hundred by two-hundred meters, behind a six-foot-high sand berm. I could see abandoned oil equipment and buildings within the walled compound, and I started to maneuver the section farther to the west to stand off from the potential danger—it was only about a hundred meters away.

Suddenly I saw a head bob behind the sandy berm of the gathering center. I immediately radioed the contact and turned the vehicle to face the threat. I gave the gunner a fire command for the coax machine gun and told him to stand by to fire. I told PFC Dudley to back up, and we moved back about a hundred more meters.

I looked to my left and saw that Matlain was doing the same thing. Tice was coming up behind us and wanted to know what was going on. In the process of dismounting my scouts, I didn't immediately respond. When the scouts were out, white flags started appearing on the top of the berm. I shouted to Corporal Tanner, my scout team leader, telling him to link up with Matlain's scouts and collect the prisoners. I ordered Matlain to provide overwatch with me while the scouts moved forward.

Before Tanner left, he tried to get a check with me on the scout radio. I didn't hear him. His portable SINCGARS, unlike the one in the vehicle, had not been used since the ground war started. He had the required fills in the radio but had fallen out of the time window required to use the frequency-hopping net: the scout radio was in the standby mode and stored in the back of the vehicle. Because of that, the radio didn't receive the time carrier from the master station, and therefore it had fallen out of time sync.

I was somewhat upset. We knew fully well that this was a problem with the scout radio. We had trained for six months in the desert knowing that the scout-team leader had to operate the radio periodically in order to stay in the proper time sync. I knew what the problem with the radio was immediately, and I had no choice but to send the team out with no communications. I could have tried to get Tanner entered late in the platoon net, which may have taken a while, or I could have sent him without the radio. Due to the urgency of the situation, I chose the latter option. I could observe the scout team's movement all the way up to the sandy berm surrounding the complex, and I knew I could move around to the left, where there was a break in the berm to support them when they moved inside.

When the scouts were on the way to the surrendering Iraqis behind and on the berm, I told Uke to watch them with the coax. I told Dudley to take us around to the left, and I told Matlain to remain in place to overwatch from this side. When I had everyone where I wanted them, I heard Lieutenant Tice trying to call the scouts on the platoon net. I called the platoon commander and told him the situation. Tice was not pleased that they were without a radio. I knew he wouldn't be, but I felt confident in my decision anyway. I could have spent five or ten minutes trying to fill the radio and then they would have had one, but I didn't feel I could spend the time. I relayed this to the platoon commander, who acknowledged my transmission. He still wasn't happy, but neither was I, and the scouts were still out doing business.

About an hour later the scouts cleared the compound and gathered the two dozen EPWs that had surrendered. When the prisoners were put into formation, I positioned my section within the walls of the compound, oriented north. The berm provided the best situation I had during the entire war: when I pulled in, I had a perfect hull-down firing position and felt very comfortable about fighting the vehicle from behind the protective walls of the compound.

It was at this compound that I saw one of the most courageous acts I witnessed during the deployment. Remarkably this act did not include a direct engagement with the enemy. Our EPW collection was growing larger every time we moved forward. We had no way to transport the prisoners as the company moved. Corporal Reese, our forward observer, had been riding in the LAV-C2 up until this point. When he got to the gathering center, he boldly remedied our transportation problem.

Reese found an Iraqi bus and figured out a way to start it. Before I knew what was going on, he had gotten the bus running, picked up the EPWs collected by our platoon, and driven off to pick up the rest of the prisoners. I was truly amazed. We had a problem with our aircraft's thinking we were the enemy, and there was Corporal Reese driving around in a captured piece of Iraqi equipment without a care in the world. I am sure any aircraft that spotted the vehicle would have quickly recognized the Cyrillic characters on its side and roof and would have jumped at the chance to deliver ordnance upon it. As far as I was concerned, Reese had demonstrated valor in his actions. It may not sound like much, but he had definitely put himself at severe personal risk.

My scouts collected enemy weapons and ammunition while the vehicle crew watched to the north from the compound. We captured a 14.5-mm machine gun that had been mounted on top of an enemy maintenance vehicle. We found a two-thousand-round case of NATO 7.62-mm ammunition that was in very good condition. I mounted the box on the outside of the vehicle because it fit our weapons and we were short on that type of shell.

We didn't stay in that position for more than an hour. The company was called back to refuel at the company trains' position. I moved my section back to the trains, which were located to the southwest. We had to travel down an improved-surface road that threaded between the burning well caps. We passed two burning well caps on the way. Although we were a hundred meters away from them, the heat was so intense that we were forced to button up inside our vehicles to avoid being burned.

We turned in the 14.5-mm machine gun, refueled, and headed back to the compound. When I looked in back of my vehicle, I saw that each of the scouts now toted an AK-47. I asked them where their M-16s were, and they replied that the AKs were better weapons. Pointing at the bandoleers of AK ammunition, they added that they had a good supply of ammo for them.

I understood that the scouts were very much impressed with the "new" weapons they had captured, but I couldn't let them run around with AK-47s. I don't think they were very happy when I told them that their primary weapons were the M16s. They wanted to keep the AKs to take them home. I told them that they could keep them on the vehicle, but they would probably have to turn them in at some point.

The scouts were not a happy bunch. I was certain that they did not know how to operate these firearms safely. And I knew that the weapons were crap compared to the M16s the team had been issued. These things weren't important to them at the time, however. It was tough to make a decision that made everyone angry with you, but I think I did the right thing. I had to remind myself that I wasn't there to make marines happy; I was there to lead them.

14

AT ABOUT 1500 on 26 February, Alpha Company received orders to move again. I had expected to sit in the screen where we were, just as we had done the two previous nights, and I was surprised that we were finally continuing our drive toward Kuwait City, the symbol that in my mind represented freedom for the thousands of displaced Kuwaitis. I knew that within Kuwait City was the U.S. Embassy. For me the American flag's riding to the top of the pole in the embassy compound would signify that Kuwait was free. Iraqis would still be in their country, but with our flag flying there, it would quickly and logically follow for the Kuwaitis to be flying their own flag atop their capital building. After that, everything was academic.

Again 2d Platoon led the company northward. We didn't travel in a company march column. The restrictions of the oil fields forced us to create a single column that threaded along the network of hard- and improved-surface roads leading to the city. The vehicle commander directing the company's movement was Corporal Royster, who boldly guided the high-speed column northward along the winding route.

Five kilometers north of the gathering center, Royster led the convoy through an abandoned Iraqi defensive position of tremendous size. We had traveled through many of the company- and battalion-sized positions before, but they paled in comparison to the Iraqi armor we now encountered just south of Kuwait City. All around us on the sandy earth, as far as the eye could see, were entrenched Iraqi tanks, trucks, and personnel carriers—all without crews. We traveled due east across the breadth of the formation—which, by my calculations, covered at least ten square kilometers and contained almost a thousand vehicles.

Corporal Royster continued the company charge past the abandoned equipment with extreme prowess. I can only imagine what went through his head at each turn in the road. Everywhere he looked was a piece of enemy equipment that could instantly destroy him. It took only one unseen Iraqi soldier out of the thousands needed to man these machines of war to vaporize Royster's vehicle instantly.

When I snaked through the area behind 2d Platoon, I was amazed at the elaborate pains the Iraqis had taken to shelter their equipment from our devastating air campaign. I remember driving and seeing nothing. And then in an instant a deep path appeared: it led to an individual Iraqi vehicle position dug deep into the ground. There was no way that an aircraft could spot most of this camouflaged equipment, and there was very little chance that we could have spotted it in time to react if the Iraqis were in fact there.

When we had crossed the huge Iraqi position, the windy trail led us to the north, and for the first time I could see the outskirts of Kuwait City. We were just south of the Kuwait International Airport—far enough away from the city that we couldn't see its big buildings but close enough that we were confronted by the network of roads that supported the urban area.

The head of the column stopped. Company movement was halted by a chain-link fence with triple barbed-wire strands that straddled a hardsurface road immediately in front of 2d Platoon. Unable to see the fence from my position, I listened to the radio traffic intently in an effort to create a mental picture.

"Blue 5, this is Blue 1, over." Lieutenant Tice was calling me on the platoon radio net.

"Go ahead, Blue 1."

"Blue 5, there is a gap in the fence in front of 2d Platoon, break." I tried to add this feature to my mental picture. "I want you to take your section through and secure the far side so the company can pass through, over."

Telling Dudley to move, I looked at Matlain, who was already following when I responded, "Roger, Blue 1." Then I noticed that the battalion command group was behind me. Sergeant Ramirez's security platoon was leading them, and they had fallen in behind Alpha Company.

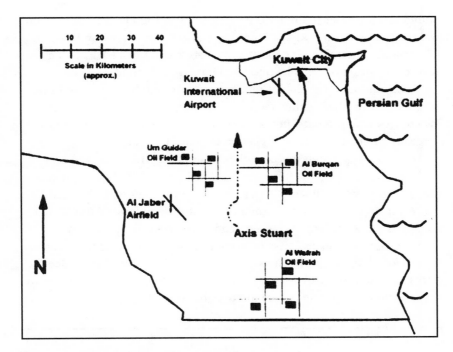

Figure 7. Route to Kuwait City on 26 February.

I darted my section forward and crested a small rise. I saw immediately what the lieutenant was talking about. Perpendicular to the company's axis was a hard-surface road. Directly in front of our lead element was an intersection. On the opposite side of the road was a chain-link fence that ran parallel to the entire length of the road, except for a twenty-foot gap directly opposite the intersection.

I continued to move swiftly, guiding slightly to the left to the center of the gap. I passed 2d Platoon, which had moved up on line to overwatch the far side of the obstacle. The road surface had a slight crown, and I felt my vehicle almost go into the air when we crossed the apex. I shot through the gap and moved fifty meters forward and twenty-five meters to the right and oriented north. In front of me, a huge compound of vehicles—it appeared to be a city-maintenance facility—sat behind a fenced-off enclosure. To my right the improved-surface road continued to wind into the city.

As soon as I set into position, Uke came over the intercom and told me he had spotted a sandbagged bunker at the top of a tower inside the compound. On my order to fire HE, he pumped three rounds into the earthen walls of the structure. Alpha Company started to move behind me, and Uke scanned the compound for other threats. He found a BMP among the rows of construction vehicles and filled it full of AP rounds.

Three minutes later Alpha Company was through the fence, and I was satisfied that we had eliminated any threats from within the compound. When 1st Platoon passed my position, I fell in behind them. Behind me Sergeant Ramirez and security platoon fell into the column.

The terrain suddenly became very restrictive. The improved-surface road wound tightly to the left around a small building and then ran north along a set of power lines. We were forced to turn left with the road because a main freeway with abutments was directly in front of us. We were canalized to travel along the access road underneath the power lines.

After Alpha Company passed through the fence, and before I was able to turn left along the power lines, the column stalled. I sat patiently, feeling very exposed in the narrow area between the maintenance compound to my left and the chain-link fence to my right.

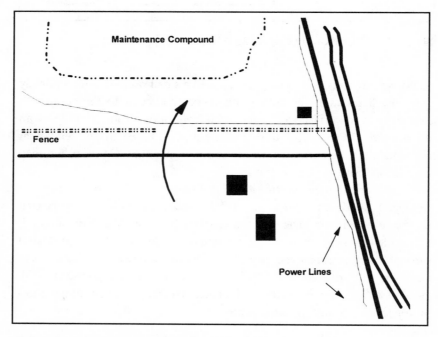

Figure 8. Restrictive area near maintenance compound.

When the column stalled, Ramirez heard the report of small-arms fire behind him. He saw the battalion S-3 firing his M16 from his vehicle at a target off to the right. He looked over in that direction and saw that eight hundred meters away, on the freeway, soldiers in a civilian vehicle were firing from their open windows at the convoy. He slewed his gunner on target, issued a section fire command, and destroyed the vehicle with 25-mm fire from two vehicles.

Simultaneously another enemy vehicle was speeding down the freeway, perpendicular to the convoy. Ramirez watched as the gunner of the LAV-25 in his sister section tracked and fired 25-mm AP rounds at it. The rounds were coming close to friendly vehicles. The gunner had started out—his vehicle in column—shooting to his right flank, but as the Iraqis moved to his left down the freeway, his cannon was firing directly over the front of his vehicle. He was directly behind my section.

I sat in my turret waiting for the company to move, and my scouts were hollering at me. I turned to them and tried to understand what they were saying. They were pointing behind us and yelling, "Sergeant Michaels, they're going to hit us!"

Just then, I caught a flash of one of the AP rounds as it passed by my head. I looked back and saw another round as it passed literally within two feet of my face. I didn't know who was shooting, and I had no idea how to get them on the radio, so I started to wave my hands frantically at the vehicle commander fifty meters behind me. His gunner was oblivious to me in his narrow gun sight, but surely the vehicle commander could see what was about to happen. Another burst went by my head.

Observing the engagement, Sergeant Ramirez could see what was going to happen. He watched the turret continue to traverse to the left, chasing the fast target, and he knew that the gunner would never see my vehicle in front of him before it was too late. Appalled that the vehicle commander would allow this to occur, Ramirez immediately got on the platoon's radio net and commanded, "Cease fire! Cease fire!"

I don't know if it was my frantic waving of arms or Ramirez's heads-up actions, but the vehicle stopped firing. Ramirez told me that for the next minute and a half, he chastised the vehicle commander and then explained to the entire platoon that indiscriminate firing was not only unprofessional but unacceptable. When I interviewed Sergeant Ramirez, I thanked him for his actions.

I didn't have much time to get angry because when I turned around, I saw a slow-moving glow approaching the column's flank from the south. It looked just like the wire-guided dragon missiles I had seen fired on ranges back at Camp Pendleton, and I immediately thought *Sagger!* I reached down to my radio control box, flipped it to the company net, and cleared the traffic with "Flash! Flash! Flash!" I followed that up with "Sagger! Sagger! Sagger! Three o'clock!"

My gunner was already looking to the right for the source of the launch when I got off the net. I watched and cringed as the missile drew closer to the head of the column. I gritted my teeth, expecting the violent explosion to occur, but it never happened. I felt a sudden relief thinking that the missile had missed or malfunctioned. Then I felt stupid. In an opening between two buildings to my left front, I saw an ambulance dart by at about fifty miles per hour. I hadn't seen the vehicle approaching on the freeway because the built-up earth on the sides of the freeway blocked my view. However, the earth was not high enough to conceal a blinking light on top of the vehicle. I had tracked the ambulance's emergency flasher, thinking it was a Sagger missile.

I felt bad that I had called in the report when it was obviously an ambulance, but I felt very good that it hadn't been a missile. We were sitting ducks at the time—and a perfect target for an angry Sagger gunner.

Alpha Company finally completed the narrow left turn to travel parallel to the freeway. I saw why the column had been so slow through that area when I completed the tight ninety-degree turn. The single-lane dirt access road that ran under the power lines was obstructed in at least a half a dozen places by fallen power lines. Dislodged from their anchors a hundred feet above, the cables dangled perilously close to the windy road. The lead vehicle of the column was forced to choose a path of safety around them. We didn't know if any electricity still ran through the heavy-gauge wires, and we didn't stop to find out. Weaving dramatically Alpha Company continued down that access trail for over a kilometer.

Finally at about 1730 we had cleared the power lines and were entering Kuwait City. The first thing I saw was two soldiers of the Kuwaiti Resistance, standing at the point in the road where the company turned off the access trail and waving their AK-47s in the air at the passing column. The pinkish armbands they wore as the mark of their organization were visible from about two hundred meters out, so I knew they were friendly to our cause. As we approached the two soldiers, I felt a sudden warmth develop in my chest.

Since the day we had seen the Kuwaiti soldiers in Saudi Arabia flying the tiny flags from their BMPs, I had felt a deep-seeded sadness for them. I had tried to imagine the pain of displacement—the burning knot in their stomachs caused by their having no home to speak of, the wondering when, and if, their freedom would be regained. Upon seeing those two resistance soldiers on the side of the road, cheering us on, I knew that freedom was at hand for the unfortunate Kuwaiti citizens.

I wondered what kind of personal hell these Kuwaitis and their brothers had gone through for almost eight months. I marveled at the sacrifices they constantly made to keep the torch of the resistance movement lit amid the thousands of Iraqi soldiers that searched for them daily. I had so much respect for their courage. That moment was probably one of the most memorable moments of my stay in the Kuwaiti theater, and I will never forget it.

As we drew even closer to the two, I tried to think of something appropriate to do that would mark the occasion. We were just passing by them on our way into the city. We couldn't stop and exchange smiles or conversation. Finally I turned to the scouts in the back and told them over the engine noise to give the soldiers our AK-47 ammo—we still had the bandoleers of ammunition we had found earlier that morning.

I passed the soldiers and saluted them from my turret. I followed the gesture of respect with a dual-handed thumbs-up. When we passed, I looked back and saw the scouts handing them ammunition on the fly. Bandoleer after bandoleer was hurriedly passed. Additionally, from the back of my vehicle, AK-47s found their way into their hands. As the men faded from my view, I hoped our gestures and offerings were to them an adequate symbol of our commitment to their cause. I hoped the soldiers left with the same warm feeling I had, and, most of all, I hoped they understood why we couldn't stop and embrace them.

A few kilometers north of the resistance soldiers, the company stopped in a large field directly northwest of a cloverleaf in the freeway. Captain Shupp ordered the company to assume a screen-line position, orienting north off of the cloverleaf—2d Platoon would cover the western portion of the field we were in, and 1st Platoon would cover the remaining portion to the east and the freeway northward from the cloverleaf. My section was assigned the task of actually occupying the cloverleaf and watching the high-speed avenue of approach that the freeway presented. I was given a section of LAV-ATs to aid me in my task.

It was dark when I left the company coil with my orders. The trip to the east-west road of the cloverleaf was only five hundred meters. I traveled south, turned left, and mounted the cloverleaf.

From the top of the interchange I could see that the task of screening from this position would be difficult. The road going over the cloverleaf was divided by a concrete median that the LAV could not breach. That meant we would have to follow the posted traffic rules to get onto the freeway—there were no shortcuts.

Another median divided the northbound lane of the freeway from the southbound lane. That median consisted of a barrier of two three-foot concrete walls that ran down the center of the freeway, north and south. Between the walls was a string of seventy-five-foot light poles. The lights were out, but the poles, spaced every twenty-five meters, ran as far north as I could see.

The cloverleaf itself had four distinct loops for entering and exiting the freeway. And there were additional accesses that I never figured out. Had the concrete medians not prevented our movement along both lanes of the road on top of the interchange, I might have been able to figure out the intricacies of the structure. But in the dark it was like a real-life mind game. I was tired and totally unable to get a firm grasp of the traffic pattern.

Forgetting the cloverleaf for the time being, I told Corporal Matlain to take one of the attached LAV-ATs, get into the southbound lane, and head north. He would eventually end up facing north against the direction of travel on the freeway. I took the other AT, found the northbound exit, and took it. I moved north on the freeway away from the cloverleaf in an attempt to find a good position to observe from.

I would have preferred to use the high ground offered by the exits from the interchange to gain an observation advantage, but the freeway banked hard to the left three hundred meters north of the interchange. Because of this, our observation was limited to about three hundred meters before we were looking into the trees and light poles on the inside corner of the turn.

Having moved the three hundred meters required to see around the corner, we stopped. I could now see about fifteen hundred meters before the freeway dove from my view. For the next thirty minutes I coordinated with Matlain on the other side of the freeway. If we were abreast, he couldn't see when I could see. If we moved until he could see, then I couldn't see. I didn't want either of our vehicles too far in front of the other because I couldn't see him from my side of the highway. The brush in the median obscured my view of the opposite side. I was concerned that he might end up so far ahead of the rest of the platoon—they were on the other side of a tree line to his left, and we couldn't see them either—that he might be mistaken for an Iraqi vehicle.

Eventually we settled on positions that were slightly staggered in depth (about a hundred meters), where we both could see forward on the freeway. I ended up about five hundred meters north of the cloverleaf. The next task was preparing our positions. After telling Matlain to get to work, I radioed Lieutenant Tice that we had finally found positions but still had to prepare them.

The only position that allowed the TOW gunner a clear field of fire down the entire length of the freeway in front of us was nestled up against the protruding brush in the left lane. Even this site had problems: the huge green road signs—the same kind you find on an American freeway—totally obstructed his view and the flight of any missile he would fire. The way I saw it, there was only one thing that could be done: knock the road signs down.

I drove down the freeway to the north under constant overwatch from Matlain for about a thousand meters. There were at least six twenty-feet-high green signs along the side of the road that obstructed the TOW gunner's view. The huge steel legs of the signs were farther apart than the front of my vehicle was wide. I had to ease up to each leg one at a time and nudge it with the aluminum trim vane of my vehicle.[1]

Dudley did an outstanding job bringing the signs down without tearing off the fragile piece of aluminum. He came into contact with one leg, gunned the accelerator until the leg was starting to bend and the vehicle was riding up on it, and then he backed off. He went to the opposite leg and repeated the process. By the time both legs were bent, the weight of the sign was enough to pull it down to the ground. It took us about forty-five minutes to topple all of them. When I returned, the TOW gunner was busy drawing the range card I had asked for.

Occupying a screen line is a thankless task. There is always something to be done and never enough time to do it in. I quickly found a position for my vehicle on a slight rise among some young trees to the right of the freeway. From that position I could see the TOW busy scanning twenty feet to my left, and I could use my thermal sight to help him acquire potential targets to the north. I wasn't happy with the meek dispersion but had no choice due to the restrictions of the freeway. I marked my vehicle position. But I still was not done—I had to work on our withdrawal plan.

I radioed Lieutenant Tice and told him we were set in positions and observing. I also told him I was still working on the plan to rejoin the platoon in the event of withdrawal. My tentative strategy, I explained, was to backtrack through the cloverleaf, turn to the west, and link up with him.

Tice had seen the cloverleaf, and he didn't like the idea. He understood, as I did, how difficult the interchange was, and he was very wary of sorting out the exits from my side in the face of an advancing enemy.

On Corporal Matlain's side, it was easy. He simply turned around, headed south, and took the westbound exit. The interchange was designed for a vehicle to do that, and there was no way a mistake could be made. On my side the story was entirely different.

I told Lieutenant Tice that I had spotted a break in the median about five hundred meters to the north that would allow me to turn around if need be. I further told him I didn't want to move out beyond that break to screen because it cut my maneuver space almost in half—moving to the break was out of the question. The lieutenant responded that he wanted me to breach the median behind my position to make my own break in the median. I acknowledged and went to work.

I left my vehicle in position, gathered the scouts not on watch, and surveyed the median. We had been working for two hours on our positions thus far, and after looking at the size of the concrete blocks, I figured we had another two hours, at a minimum, remaining. Initially I thought that if we could punch a hole through the reinforced concrete, I could attach the vehicle winch to the block and pull it out of the way. The scouts got busy with a shovel and a pick and tried to make that happen.

After thirty minutes the scouts had barely chipped the concrete surface. They tried using pry bars to gain leverage on the block against the earth between the medians and the concrete on our side, but that turned out to be a fruitless endeavor. I told the scouts to keep trying and went back to my radio. I asked Lieutenant Tice for some of the C4 explosives we had in Sergeant Negron's section to bust the concrete by force. I don't know why, but he would not allow me to do that. It was clear to me, on the scene, that the median was beyond our capability to breach without explosives. He wanted it done, so I briefed the scouts, explaining the situation to them. They worked diligently for a couple of hours but never solved the riddle.

While the scouts were working, Tice called me on the radio. "Blue 5, this is Blue 1, over."

I answered, "Go ahead, Blue 1."

He gave me marching orders. "Charlie Company is set in positions to the southwest of the cloverleaf, break." I pictured the open field behind 2d Platoon near what I thought was a hospital. Tice continued, "Leave Blue 6 there. I need you to go and try to link up with Charlie Company so we can tie in, over."

I yelled at my scouts, telling them to get on the vehicle. I told Dudley to fire it up, and then I called back to the platoon commander: "Solid copy, Blue 1. Interrogative: is Charlie Company freq [frequency] hopping, over?" With the crew mounted up and ready to go, I told Dudley to get on the freeway heading south.

I knew someone would have to tell the marines of Charlie Company that I was approaching them from its flank. I would have preferred to call them myself, to tell them personally that I was coming to them. I knew if they saw a lone armored vehicle approaching their flank, it might be a *shoot first and ask questions later* scenario.

Lieutenant Tice radioed back, "Roger, Blue 5, they probably are."

Since they were frequency hopping I wouldn't be able to talk to them: I could probably get their hopset, but it would be difficult to enter their net without their sync time. That wasn't good, but I trusted Lieutenant Masters in the LAV-C2. "Roger, who is going to coordinate this, over?" I was already approaching the cloverleaf.

"Blue 5," he said, "we're working on that now."

If I had not been preoccupied with the cloverleaf at the time, that statement might have bothered me. The *we're working on it* part was not very comforting. As it was, though, I didn't dwell on the statement. For the next thirty minutes I tried to get to the southbound lane of the freeway from the northbound lane through the restrictive interchange. It was a nightmare. The median on top of the interchange prevented me from simply crossing over and taking the designated exit to the south. I went up and down the cloverleaf like a rat in a maze. No matter how many variations I tried, I could not get to the southbound lane.

Finally I got off the cloverleaf, passed the interchange heading south, went up the northbound exit of the cloverleaf heading the wrong way, dodged a bomb crater in the road, and looped over the interchange against the flow of traffic until I was finally on the south side—the side that allowed me to exit, going the wrong way again, onto the southbound lane. Once I was at the bottom and on the freeway, I was able to dart across the open field to the southwest of the cloverleaf, heading west toward Charlie Company.

It was at this point that I called the platoon commander again. "Blue 1, this is Blue 5, over."

"Go ahead, Blue 5."

"Roger, I'm heading toward Charlie now. Have you worked out the coordination, over?"

Lieutenant Tice's response really surprised me. I had spent a lot of time trying to get through the cloverleaf, and I figured that the coordination would be a done deal. He responded, "Wait one, over."

I knew this meant he was checking with the XO. Here I was, eight hundred meters away from Charlie and closing, and he had to check with the XO to see if they knew I was approaching them. I told Uke to watch very closely for any muzzle flashes, and I reached instinctively for the slim cylinder of the green star-cluster. Once I found it, I held it tightly in my hand, wondering if I would have the time to launch it if Charlie Company fired at us.

I knew that no matter what happened, we would not shoot back at Charlie Company. It would surely be in self-defense, but there was absolutely no way I could ever bring myself to give the command to fire on friendly vehicles, regardless of the situation. The only course of action open to me was this: hope that the XO got through and, in case he didn't, prepare to dismount the vehicle crew when someone fired at us. I was scared.

We moved about a hundred meters more before Lieutenant Tice called me back. "Blue 5, this is Blue 1. Go ahead and turn around and go back to your position, over."

He didn't have to tell me twice. I knew from that call that coordination had never been made, and I was glad he had decided to hold off with the mission until it had been made. I answered him and moved back to my position. I had the cloverleaf figured out by then and was able to negotiate it swiftly, heading straight back to my section.

About an hour later, Lieutenant Tice showed up at my position to check it out. He pulled up behind the TOW and dismounted his vehicle. I was standing in my turret and was about to get down to meet him when one of the scouts working on the median yelled, "Hey! We've got a vehicle coming this way!" I glanced around and saw the scouts running back toward our vehicle. Faintly I could hear a tracked-vehicle noise on the freeway behind us! I grabbed my turret hand control and traversed the turret around to face the threat. I gave a fire command to Uke and told him to stand by.

Uke came over the intercom: "Hey! I've got a flashing weapons light!" The gun was over the fire-inhibit zone in the back of the vehicle, and the light was notifying us that the weapon could not be fired—it was over the open troop hatches and, by design, could not be fired until those hatches were closed. I couldn't believe it.

We had already been through this—we had hot-wired the inhibitor switches in those hatches so the gun logic would think they were closed. The scouts had to be up and looking when you were moving, and there was no time for them to close their hatches if a contact appeared behind us. With the hatches wired, the scouts could simply duck down inside while the gun fired over their heads. It was loud, but as long as they got down—a measure we had drilled—they would be safe. Now, the wires had apparently come loose. They were working earlier in the day, but that fact did us no good at the present moment.

I saw the tracked vehicle approach. It was some sort of high-backed armored personnel carrier with a small-caliber machine gun mounted on top. I knew that he couldn't see us in the trees, so I told Uke, "Don't move the turret. He can't see us. As soon as he passes, I'll slew you back on, and we'll get him from the rear." Then I looked to the road beside my vehicle. There, standing defiantly in the middle of the road, was Lieutenant Tice, the platoon commander. I couldn't believe he hadn't mounted up on his own vehicle when we identified the vehicle to our rear. Tice walked toward the moving vehicle and tried to stop him with his 9-mm pistol. The stranger slowed only briefly and then took off heading north. I slewed the turret around, and Uke picked up the target. I issued a fire command, but I never gave the command to fire.

I don't know exactly why I never told Uke to fire. When the vehicle passed us, I tried to determine if he was a good guy or a bad guy, but in the dim light I could not tell. The vehicle was not distinctly Iraqi by model: it could have been owned by any of a number of countries, including the Allies. It was coming from the south, so the thought entered my head that it could be manned by a lost Saudi crew trying to rejoin their unit. Yet the vehicle had showed no threatening actions, passing within three feet of Lieutenant Tice (executing a bold act) and the LAV-AT on the road but never once orienting its weapon on either of them.

Looking back, I guess all those facts combined led me to neglect issuing the command of execution in the fire command. If a friendly vehicle were going to be shot, my crew were not going to be the ones doing it. If the vehicle had displayed aggressive behavior, I would have given Uke the command that would have led to its destruction. If the vehicle were Iraqi —which, in fact, it probably was—they were lucky Iraqis.

While all this was going on in my position, Sergeant Ramirez had his hands full back at the battalion CP, which had pulled in behind Alpha and Charlie Companies in an open area that Ramirez thought was near the Kuwaiti zoo. It was already getting dark, and Ramirez knew he was responsible for the security of the command group. He didn't like being in the city: the potential for the enemy to hide and ambush your positions was too high. When he saw that the CP was going to be in the open field surrounded by buildings, he made the decision to actively patrol the surrounding area.

Before the vehicles even came to a halt, Ramirez radioed all the vehicles in his security platoon and told them to send their scouts to his vehicle as soon as they stopped: he was sending out a security patrol immediately. Ramirez then waited for the scouts to arrive. Just as the final scouts were gathering, the commander of the vehicle oriented northeast called in a report to Ramirez: through his thermal sight he could see fifteen people moving west among the trees around the battalion CP. Envisioning the path the people would be taking, Ramirez realized that eventually they would reach the barracks-like building only a hundred meters behind him.

Ramirez also saw that on the western edge of the CP, the people would have to cross a road, an open area, before darting back into the concealment of the trees. Having no time now to waste, Ramirez realized how lucky he had been in ordering that the scouts be sent to his position the moment they had stopped.

The scouts all looked up to him when he dismounted the vehicle. He issued them a FRAGO, and the group of marines stepped off toward the point where the Iraqis would have to cross the road. Sergeant Ramirez led the patrol personally.

The marines moved swiftly and set up positions in the trees on the south side of the road. They waited and were soon able to confirm the group as Iraqi. In front of the marines, on the opposite side of the road, an enemy squad was moving with stealth through the trees. The soldiers were carrying rifles, mortars, and RPGs. Sergeant Ramirez wasn't sure of their intentions, but those details were irrelevant: they were moving like a military unit with a purpose.

When the Iraqis got into the open road where he could see them all, Sergeant Ramirez hollered, "Halt! Put your hands in the air!" Next to Ramirez twelve nervous marines lay in overwatch looking for a reason to fire.

Genuinely surprised, the Iraqi troops dropped their weapons to the deck and immediately surrendered. Ramirez and the scouts then went about the laborious task of processing them as EPWs.

When Ramirez had cataloged the load of weapons and ammunition the soldiers carried, he moved the marines to clear the building behind them. Inside the structure they found a cache of weapons and ammunition that the Iraqi soldiers could have used, had they gotten that far. Sergeant Ramirez could not believe this additional stroke of good fortune. If he hadn't instinctively gathered the scouts to conduct security patrols, the Iraqis would have reached the building. If the Iraqis had been allowed to enter that building, there was no telling what would have happened to the battalion CP.

15

WHEN THE wandering tracked vehicle had left to the north and Lieutenant Tice finished inspecting my position, he agreed it would be impossible to breach the median with the resources we had available. The scouts were very glad to hear this: they were worn out from trying to accomplish the impossible task, and they were finally able to come back to the vehicle to augment the security of our position. Lieutenant Tice was happy with the position; he had confidence that I had beaten the mystery of the cloverleaf and that I could get back to the platoon if we had to withdraw. He left us, and we settled in to watch the freeway until morning.

I had one last task to finish before we were entirely set, though. The LAV-AT attached to me was not equipped with a SINCGARS radio. The whole evening I had been pondering how to work with this crew in the absence of the frequency-hopping radio. Up until this point I had simply spoken face to face with the vehicle commander; he was close enough to my position for this to be the easiest way to conduct business. Now that the position was all but set, I wanted to make sure he could communicate with us in the middle of the night if he saw something.

I made a final walk to his vehicle to talk to him. I asked him for his single-channel frequency, and we devised a plan that would allow us to reach each other. I told Corporal Matlain to change his radio with the company frequency loaded to the frequency used by the TOWs. The TOWs talked to

Matlain on that frequency, and he talked to me on the frequency-hopping platoon net. I listened to Matlain on the platoon net, and I could eavesdrop on the company net. We were set.

The only reservation I had when I walked back to my vehicle was that I didn't know the marine who was commanding the TOW vehicle. I don't believe I even knew his name, just his call sign. That was one of the problems with having a weapons company: you never knew the marines you were working with—never saw them make decisions, never knew how they thought. But I was happy just to be able to communicate on the radio with this vehicle commander, and finally I was able to assume my watch.

We had worked for more than four hours to get that position completely prepared. And then, after all we had done, we didn't use it. At 2230, thirty minutes after we were set, the platoon commander called us all back to the company CP to receive an order: Task Force Shepherd, Alpha and Charlie Companies, had been given the task of securing the Kuwait International Airport. The airport had actually been assigned to another unit initially, but that unit was still bogged down all the way back in the al-Burqan oil fields. The enemy pockets of resistance, the rapidity of our movement, and the lack of ground transportation to enable the unit to catch up meant that it was out of the picture.

When we arrived at the company coil, I went off to receive the order, and the crew stayed with the vehicle, tuning their portable radio to the Armed Forces Network. While the platoon commander told the vehicle commanders what we had to do, my crew listened to the news: a fierce tank battle was being waged at the Kuwait airport.

We huddled around the platoon commander's 1:50,000 map and watched as he outlined the company plan. We were going to drive on the freeways to the south entrance of the airport. The order of march was Alpha Company, Charlie Company, and then the battalion command group. Within Alpha it was 1st Platoon followed by 2d Platoon. It was about an eight-kilometer movement from where we were to the south end of the airport.

Kuwait International was laid out in an H-shaped configuration, with the runways—oriented slightly northeast and separated by a distance of about fifteen hundred meters—forming the two parallel sides. The terminal and airport facilities were located at the northern end of the layout, and numerous other small buildings and structures bordered the runways.

Where we were entering—between the south end of the runways—an access road bisected the runways. On both sides of the road ran two parallel rows of ten-foot chain-link fence with triple strands of barbed wire across the top, each row separated by about eight feet. The design led me to believe this was an area the airport police used to patrol the perimeter. Complicating the situation were additional lengths of the same type of fencing running perpendicular to the parallel rows and dividing the area around the airport into odd-shaped boxes of fenced-in terrain.

The plan was for Alpha Company to move up the access road about fifteen hundred meters and then blast through the fence to the west so we could come on line facing north—oriented on the western runway—with 1st Platoon on the right and 2d Platoon on the left. Charlie Company would repeat the process on the east side of the access road, and when the two companies were on line, the battalion would sweep through to the north end of the airport. It was a simple plan, except that a tank battle was going on there.

Lieutenant Tice followed the company plan with the platoon scheme of maneuver. He would lead the platoon movement, followed by Sergeant Negron. When the lieutenant pulled off the access road, Negron would pass him, go the fifty feet to the fence line, and burst through the chain-link mesh, using his LAV. NCO Jones, and then my section, would follow Negron through the fence and spread out laterally at fifty-meter intervals oriented north. Then 2d Platoon would pass through us and fall in at the same interval on our left flank.

From those positions we would advance—company on line—to the north, putting 25-mm rounds into every window of every building we passed en route to the terminal. Lieutenant Tice knew we didn't have enough manpower to clear any buildings; we would be forced to clear them by gunfire. The terminal was the objective: when we took it, the mission would be complete. The last thing he passed on to us was that there were Avgas (aviation gas) fuel tanks in our sector. He cautioned us about shooting at or toward the tanks—if we hit them, they would explode with such fury that we probably wouldn't be able to get past them. I left the order and went to brief my crew.

Organizing the Task Force Shepherd column took forever. I can remember waiting an incredibly long time before Charlie, Alpha, and the command group were ready to go. I was growing impatient; I think we all were.

Early in the morning, before light, the column finally started to head south on the freeway toward the airport. It was very difficult to maintain proper dispersion in the column. I had to fight the natural urge to race forward to the head of the column, to get to the action. We first traveled south and then east, toward the airport. When we made the turn to the east, I listened to reports coming in from 2d Platoon: the unit was receiving small-arms fire from the sides of the road. I looked cautiously to the road sides and hoped we were moving fast enough to avoid being shot.

Sergeant Ramirez, behind the lead element of the airport convoy, would have felt fortunate if all he had received was small-arms fire. Out of nowhere a Sagger missile was launched at the column from close range. Ramirez saw the missile approaching from the left, but he didn't have enough time even to transmit an alert before the projectile crossed directly in front of his vehicle. Rocketing through the column, the Sagger exploded off to the right. There would have been nothing Ramirez could have done if the Iraqi gunner had been on target.

At the head of the column we turned north along the access road at the airport, and I watched Lieutenant Tice pull off the road and orient north. It was then I noticed that the fence line was more than a hundred meters away from the access road—not fifty meters, as we had been briefed. I knew that Negron would pull fifty meters to the left of Lieutenant Tice and wouldn't reach the fence to breach it.

Sergeant Negron oriented north. I followed NCO Jones, and I assumed he would breach the fence, but he didn't. When he pulled up to the fence, he turned abruptly north—parallel to the fence, about three feet from it—and radioed the platoon commander: "This is Blue 4, I am at the fence. I say again, at the fence, and it is not breached, over."

I stopped about twenty-five meters behind him in disbelief. It was obvious that he was supposed to take on the job of breaching the fence, once Negron had been denied the task. I started moving toward him to do it myself. He was back on the radio, muttering something about how the fence had to be breached, when I pulled right behind him. He was directly in the path I needed to take to hit the fence squarely.

I looked behind me at the rest of the company, who were halted and waiting, and I thought *Oh, this is just great!* I broke in on his transmission to Blue 1: "Blue 4, move out of the way, pull forward."

NCO Jones came back on the net and said, "I've got to reposition my vehicle to break through."

I said firmly, "Blue 4, just get out of the way. I've got the fence." I don't know what was going on in his vehicle at the time, but he had put himself in a terribly awkward position—parallel and adjacent to the fence. His inability to act infuriated me.

Jones finally moved his vehicle forward, and PFC Dudley eased the vehicle to the fence. I ducked down inside the turret to avoid the barbed wire, and Dudley rolled over the first fence. When I popped back up, I noticed that directly across the second fence a perpendicular fence line married up to it. We would be hopelessly tangled if I tried to breach the second line where I was. I told Dudley to guide right ten feet—past the perpendicular fence line—before breaching the second fence.

Captain Shupp came over the radio demanding to know what was taking so long. He was his normal, intense self. I knew the platoon commander couldn't see what was going on, so I answered the captain. "Black 6, this is Blue 5, give me a minute. There is a third fence connecting at the breach point that I am trying to get around."

The captain replied, "Hurry up!" I smiled. That was exactly what I expected of him. He was true to character—no mission was too tough; just get it done.

I broke through the last fence and pulled into the open field. The time was 0330. I moved in about twenty-five meters and turned to orient north. Suddenly it seemed very dark: I literally could not see ten feet in front of the vehicle. I had been so intent on clearing the fence that I hadn't noticed how poor the visibility had become. The company poured through the breach behind me and spread out laterally in the surreal darkness.

The visibility was now so limited that one of the attached TOW vehicles actually hit Jones's vehicle when he went by—not hard but hard enough to cause us to put chemlights in our side-vision blocks so we could see each other.

It was 0430 when Alpha and Charlie Companies were set for the attack. Sergeant Hernandez and Charlie had gone through the same motions on the east side of the airport that Alpha had on the west side. It was just as dark where Charlie was. Only fifteen hundred meters separated the two companies, but we may as well have been a world apart.

With the companies set, the battalion commander launched the attack, but he stopped when he found out that Alpha's 2d Platoon had taken up positions that straddled Iraqi land mines. Those mines and the poor visibility, coupled with the fact that we had encountered zero resistance, caused the commander to delay the attack until dawn.

Delaying the attack was a very good call, I felt. We couldn't see very far at all in the darkness, and any movement forward would have been made at great risk, considering the situation. Had there been resistance, the situation would have changed, I'm sure, but there was none, and consequently we waited until dawn.

At 0630 there was enough light to see almost a kilometer, and the order

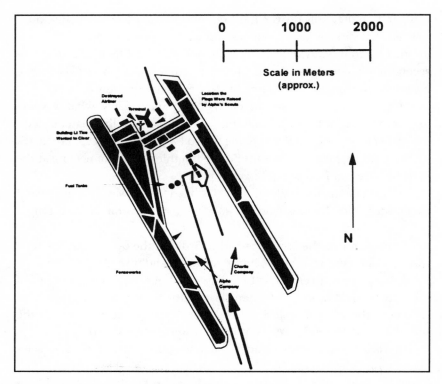

Figure 9. Kuwait International Airport.

was given to commence the assault. We moved out on line and advanced unimpeded to the airport terminal. The Avgas tanks were only five hundred meters in front of me, and I couldn't see anything past them, so I just stayed in the formation and watched what I could.

When I passed the fuel tanks, I could see the white airport terminal twelve hundred meters to my front. Common sense and lack of resistance told us that, despite our plan, we didn't need to fire into the windows of all the buildings we went by, so we advanced without the accompaniment of gun fire. About a thousand meters from the terminal, Uke saw a muzzle flash coming from it. I saw the flash too, and I directed Uke to fire a burst of 25-mm at the source. When I got closer, I realized that the flashes were the oil fires far to the south, reflecting off of the vibrating Plexiglas windows of the terminal. I felt stupid again, but I also felt it was better to be safe than sorry.

All the vehicles in 1st Platoon pulled up directly toward the terminal. When we were about two hundred meters away, Captain Shupp directed Lieutenant Tice to dismount scouts and clear the terminal. What followed was a five-minute conversation between the captain and my platoon commander.

The airport terminal—with the destroyed Boeing 747, to which the press had given so much attention, sitting in front—was a multistory state-of-the-art structure. An immense building, it was almost five hundred meters long and three hundred meters wide. It appeared to me that it would rival, in size, just about any terminal I had seen in the United States. The size of the building alone prohibited a deliberate search-and-clear by a force smaller than a company or more of infantrymen.

Lieutenant Tice was on the radio, trying to tell this to the captain. What the lieutenant wanted to do, if he *had* to clear a building, was to clear the control tower just to the south of the terminal. The tower was probably fifteen stories high, but each floor was only twenty-five meters square. To clear it would be an immense task, to be sure—but a much more manageable one with our assets than the terminal proper would be.

But the captain wanted the terminal itself, and no amount of arguing by Lieutenant Tice could convince him not to take it. The lieutenant therefore came over the platoon net and ordered the scouts to clear the main terminal building. Sergeant Sweeny, the senior scout, was ordered to take charge and carry out the task.

I filled my scout-team leader in on the plan, and he took the team to find Sergeant Sweeny. There was really no way to overwatch the scouts as they cleared the building: once they were inside, radio communication with them was lost, and we couldn't see them—they were on their own. Lieutenant Tice moved my section to the north side of the terminal to overwatch for an Iraqi counterattack while the scouts moved through the huge structure alone.

We moved to position, but the whole situation was uneventful. The one thing I remember about waiting for the scouts to clear the building was my impression of the rape of the country that was displayed all around me. This was my first real view of Kuwait City in the hours of daylight. Cars and buildings had been vandalized and destroyed. Almost every car was up on blocks with the tires removed, hood open, and engine stripped. Each building was punctuated by broken glass and doors falling off their hinges.

It was really disgusting. The Iraqis had taken everything of value within sight. Knowing that the Kuwaitis were finally getting their country back left me with mixed emotions. On the one hand they were free, but on the other hand they had a long road ahead in recovering their lives. It was a shame that the leader of Iraq didn't pay the ultimate price for his role in the utter violation of Kuwait.

At 0657 the scouts reached the top floor of the terminal, where the Iraqi flag was flying on a short flag pole. I watched as one of the scouts ran down the Iraqi flag and in its place raised the American, Marine Corps, and Kuwaiti flags: *honor, courage, commitment.*

I had to choke back the urge to cry when I saw the flags rise and flap gently in the breeze. From my position they waved in a small patch of blue amidst the overcast sky. It was so satisfying to see the flags replace the gruesome Iraqi flag, the symbol of oppression. Right then and there I knew that Kuwait was free. Things still had to run their course, but Kuwait was free. We knew it, and we had been part of it. That moment is as much a part of my being as any part of my life is. I write this book today because of moments like that.

Only one thing that happened had the potential to ruin that perfect day. An OV-10 pilot had to make an emergency landing at the airport for some reason—he just wanted to be the first pilot to land there, if you ask me. The problem was that the runways were mined. To Captain Shupp, this was an easy fix: "Clear the runway, 2d Platoon." He ended our actions in the deployment true to form: no questions asked, accomplish the mission. We later learned that the OV-10 went somewhere else to land, but 2d Platoon was ready to carry out the task nonetheless.

After that aborted assignment we pulled into a fenced-in compound immediately south of the terminal. Friendly forces appeared out of nowhere, and soon the airport was crawling with activity. No one saw us, though. Alpha Company was out of sight, backed up to a large warehouse in the compound. And that's where the conflict ended for us.

When the word for an offensive cessation came, we already knew it was over. We watched from our compound as the airport became the hub of the division's operations. We sat back against the walls of the warehouse, thankful that Kuwait was free and wondering when we would go home. We smiled, we laughed, we patted each other on the backs. The war stories started in earnest as each crew told its tale of heroics to the other crews.

Captain Shupp passed the word to turn in all captured enemy weapons and equipment to the company gunny. An hour later only two or three weapons and a handful of ammunition had been piled behind the gunny's LAV-L. Everyone was intent on keeping the captured gear a secret in hopes of being able to take it home. The captain spoke at great length in conveying to the company his displeasure over this matter. When he was done, the pile of weapons behind the LAV-L grew enormously, with hundreds of weapons, dozens of ammunition bandoleers, and a mass of assorted gear having appeared from nowhere.

Lieutenant Tice was talking to each vehicle commander individually, and it was my turn. He called me behind the warehouse. For the first time, I saw no tension in the leader standing before me. A huge weight had been lifted off his shoulders. While he led 1st Platoon, his ethical and moral value-system had played havoc with his warrior system. With the hostilities ended, I was finally able to see him as the man behind the marine leader. I felt sorry for him.

Everyone took responsibility seriously, but I could tell that to Lieutenant Tice, the responsibility of his marines was beyond serious: their lives were his sole thought. Although he would have continued to function as a leader, I am sure that if a marine in our platoon had died, Lieutenant Tice would have gone to his grave with the responsibility of that death set squarely upon his shoulders, regardless of the situation. I could see that he knew it as well. He knew it all too fully.

We talked about the previous four days for half an hour or so. He first asked me if I had anyone whom I would recommend for commendation. I told him my entire crew deserved commendation, but in truth, no single individual had done anything that was more worthy of commendation than what any of the others had done. I told him Matlain had performed with confidence, proficiency, and professionalism. I don't want to belittle the awards system, but my feelings were quite clear about this. Every citation I had ever read from past wars had one thing in common: the marine receiving the decoration had always been issued a Purple Heart. Alpha Company had some hairy moments, but nothing very singular or dramatic had occurred beyond that. As a crew we deserved every measure of honor as far as I was concerned, but as individuals we deserved a trip home, and that was it.

Lieutenant Tice and I talked for a little while longer. He told me he had been impressed with my handling of the Charlie Company linkup debacle, and I told him the horror story of the cloverleaf. We touched briefly on the staff sergeant issue, and he nodded in understanding. We shook hands, and I left. The lieutenant then went off to speak with another of the vehicle commanders.

There was one incident in the compound that ruined the moment. Sergeant Griswald—the same caring NCO I had talked to in first class during the flight over—was clearing the vehicle weapons and discharged a 7.62-mm coax round into the air. The platoon commander's gunner, he was reaching across to the weapon from the gunner's seat when it happened.

Our coax machine gun has a critical problem. Sometimes when it jams, a round is lodged above the chamber with its pointed projectile tip levered against the chamber guide. With the pressure of the feed-tray cover on the back of the round and the tension of the drive spring on its base, the round will not chamber and the weapon will not fire. Unfortunately when the feed-tray cover is lifted, the tension on the system is released, the round tilts nose down, and the bolt chambers the round and fires it.

This is exactly what happened to Sergeant Griswald. He was lifting the feed tray to clear the weapon and did not know there was a round above the chamber. Unfortunately the rules are clear concerning unauthorized (accidental) discharges, and Sergeant Griswald left with a mark on his record after seven months of deployment. It is ironic that after all the difficulties we had been through during our operation in Saudi Arabia, one of the things we had tried the hardest to avoid took place on our final day.

Epilogue

TASK FORCE Shepherd left the Kuwait International Airport on the morning of 1 March 1991. The trip through the city was memorable. Our long column of vehicles used the main freeways to travel south toward Manifa Bay. I had attached the American, Marine Corps, and Kuwaiti flags—the latter recovered from a garbage heap at the airport—to my antenna mast, and the three flapped loudly in the wind behind me as we drove south.

The streets were flooded with Kuwaiti men, women, and children. They all were waving American and Kuwaiti flags and blowing us kisses as we passed by. Cars joined our convoy, their occupants hanging out the open windows and expressing their thanks to us for their freedom. I thanked them back for being so patient. The whole trip seemed like an ad hoc parade that the citizens of Kuwait had decided to sponsor upon our departure.

When we left the celebrating Kuwaitis behind, I knew I wouldn't see them again. It was like watching old friends pass in the distance. We had spent so much time committed to one goal that it seemed strange finally to be leaving with that goal having been accomplished.

Since the war I have had the opportunity to review a great number of the documentaries and news stories dealing with Desert Storm. Having finally been able to see the magnitude of our mission, I have realized that Alpha Company was a very small part of a big campaign. We were but one cog in the wheel of the war machine that ousted the Iraqis from Kuwait and chased them across their own deserts.

Looking from this side of the world, Task Force Shepherd seems so insignificant. Even so, when I was a part of that one cog, we were everything. We were significant. The officers, SNCOs, and NCOs who drove Shepherd through the blackness of al-Burqan displayed honor that bordered on chivalry. Through various actions against the enemy they displayed courage that belied their small part of the whole operation. Throughout the entire deployment they were committed in heart and in soul to one common goal—to free Kuwait.

Afterword

WHEN I ARRIVED back in the United States, I had one thing on my mind: reuniting with my one-year-old son and loving, supportive wife. The long flight home was worse than the entire deployment. One thing I did not expect, though, was the overwhelming support from the citizens of America. I guess I was so used to seeing all of the cynical reactions of Americans in the press that I didn't expect to experience anything positive at this point. Was I ever wrong!

We arrived in Bangor, Maine, on our C-5 flight from Spain sometime in the middle of the night. We had to stop there for our plane to be refueled and serviced, so we begrudgingly interrupted our freedom flight to board a bus that would take us to a waiting area. A marine sergeant major stepped aboard the bus and told us there were some people who wanted to see us. He said he understood that we were tired and wanted to go home but it would really mean a lot to these people if we would agree to meet them. We smiled and nodded half-heartedly—what else could we do?

The green military bus drove us to a large warehouse about ten minutes from where our plane was parked. It was biting cold as we walked toward the building. But however low the temperature outside was, it did nothing to stifle the warmth we were about to feel. When I stepped into the warehouse, I stopped in my tracks and my jaw dropped to the floor. In front of me was a hundred-foot length of red carpet bordered by plush velvet ropes and brass poles. Behind those poles were hundreds of people clapping their hands and smiling at us. From somewhere deep in the building, Lee Greenwood's "God Bless the U.S.A." blared through a tremendous sound system.

With the deep power of the music grasping our souls, we moved down the carpet and shook hands with the people who had wanted us to come here. I looked from face to cheering face and thanked these individuals for their support—every set of eyes I met and every hand I shook was warm, approving, and friendly. Children were grabbing at our pant legs, begging for attention. Those people who weren't smiling were crying.

The music and the genuine warmth of the crowd got to me, and a tear rolled down my cheek. I was so overwhelmed by the whole situation that I couldn't control my emotions anymore. As I listened to the words in Greenwood's song— "I'm proud to be an American, where at least I know I'm free, and I won't forget the men who died who gave that right to me" —I started to shake, and I struggled to wipe my eyes. At that moment I was very proud to be a marine, even prouder to be an American, and most of all I was happy to be home.

When I got to California and was reunited with my family, there was closure for me. It was finally all over, and I could begin the transition back into a normal life—which was not always an easy task, by the way. But my wife was ever supportive, and because of that fact I can now finish this book, which I end with these words: God bless America.

Notes

Chapter 1

1. Today 1st LAI Battalion is located at Camp Pendleton, California; 2d LAI Battalion is at Camp Lejeune, North Carolina; 3d LAI Battalion is at Twentynine Palms, California; and 4th LAI Battalion (the reserve battalion) is at four separate sites: a company each in California, Utah, Louisiana, and Maryland.

2. At this time an LAV company was attached to the Marine Expeditionary Unit (MEU) for a six-month deployment.

3. The operations officer, or S-3, is the battalion commander's operational planner. His duties include oversight on training scheduling and management, generation of operational orders, command and control functions, and coordination of the battle.

4. SINCGARS is the type of radio that was mounted in all of Company A's vehicles. A dual-function radio, it works as a standard VHF-FM radio and, in a special mode, as a frequency-hopping radio for secure transmission.

5. In addition to the 25-mm chain gun, the LAV-25 is equipped with a 7.62-mm coaxially mounted machine gun (mounted coaxially to the chain-gun barrel) and a 7.62-mm pintle-mounted machine gun (mounted on top of the vehicle in front of the commander's position).

6. The MPS is a squadron of merchant vessels that is capable of moving marine combat equipment to a crisis area very rapidly. The equipment is preloaded, and occasionally it is off-loaded for service and maintenance. Some of the NCOs in Charlie Company, including Sergeant Hernandez, had conducted these off-loads in the past.

Chapter 2

1. Each member of the company was required to sign out every time we left the company area. We left phone numbers where we could be reached in the event that the commanding officer "recalled" the company to deploy.

2. Shelter halves are canvas pieces used to construct tents, field jackets are heavy coats, and woolly-pullys are heavy wool sweaters. These items of equipment are normally packed when marines are deployed to areas where inclement weather is expected. We couldn't see the sense in taking them to the desert, however.

Chapter 8

1. This was one of the few operations orders we received during the deployment. Usually Captain Shupp moved us with FRAGOs, which are short, abbreviated orders passed over the radio.

2. A coil is a wagon wheel of sorts, which is created when each vehicle in the company pulls in and faces outward. The end result is a large circlelike formation with 360-degree security.

Chapter 9

1. An OV-10 is a small propeller-driven aircraft. While the pilot flies the plane, the backseater, or FACA, watches the battlefield. The FACA uses the aircraft's radios to communicate with ground forces and to guide attack aircraft onto targets. The OV-10's good vantage point in the air, its slow speed, and its time on station allow it to serve very effectively as the controller of all air assets for any particular tactical situation.

2. The AT-3 "Sagger" missile is a wire-guided antitank missile that can be fired from either a hand-carried platform or a vehicle-mounted platform.

3. The Cobras were affected by the darkness as well. They didn't have an incredible amount of success; however, they were able to destroy one T-55 with a TOW missile—the first tank kill by an AH-1W Cobra gunship ever to occur.

4. This was common with the BGM-71As, an older version of the TOW missile. The BGM-71Cs, a newer version, worked very well from the hovering Cobra platforms. The 71As were used extensively because they were still in stock and the 71Cs were expensive.

Chapter 11

1. The artillery battery picked up the incoming enemy artillery on radar and used the trajectory of those rounds to determine the location of the enemy firing battery. Once that location was known, the friendly fire-direction center directed friendly artillery to fire on the enemy battery's location.

Chapter 12

1. The command groups are a pair of LAV-C2s augmented by a dozen specially equipped HMMWVs. Together the vehicles provide the battalion commander with a mobile platform from which to fight the battle. The battalion staff mans the radio banks in the back of the LAV-C2s and coordinates all aspects of the battle, using map boards and blue and red felt-tipped pens. The Alpha Command Group is the primary command group, and the Bravo Command Group—which mirrors in composition the Alpha Group—stands by to assume control of the battle if the Alpha Group is unable to do so.

2. In a polar mission the fire-direction center plots the data for the indirect fire from a known location—that of the observer. This type of mission is extremely accurate but only if the fire-direction center knows the exact location of the observer.

Chapter 13

1. The tracer element in the AP rounds burns out at about seventeen hundred meters. The round continues in its flight, but without the glow of the burning tracer it is very difficult to observe the round's impact.

Chapter 14

1. The trim vane is a quarter-inch sheet of aluminum that is attached to the front of the vehicle. It serves as a bow for the LAV in the event that the vehicle has to swim across a body of water. The driver uses a pneumatic lever to raise and lower the trim vane as required.

About the Author

The author, currently an active duty master sergeant in the United States Marine Corps, lives in Indianapolis, Indiana, with his wife Angie and their three sons: Alec, Christopher, and Nicholas. Master Sergeant Michaels spent sixteen years in the Light Armored Vehicle Community, serving in virtually every enlisted billet. After his final tour as Company Gunnery Sergeant of Weapons Company, 1st Light Armored Reconnaissance Battalion, he was ordered to recruiting duty, where he has since served. Currently he is the recruiter instructor for Recruiting Station Indianapolis.

About the

The Naval Institute Press is the book-publishing arm of the U.S. Naval Institute, a private, nonprofit, membership society for sea service professionals and others who share an interest in naval and maritime affairs. Established in 1873 at the U.S. Naval Academy in Annapolis, Maryland, where its offices remain today, the Naval Institute has members worldwide.

Members of the Naval Institute support the education programs of the society and receive the influential monthly magazine *Proceedings* or the colorful bimonthly magazine *Naval History* and discounts on fine nautical prints and on ship and aircraft photos. They also have access to the transcripts of the Institute's Oral History Program and get discounted admission to any of the Institute-sponsored seminars offered around the country.

The Naval Institute's book-publishing program, begun in 1898 with basic guides to naval practices, has broadened its scope to include books of more general interest. Now the Naval Institute Press publishes about seventy titles each year, ranging from how-to books on boating and navigation to battle histories, biographies, ship and aircraft guides, and novels. Institute members receive significant discounts on the Press's more than eight hundred books in print.

Full-time students are eligible for special half-price membership rates. Life memberships are also available.

For a free catalog describing Naval Institute Press books currently available, and for further information about joining the U.S. Naval Institute, please write to:

Member Services
U.S. Naval Institute
291 Wood Road
Annapolis, MD 21402-5034
Telephone: (800) 233-8764
Fax: (410) 571-1703
Web address: www.usni.org